Emily Dickinson & the Image of Home

Emily Dickinson & the Image of Home

by Jean McClure Mudge

The University of Massachusetts Press   Amherst 1975

Acknowledgment is made to the following publishers for material reprinted
with permission.
Harvard University Press, for material reprinted by permission of the publishers
and the Trustees of Amherst College from Thomas H. Johnson, Editor, *The
Poems of Emily Dickinson*, Cambridge, Mass.: The Belknap Press of Harvard
University Press, Copyright, 1951, 1955, by The President and Fellows of Harvard
College; and for material reprinted by permission of the publishers from *The
Letters of Emily Dickinson*, edited by Thomas H. Johnson and Theodora Ward,
Cambridge, Mass.: The Belknap Press of Harvard University Press, Copyright,
1958, by the President and Fellows of Harvard College.
Houghton Mifflin Company, for material from *Emily Dickinson Face to Face*,
by Martha D. Bianchi, copyright 1932 by Martha Dickinson Bianchi. Renewed
© 1960 by Alfred Leete Hampson. Reprinted by permission of Houghton Mifflin
Company; and for material from *The Life and Letters of Emily Dickinson*, by
Martha D. Bianchi, copyright 1924 by Martha Dickinson Bianchi. Copyright
renewed 1952 by Alfred Leete Hampson. Reprinted by permission of Houghton
Mifflin Company.
Little, Brown and Company, for material reprinted from *The Complete Poems
of Emily Dickinson*, Edited by Thomas T. Johnson, by permission of Little,
Brown and Co. Poems originally published under the title *The Single Hound*
copyright 1914, 1942 by Martha Dickinson Bianchi. Poems originally published
under the title *Further Poems* copyright 1929, © 1957 by Mary L. Hampson.
Poems originally published as *Unpublished Poems* copyright 1935 by Martha
Dickinson Bianchi, © 1963 by Mary L. Hampson.

For my parents, Eva C. & Robert B. McClure,
   whose several homes, some overseas,
   have always been real ones,

And for my family, Lew, Bob, Bill, & Annie,
   whose activities have enriched as
   they have postponed these pages.

. . . a human work is nothing other than a lengthy journey to recover by the detours of art the two or three simple and great images by which the heart was first opened.

CAMUS

Home is the riddle of the wise — the booty of the dove.

EMILY DICKINSON, 1881

Contents

List of Illustrations

Preface

A number of assumptions underlie this study. The first and most central one is that even for a highly imaginative mind, such as Emily Dickinson's, earliest encounters with the concrete world during childhood and adolescence are of primary and lasting importance. New worlds of delight and despair may arise from the artist's consciousness, but those worlds have their beginnings in the awareness of particular places and objects of meaning. It might be said that these scenes and things groove the psyche. More exactly, mind and object combine so that the perceiving "I" participates in the things upon which it focuses. When Whitman tells us, "There was a child went forth every day / And the first object he looked upon and received with wonder or / pity or love or dread, that object he became," and adds that this object and its successors "became part of him" for his lifetime, he describes the enmeshing of perception and the thing perceived in the formation of an individual mind. In our day, the philosopher Merleau-Ponty succinctly states, "J'en suis," literally, "I am of it [the world]." Subject and object find a co-terminus in consciousness.

My initial attention, then, to Emily Dickinson as a physical being and to her houses, the first objects in her world, is in order to explore an early, fundamental part of her sensitivity to space. This sensitivity leads to her self-estimate and eventually to her concepts of "center" and "circumference." Ultimately, it affects her attitudes toward all of life and to a life beyond.

In his *Autobiographic Sketches* (1853), Thomas De Quincey speaks to this subject in a discussion about why death is more affecting in summer than in any other season. Emily read this book, frequently pencilling it, and in the right margin of the following passage, she marked the last sentence:

> But, in my case, there was even a subtler reason why the summer had this intense power of vivifying the spectacle or the thoughts of death. And, recollecting it, I am struck with the

truth, that far more of our deepest thoughts and feelings pass to us through perplexed combinations of *concrete* objects, pass to us as *involutes* (if I may coin that word) in compound experiences incapable of being disentangled, than ever reach us directly and in their own abstract shapes.[1]

De Quincey provides a double testimony, first to the centrality of the impressions made by the phenomenological world, and second, to their myriad interweavings to become complex and involved, in short, "involutes." Actually, he makes a third observation when he says that these packages of perceptions affect our minds in greater number than do abstract ideas. He implies that concrete experiences may provide us material for our thoughts, that is, abstractions are dependent upon such perceptions. Surely this must be his intent if the subject is the increased poignancy of death in the summer as opposed to other times of year. He probes the sources of this emotional reaction and discovers that his memory of reading the Bible before the nursery fireplace may have had a conditioning effect, for he associated tropical climes with Jerusalem, the scene of the Crucifixion. Interestingly, he emphasizes that Jerusalem became, for him, the *omphalos* (navel), or physical and spiritual center of the earth, because here mortality was put to death. Yet a man had to die before he could rise, and the ambiguity of Jerusalem's promise bothers De Quincey. Nonetheless, his major point is this:

Summer, therefore, had connected itself with death, not merely as a mode of antagonism, but also as a phenomenon brought into intricate relations with death by scriptural scenery and events.[2]

De Quincey's particular emphasis upon the accentuated relation between summer and sorrow is a combination quite familiar to Dickinson. Summer for her was the season of apex, a noon or high time of great promise, and in retrospect, profound despair. Well over a hundred of her poems are about summer, and in one she equates her writing with it: "My Art, a Summer Day – had patrons."[3] In another, she seems to echo De Quincey's combination of specific and general observations about summer, death, and the concrete nature of lasting impressions, although Emily's death is in this life:

When I hoped, I recollect
Just the place I stood –
At a Window facing West –
Roughest Air – was good –

Not a Sleet could bite me –
Not a frost could cool –
Hope it was that kept me warm –
Not Merino shawl –

When I feared – I recollect
Just the Day it was –
Worlds were lying out to Sun –
Yet how Nature froze –

Icicles upon my soul
Prickled Blue and Cool –
Bird went praising everywhere –
Only Me – was still –

(768)

.   .   .   .

Here the poet has emotions ostensibly inappropriate to the seasons. Hope in winter keeps her warm, but fear in summer freezes her when all of nature is "out to Sun." In this season, "Bird went praising everywhere," but Emily, by contrast, bears the pain and fright of the "Blue" and "Cool" icicles which prick her soul. Most important, the poet recalls the specific stances and places she took in each mood, that is, the particulars of her situation. She thus illustrates De Quincey's point that one's mind is profoundly affected by discrete, felt experiences in concrete environments. This mode of thought may be found repeatedly in Emily's letters as well as her poems and will be touched upon in appropriate parts of this study.

The poem above also exemplifies a second assumption, one pertaining to the speaker of the poetry. Emily Dickinson wrote to Thomas Wentworth Higginson in July 1862, "When I state myself, as the Representative of the Verse – it does not mean – me – but a supposed person."[4] Yet a month earlier she had admitted to him, "I felt a palsy, here – the Verses just relieve,"[5] a process which this poem may have accomplished. Since she uses the first person pronoun 1682 times in the poetry,[6] "my" and "me" 755 and 616 times respectively, "mine" 107 times, and "myself" 80 times, her

June comment seems more accurate than her later one.[7] But perhaps she was not wholly wrong about who was the "Representative of the Verse," because when she uses "I," it may denote one of her several selves. Emily's divided psyche will be discussed in chapter 2, and at this moment, it is enough to recognize that she may refer to one or another side of herself, or unite those sides, when she refers to "I." Each instance needs separate treatment.

Whether or not the first person pronoun signifies a united or divided self, it was a consciousness which had chosen "polar privacy." Though perhaps at one time Emily hoped to publish, especially some of the poems she sent to Higginson in the early 1860s, she retreated from that wish in her lifetime, putting half the poems, probably her preferred ones, in fascicles of about twenty poems each, leaving the others in various stages of completion. In short, the speaker of the poems was not expecting to be scrutinized in the same way a publishing poet might be; thus "I" could reflect herself as closely as she allowed, or might even reveal more than she would wish. In addition, the facts that Emily often enclosed poems within letters to friends, such as Samuel Bowles or the Josiah Hollands, which continue the sense of the particular letter, or speak of her known interests, and that these letters and poems were not meant for publication are further evidence that "I" is safely assumed to be one of the facets of Dickinson's consciousness.[8]

Despite this evidence of the probable use of "I" to describe the historical person Emily Dickinson (more convincing in Dickinson's case, for the psychological, publishing, and circumstantial facts given above, than in most other cases), the question remains of the full nature of the being referred to by this personal pronoun. Who is the poetry's "I" in truth? The poet's self-image, which often strays from reality, and her tendency toward hyperbole are at least two reasons why "I," "me," and "myself" must be read as something different from the flesh-and-blood poet. The personality whose experiences are espalied with such precision in the garden of this poetry enjoys not only the rich resources of its author's experience but also the heightening effects of its creator's imagination. The "I" then is a hybrid self, derived from both the poet's life and her poetic invention. It is a being at once existential and literary. For this reason, the biographical information of the first two chapters of this book takes on a value beyond biography. It attempts to show the empirical sources which are simultaneously

historical events in the author's life and items reworked by her
artistic intention.

Still another more general thought underlying this exploration
of the poet's consciousness of space is the universality of Dickinson's situation, which was sometimes, if not gnawingly, to feel out-
of-place as woman and writer, in short, homeless. Not only was this
true for other writers of her era (to be discussed in chapter 4), from
those of stature like Hawthorne and Melville to popular writers
like Horatio Alger,[9] but it seems to be the hallmark of our own
day, if Susan Sontag is correct:

> Most serious thought in our time struggles with the feeling
> of homelessness. The felt unreliability of human experience
> brought about by the inhuman acceleration of historical
> change has led every sensitive modern mind to the recording
> of some kind of nausea, of intellectual vertigo.[10]

Erik Erikson makes the same point but on an opposite note, observing that the optimum sense of identity is to possess a feeling of
at homeness. Thus when Dickinson uses house and home imagery
to surmount her situation and find a place, she speaks to the present
as much as she would have liked to speak to her own generation.

Finally, this study makes a minimal use of selected materials
from psychology and psychosociology relevent to Dickinson's life
pattern as reflected in her architectural imagery. Freud and Erikson are the major figures who are touched upon, generally in chapter 1, more particularly in separate sections of chapters 2 and 3. In
these introductory pages it seems fitting to place Carl Jung's observations, since he has a significant but short word to add. In a
preliminary note to Jung's *Psyche and Symbol,* a book which omits
any attention to the house or home symbol, Violet Saub de Laszlo
comments about his work on personality types, offering a précis of
Jung:

> It is characteristic of the introverted intuitive personality that
> the inner image constitutes the most convincing aspect of the
> totality of his life experience. This inner image, the symbol,
> carries for the intuitive introvert more than for any other per-
> sonality type the essential meaning of existence.[11]

Her discussion continues on the subject of Jung's archetypes, but
the passage just quoted is pertinent to Dickinson, who cherished

her "introverted" and "intuitive" identity. Jung's understanding of the symbol seems even more applicable to the image of house and home, for it is not only an inner figure, that is, a symbol, but a symbol of innerness. Perhaps in Dickinson's work it exhibits the poet's understanding of life with double strength.

Assumptions outlined, techniques deserve a word. "Image" seems to me the best term to use in this study for a primary reason: its quality of instantaneously indicating a number of significations at once. Not only does Emily Dickinson describe physical views of her house and home, fulfilling the common first understanding of the word image as something seen or represented, as in a painting. She also packs into these words her felt life and her memories, expanding the sense of image beyond the visual to the experiential and the remembered. Image thus performs an enormously weighty service for the poet, and it does so whether she is apparently merely referring to her house or home in a letter or making clear figurative use of these words in poems. Observe, for example, the prepoetic symbolizations she makes in prose passages about her Pleasant Street house, as discussed in chapter 2. In the poetry, of course, simile, metaphor, symbol, synecdoche, or emblem may be distinguished. But image as a generic term includes all these figures and also signifies the simple facts of Dickinson's actual house or home. The particular figure of speech becomes important only when the single text, of poem or letter, is under scrutiny. The "Image of Home," then, seemed a comprehensive critical banner under which I could pursue Dickinson's wide reach of meaning without missing the poetic condensations of her prose in their less obvious places or the specific formal techniques of her poetry.

The Harvard variorum volumes of Emily Dickinson's letters and poems have been referred to so extensively that I had to devise a shorthand for identifying them to reduce footnotes and facilitate reading. The letters are always footnoted with volume, letter, and page numbers, except where several related letters are mentioned: then only page numbers are given. When quoted in the text, poems are identified by their Johnson number (not page number) in parentheses on the last line. In the notes, they are referred to by volume, poem number, and page number if the references are limited to one or two poems. Above that, only the volume and poem numbers are designated. The notation PF identifies prose fragments.

The pencilled markings attributed to Emily in her father's or sister-in-law's books may be distinguished from the owners' in at least two ways. First, the poet's touch is lighter than Sue's, whose pencil seems guided by a weight of confidence or acclaim, perhaps because she intended to guide Emily's attention to the passage in question. Unlike Sue, Edward did not generously mark his books, or at least the ones in question here. Second, Emily occasionally makes a cross mark in book margins which is identical with such marks on holograph poems, indicating word variations or substitutes. Sue is not known to have used such a notation. The two types of markings may be compared in Sue's and Emily's copies of *Aurora Leigh,* where Sue's is heavily pencilled by both women and Emily's only by her. Despite these distinctions, it is sometimes impossible to tell beyond doubt if a pencil line was drawn by the poet. Nonetheless, since Sue and she intimately shared reading interests, one may at least assume Emily read certain works in light of evidence indicating her knowledge of them.

Close readers of Dickinson's work will be bothered by a consistent punctuation error she makes with contractions, as in "must'nt," or with contractions as substitutes for possessives, for example, "it's" when she means "its." So common is this mistake in her lines that mentioning it here will eliminate the need for using *sic* at the many necessary places, which would only interrupt the pleasure of a connected reading of her verse or prose.

Beyond preliminaries are acknowledgments, and I would first like to mention Emily's grandfather, Samuel Fowler Dickinson. This is not to confuse a figure properly in the text and now deceased with ones related to this study and very much alive. S. F. Dickinson deserves attention for his role as the first owner of the Dickinson homestead and the builder of its Mansion, where the great majority of Emily's extant poems were written. Aged, infirm, and in penury, Mr. Dickinson died away from a home to which his children strangely did not help him to return, despite his fervent wish to do so in the few years before his death. It was his house above anyone else's for he chose the design, perhaps selected the brick from the South Amherst brickworks, and made minor changes to the property during his residence, as he reported to his son and Emily's father, Edward, then a student at Yale. When one examines the Mansion in the pages and photographs to follow, the spectre of Samuel Fowler Dickinson should be the first imagined to be haunting the place, grumbling perhaps about the impoverishment of appearance that technological improvements have brought to his property, shaking a cane at an innocent tourist.

Leaving history to speak of the present, I am pleased to acknowledge assistance from Sydney Ahlstrom, Millicent Todd Bingham, William H. Bond, Charles Feidelson, James Gerhard, Mary L. Hampson, Carolyn Jakeman, Leo Marx, Floyd S. Merritt, Priscilla Parke, J. Richard Phillips, Winifred Sayer, Daniel P. Schwartz, Richard Sewall, David Sofield, Leone Stein, and Sarah Upton. Most especially, I am indebted to two advisors, R. W. B. Lewis and J. Hillis Miller, whose criticisms have led to improvements on every level of the work which follows, while they are in no way responsible for any of its arguments or, needless to say, its errors.

The credit ordinarily due spouses in a work of this sort for patient attention to endless discussion about it is, in this case, considerably increased by my husband's skill in taking many of the photographs reproduced here. Further, he taught me a new pleasure of a dark room: how to make prints . . . and in the Dickinson's former bathroom in the Mansion. From ideas to objects, then, Lew Mudge is present in this study with deceptive unobtrusiveness.

Chapter 1
Inscape and the image of home

Emily Dickinson's image of house or home, touching the poet's tangible and imaginative worlds at once, is perhaps the most penetrating and comprehensive figure she employs (see Appendix). Of course, the frequency with which this image recurs in her work is not my point. Further, I am not arguing that it is her only major figure of speech, nor that it absorbs all other patterns of images. Her lyric life is embodied in the language of nature, royalty, and lapidary art, of science, religion, politics, history, literature, and geography. She practices "gem-tactics," using a wealth of words to suit her subjects. But her largest fund of expression, second only to a penchant for technological terminology, derives from the domestic scene she intimately knew. This leaning illustrates the physical character of her favorite words and her preference for the concrete symbol.[1] The poet uses household terms – from architecture to such humble objects as the cup – the image of house and home *per se* or its corollaries and surrogates, to treat all of her most pressing concerns, concerns which relate to her place in the universe. *Home* thus reflects her inner landscape, which may be called her *spatial inscape,* a sensitivity to space dependent on both personal and social factors. At the same time, this figure emerges as a unique and unifying touchstone to several facets of the poet's consciousness, that is, to her choice of subject, mood, or style.

The coalescing nature of the home image gives the critic both a promise and a problem. It promises a way of observing, separately and together, the diverse perceptions which combined to illustrate Emily Dickinson's first subjects, perceptions of her body, of the architecture of her two literal homes, of historical events in family and town life, and of cultural and literary influences. Yet this wealth of phenomena immediately poses a problem of method. In what way may such experiences be treated, adequate to the complexity of their absorption in the poet's mind? How do they converge in her house and home language, or is it possible to say exactly by what means an affecting observation, fleeting glance, or cultural influence actually meshes in first consciousness, then expression? How, for example, could the steps leading to one of her least tangible statements, "Home is the definition of God," be traced? At this moment, a discussion of my approach seems best postponed until the chapter's end after evidence has been adduced to illustrate the depth and breadth of meaning Dickinson attached to home. Its consecration and ubiquity in her work bear upon my type of analysis and its limits.

I.

"Home is a holy thing . . ." Emily Dickinson once wrote her brother Austin. The adjective is extravagant for one noted for her consistent heterodoxy. She would have saved "holy" for an item of ultimate value. Home earned such an accolade. Why? Was she simply echoing the spirit of her times in which Home, Flag, and Mother figured first among the country's loyalties? The contemporary motto "Home, Sweet Home!" cross-stitched, framed, and exhibited in middle class parlors in two dimensional rigidity, obscured, in its banality, the heartfelt sentiment which first inspired it. Was Dickinson, like Hawthorne, Melville, Poe, Alger, and others, expressing a cultural and literary theme readily at hand? In part, indeed she was. But she also had a unique perspective on the subject. Alone among American authors, Dickinson spent her life almost exclusively at home, gradually withdrawing into near seclusion in the grounds of the Dickinson homestead on Main Street in Amherst. It seems not only natural, but even conditioned, that she should speak fervently of home.

At forty, the proverbial age at which one makes a retrospective analysis of one's life and perhaps also finds that "life begins at" this momentous year, Dickinson wrote the following poem:

> Remembrance has a Rear and Front –
> 'Tis something like a House –
> It has a Garret also
> For Refuse and the Mouse.

> Besides the deepest Cellar
> That ever Mason laid –
> Look to it by it's Fathoms
> Ourselves be not pursued –   (1182)

Looking back, Dickinson metaphorically set her memories where most of them actually originated, in a house, thus choosing the most apt image to embody the whole package of her past. Doing so, she suggested how acutely her consciousness of space, especially enclosed space, may have dominated her sensibility.

The poem's architectural features seem general enough to apply to any house, whether it was Emily's or another's. But, in fact, they fit the features of the Dickinson Mansion quite well. Front and back doors face each other across a long hallway in the main rectangle of the homestead. Its garret is ample now and was even larger in Emily's time before it was finished to form three additional rooms. And its cellar, still of the same dimensions as a hundred years ago, is notably deep, a sign of wealth in the nineteenth century,[2] and the one distinguishing reference which strongly hints that the house she had in mind was the one she knew so well. The granite and brick foundation of the homestead is over six feet deep.

What does Dickinson do, then, with the empirical facts of a house which was probably her family's? She makes them fit her subject – memory or the mind's present contents – by describing it as a house seen displayed on a drawing board in vertical cross section. Certain retained thoughts have particular places suitable to their nature. "Front" ones, those with the least history, are recent, while "back" ones are "antiquer," an adjective Emily once uses in a poem. In the attic are those memories left over or not in use, including herself *per se* ("Mouse" occasionally represents the poet elsewhere[3]), and their value remains ambiguous. But in the deep cellar are a wealth of horrendous thoughts of which she may not be thoroughly conscious except for their power to evoke fear. In an earlier version of the poem, Emily's last two lines revealed the intensity of her fright, "Leave me not ever there alone / Oh thou Almighty God!"

A real or ideal house used as the structural model for "Remembrance has a Rear and Front" suggests, as I have said, that Dickinson's actual surroundings and her reaction to them find their imprint in her poetry. Perhaps they do so in ways more subtle than aesthetic design, especially in light of her increasing seclusion at home. This hypothesis does not imply that the poet's mind was a tabula rasa dependent upon sense experience for its sole source of inspiration. The autonomy of poetic imagination never seems stronger than in this poet, an imagination which appears to be independent of perception, memory, or even the deepest, unconscious forces, so private is her language at times. Yet in one who chose withdrawal, indicating her acute sensitivity to space, it would seem more than likely that her immediate environment might contribute to her subject matter, her figures of speech, and even to her style. That it could also shape her understanding of the nature of art and of the limits of her own mind may seem less obvious. But in fact, she uses architectural imagery to speak of these central matters, epigrammatically to be sure, but with a heightened intensity, it seems, by fitting them to the imagery of house or home.

This poetic dependence upon home will be illustrated in the next few pages where I shall overview the nature of Dickinson's two houses, her shifting inner world, her assumptions about art, and her definition of her own consciousness. In another section, I shall move from the outer evidence of the poet's architecture – selected comments about home in prose or poetry – to examine her inscape. From here, I shall turn to Dickinson's variations on the home definition played against those found in the family's 1844 edition of Webster's. On the subject of vocabulary, the reader is invited to consult the Appendix, which describes the extent and nature of Emily's use of key words relating to space. A final part of the chapter opens with a discussion of four theorists' views of the symbolic significance of houses; it closes with a description of my own method.

II.

Since all but five of Dickinson's remaining poems were written at the Dickinson homestead, it is easy to forget that the poet had two houses to call home during her lifetime. For fifteen years (1840–55), from ages nine to twenty-five, she lived in another house besides her birthplace, a house on Pleasant Street (then North Street). The signal importance of this house is its influence in forming Emily's ideas about the idyllic possibilities of home, despite moments of despair and frustration she suffered there. This conditioning environment impressed on her memory indelible concepts about home, in effect molding her spatial awareness with singular force. When Emily wrote Austin, "Home is a holy thing . . ." she was speaking of the Pleasant Street house.

It is hardly surprising, then, that she was more melancholy than whimsical in reporting the family's return in 1855 to the homestead, or "The Mansion," as it was called.[4] Her letters after the move repeat the home-centeredness she had developed at the Pleasant Street place, but with certain crucial alterations, to be considered in chapters to follow. This attachment to home, almost involuntary in its intensity, one senses, was dramatically apparent eight years before the "transfer," as Emily labelled the move to Main Street. She could tolerate only two semesters at South Hadley Seminary (Mount Holyoke) in 1847 and 1848, as much as she enjoyed certain aspects of life there. After her return, while still in her twenties, she infrequently visited friends or relatives outside Amherst. By the time she was thirty-eight, after thirteen years in the Mansion, she confided to a friend, "You noticed my dwelling alone – To an Emigrant, Country is idle except it be his own. . . . I do not cross my Father's ground to any House or town."[5] Evidently, her "Country" could be approximated only at home, and to leave it would be as radical as emigration.

In later chapters, the architectural details of both the Pleasant Street house and the Mansion will be discussed to set the stage for particular poems in which Dickinson expands the value of concrete space. Now, however, my purpose is to note that in a significant number of her poems, the house or home figure synthesizes architectural reference, even description sometimes, with the revelation of mental or emotional states, at once giving a visual and figurative view of the poet's inner and outer worlds. Dickinson's precise focus is upon this latter world, the nuances of her inner life, not upon the design features of her actual house inside or out. But the family home repeatedly appears to serve as a reference at hand, revealing the significance she found suggested by the house itself or by its parts.

Many poems enlarge architectural fact to fit Emily's mood, as in "I dwell in Possibility / A fairer House than Prose," "I learned – at least – what Home could be," "I was the slightest in the House,"[6] but each varies the angle of approach, illustrating a particular nuance of meaning. Later on, these several angles will be separately treated, showing Dickinson's skill in varying her general pattern of borrowing elements from the house she knew to provide a scaffolding for her emotional, mental, or spiritual life.

Even when she speaks more broadly of art, elliptically referring to her poetic purpose, she also draws upon the house image. "Nature," she once observed, "is a Haunted House – but Art – a House that tries to be haunted."[7] This statement echoes many of Emily's encounters with spectres (sometimes, colloquially, "buggers") which began with close friends like Abiah Root and progressed inward until she realized that "One need not be a Chamber – to be Haunted."[8] Whether fearsome or not, at least such spectres were alive by the grace of the perceiver. Just so, Emily wished to build a house of poetry equally haunted by a life borne of her imagination.

At the center of her perceptions, consciousness itself, Dickinson again relied upon house and home imagery. The process by which this figure moved from exterior to interior, enhancing its importance as it increasingly became an essential part of the poet's psyche, appears at an apex in a comment Dickinson made at age forty-eight, seven years before her death: "Consciousness is the only home of which we *now* know. That sunny adverb had been enough were it not foreclosed."[9] The foreclosure, of course, was simply the end of life. By emphasizing *now,* Dickinson by contrast alluded to eternity, that "Bareheaded life" under the grass which worried her, she once said, "like a Wasp."[10] And the worrying began early, continuing all her life. Regardless of period, death stalks her work as either subject or assumption. So pervasive is the theme that she actually dwells in death or a deathlike life. It is an alternate shelter to her literal home. With this apprehension permeating her consciousness, no wonder her motifs of enclosure often echo that final closure or the emotional closures effecting a death-in-life.

But why did Dickinson feel that her *only* home in life was such a private one? Her poems and letters indicate that the gradual self-incarceration at home was much more complex than a withdrawal into certain, peaceful solitude. In more than one instance, she pointedly referred to the homestead as "father's house," implying it was not truly hers.[11] Even in her own bedroom, she confessed, "Sweet hours have perished here, / This is a timid room."[12] If her immediate setting was possessed by others or threatened by enfeebling projections ("this timid room"), no wonder Dickinson found her surest home to be exclusively her own intricate mind.

"Consciousness is the only home of which we *now* know" was probably a long time being born, cultured, sometimes unconsciously perhaps, through a series of experiences of which death was only one factor. Years before affirming that only the psyche could provide a home in this life, the poet probably intuited the idea. She was proud to be a Dickinson, to be someone quite distinctive from other folk, even certain relatives. She had only her immediate family in mind when in 1853, at twenty-two, she wrote her brother, Austin, "I think we miss each other more every day that we grow older, for we're all unlike most everyone, and are therefore more dependent on each other for delight."[13] A few weeks later, upon meeting her Newman cousins for the first time, she wrote Austin again: "The Newmans seem very pleasant, but they are not *like us*. What makes a few of us so different from others? It's a question I often ask myself."[14]

When Austin married three years later, though he lived next door, Emily may have felt "home" was much diminished by his leaving and she must thereafter rely more upon herself. In any case, these prose samples seem to illustrate in nascent form the arch-exclusiveness of a consciousness poetically confirmed a few years later:

> The Soul selects her own Society –
> Then – shuts the Door –
> To her divine Majority –
> Present no more –

"Unmoved," she continues in the second stanza, by the passing world of event or man, she announces in the third:

> I've known her – from an ample nation –
> Choose One –
> Then – close the Valves of her attention –
> Like Stone –
>
> (303)

The "One" may have been someone other than the poet. But Emily's early recognition of two selves, "me" and "my spirit," may have meant that her second consciousness was the one she chose for a sole companion.[15]

Beyond this poem, the epitome of the poet's mind at home only with itself, Dickinson's search for a meaning for *home* and her several uses of the word *house* indicate a consistent faith in a reality she defined somewhat differently from the common understandings of these seemingly simple words. For by equating home with consciousness, Emily did not solve a problem; she set herself one. She well knew that the mood, direction, and focus of her mind fluctuated, that her interior world turned, shifted, rose or sunk, that, in brief, it was in constant motion and change. She thus had a ceaseless quest: to explore for that place beyond all places, a true home. The central struggle of her life finally became, in effect, an endless pursuit of this ever-elusive locus.

Not only house and home but their corollaries – garrets, chambers, rooms; corridors, doorways, windows; and miscellaneous furniture (especially objects which are containers) – project the form of the poet's mind and thus bring us close to Dickinson's evolving "place," as person and poet. Other images also objectify her inner life but usually without the richness of overtone, or, more particularly, the range of subjects, incorporated in this one. They include all of her major concerns: self, family, faith, love, loneliness, madness, renunciation, nature, God, death, immortality, eternity, and of course, poetry. The image of home, taken from the poet's prose as well as her poetry, becomes a small but forceful expression of the most significant aspects of her sensibility.

III.

How close may we come to Dickinson's professed home, that interior world of which the soul and itself are the only society? Environment, obviously, is a key concept in a study of the poet's actual and poetic home. And the point at which the physical building as a perception joins the idea of home in her mind is an environment of a psychic sort, as "Remembrance has a Rear and Front" and the other poems mentioned above suggest. The word *inscape,* by which I mean an inward view or scene (to alter G. M. Hopkins's definition, to be discussed below), helps to define this composite of outer and inner realities and also to measure our distance from the poet. Encompassing two worlds, the word is akin to Erik Erikson's concept of identity, which, he insists, is intimately and constantly related to one's concrete environment, itself nothing less than "a pervasive actuality."[16] Inscape, then, may be used as a critical term designed to study a work of art as a product of its several sources of genesis, within and without the creator. Though it is "within" the mind, inscape contains a sociological as well as a psychological dimension. It thus encompasses the twin emphases upon a particular mind and its physical and cultural situation made by contemporary social science in defining identity.

Actually, the terms *identity, inscape,* and *imagination* appear to have a core meaning in common, though each may develop in separate directions from this shared center. Considering identity as "at homeness" in the world, psychologists and psychosociologists have increasingly recognized the importance of a realm of reality lying between the subjective and objective, a third "transitional" or "intermediate" area in which the first two are fused. Here Emerson's "Me" and "Not Me," man and nature, coalesce, and fantasy and fact unite.

Psychology sees the mother's role in reaching this transitional realm to be a crucial one; she must mediate between inner and outer worlds to preserve her infant's illusion of subjective creation of an object to a degree short of nurturing solipsism but extending to the vital function of fostering self-confidence in a world which shows itself potentially hostile. It is not hard to see the affinities this analysis has with concepts of inscape, as just described, and with classic views of the imagination. Charles Rycroft, a contemporary psychologist whose comments are the basis of the paragraph above, has recently remarked:

> Although this concept of a transitional reality, which mediates between the private world of dreams and the public, shared world of the environment, is perhaps the most important contribution made to psycho-analytical theory in the last thirty years, it must be admitted that from a general, cultural point of view it is not entirely original. It is, after all, what the poets call Imagination, that "intermediate faculty" (Coleridge), which enables its possessors to inhabit a world of "both what they half-create and what perceive" (Wordsworth), to "half-create the wondrous world they see" (Young's *Night Thoughts*, vi, 424).[17]

But inscape denotes a pattern or blueprint of the mind more general than identity or imagination, though all three may derive their materials from the same sources. The general classifying nature of inscape, in fact, was one of the qualities stressed by Gerard Manley Hopkins, who originated the term. After distinguishing at least three inscapes – of nature, of words, and of the poet – Hopkins finally found these undergirding forms gave a cosmic, ultimately Christological unity to the diversity of creation. So far did Hopkins carry the applicability of inscape that, for him, man was a "scape" for Christ, and conversely, Christ the inscape for humankind.

I shall continue to think of inscape as a structuring design of the mind which transcends or underlies any particular expression of ideas, but which is neither cosmic nor Christological in its extent. It is more like Hopkins's discussion of inscape in relation to the poet alone. J. Hillis Miller describes Hopkins's views:

> In writing poetry the poet expresses the innate pattern of his inscape. Poetry, like other arts, is creative not in the sense that it makes something out of nothing, but in the sense that it imposes upon the raw material of its art, words, a distinctive and highly pitched pattern. This pattern is a copy or echo of the pattern of selfhood in the poet. . . .
> . . . The artist and his work are different versions of the same inscape. They rhyme. Like a man who leaves his fingerprints on everything he touches, the poet makes his poems, whether he wishes to do so or not, in such a way that they match the pattern of his individuality. The poet is like a stamp or mold which shapes everything according to its design.[18]

Paradoxically, then, though the inscape is generic to the poet as a code or psychic switchboard, it is highly idiosyncratic to each artist. Hopkins appears to clarify this combination of particularity and generality in inscape when he speaks of it in relation to poetry or music. The following quotation also emphasizes the manner in which this stamp of selfhood makes itself known. Here Miller uses Hopkins's own words:

> . . . the inscape must be understood as so standing by itself that it could be copied and repeated. If not repetition, *oftening, over-and-overing, aftering* of the inscape must take place in order to detach it to the mind and in this light poetry is

speech which afters and oftens its inscape, speech couched in a repeating figure and verse is spoken sound having a repeating figure.[19]

In repetition, in fact, I find the most convincing reason for adopting and altering, for application to Dickinson, Hopkins's understanding of inscape. I do not think of inscape as an unquestionable entity, as he sometimes does. Rather, Dickinson's inscape (and in this case, her inscape of space) seems to me better approached as an "as if" phenomenon, pressing for recognition largely by the poet's characteristic return to motifs of enclosure and closure as seen in her poetics of house and home. These repetitions seem to point beyond themselves to what may be a psychic spatial formula or unifying form whose effects appear as an "oftening" or "aftering" in her work. Her inscape of space may not be something to be magnified under a microscope and "proved" to exist but only hinted at by its recurring reflection in her imagery. Thus, when the poet's inscape may appear in her house figure, we have only touched but not fathomed her sensibility.

When Dickinson uses *house* or *home* in letters or poems she may refer to actual buildings, or simultaneously to something much more, usually to a beloved, security, fulfillment, immortality, a state of peace or rest – or their reverse. Further, the two words may be synonymous but are not necessarily so. *Home* often appears to be a richer term than *house*. And that possibility emerges from its original definition, to which Emily probably never referred. Yet its dictionary meaning gives us a touchstone against which to test her understanding of the word.

In the Dickinson family edition of Noah Webster (Amherst, 1844), *home* bears at least five meanings. First, and most commonly, it signifies "a dwelling house; the house or place in which one resides. He was not at home." Significantly for Emily's attachment to the word, its basic sense is "probably to inclose, to cover or to make fast," in short, to secure in peace. Second, home is "one's own country." Third, "the place of constant residence; the seat." Fourth, the Christian concept of the "grave, death; or a future state." Here Webster quotes Eccles. 12:5, "Man goeth to his long *home.*" Fifth, it means "the present state of existence," illustrated by 2 Cor. 5:6, "Whilst we are at *home* in the body, we are absent from the Lord." Finally, as a related term, Webster defines homestead, "the place

of a mansion house; the inclosure or ground immediately connected with the mansion," which also means, especially in America, one's original place of residence.[20] The Dickinson homestead
was just such a place for Emily and her father. Both were born in
the family mansion (Edward in 1803, Emily in 1830).

Repeatedly the poet draws upon these definitions, giving them
her personal stamp. The concrete meanings of home, Webster's
first and third definitions, she uses as they are. But with "one's own
country" she expands the literal and finds both narrow and broad
significance. Her "country" may merely be a "Blue Peninsula" or
it can be enlarged to encompass the whole town. When she calls
herself "Amherst," she claims the identity because she has lived
nowhere else, and consequently is thoroughly native. More, she
describes the place where she ideally is – not, surely, the Connecticut Valley or America, but rather, quite grandly, "My Country is
Truth." She reaches for this place rather than coming from it.
Beyond precise mapping, it is paradoxically supremely particular
because it is a growing part of the inner woman, the liberated self
living in a "free Democracy."[21]

Dickinson's intense awareness of the wide range of possibility in
Webster's fifth definition, home as "the present state of existence,"
is nothing less than the major reason she claims attention as a
unique interpreter of the inner life. Home fluctuated for her between a place offering protected, contented calm – "A Peace, as
Hemispheres at Home," she cosmically put it in one poem – and
an anxious, empty state which enclosed the self on all sides, no
better represented than in the poem beginning, "Doom is the
House without the Door."[22] These two attitudes delimited her consciousness as it fluctuated toward first one, then the other. Home's
most precise location becomes evident when the poet takes it completely unto herself and admits, "One need not be a Chamber – to
be Haunted – / One need not be a House." Emily could thus reverse the root meaning of home and mock its positive purpose "to
inclose, to cover or to make fast." Home, sometimes a paradise of
possibility, could be transfigured by the poet into a prison, which
she felt either as confinement or, more menacingly, as nowhereness,
"Homeless at home."[23] But the turns she was capable of making
seem endless, for sometimes liberty is shunned and encapsulation
cherished, as in "A Prison gets to be a friend."[24]

Finally, Dickinson's "long home" also shifted between positive and negative poles. The Christian hope of an afterlife hovered near as a possibility, but the conditions of that "House of Supposition" in the "Acres of Perhaps" lay only in wonder, not certainty. Further, the "long home" could be simply underground, as in the poet's description of her father's empirical state after death, "Incarceration – Home."[25]

IV.

Webster's references to his cultural heritage again remind us that Dickinson, like her literary peers, was merely drawing upon a tradition in which the figure of house and home was so basic as to be an unconscious given. But the obvious has a way of being overlooked and its deeply effecting, and affecting, influence may be missed. So it seems with Dickinson's ambivalent attachment to home. To several theorists such an observation would be no news. Gaston Bachelard, Sigmund Freud, Erik Erikson, and Kenneth Burke have made landmark statements about the significance of house imagery. I should like to examine their views, not as models for a methodology, but rather to emphasize the primary importance of the house to both literary critics and psychologists, who illustrate the several nuances of meaning, in short, the reverberatory power, of this central symbol. With each, I shall test its applicability to understanding Dickinson.

In *The Poetics of Space* (1958) Bachelard discusses natural coverings, such as nests and shells, as well as man's own imitations of nature in buildings and their parts, from cellars to attics, and in furniture, from wardrobes to drawers and boxes. Natural or manmade, all these objects illustrate the overarching importance of the house. Bachelard states:

> . . . the house is one of the greatest powers of integration for the thoughts, memories and dreams of mankind. The binding principle in this integration is the daydream. Past, present and future give the house different dynamisms, which often interfere, at times opposing, at others, stimulating one another. In the life of a man, the house thrusts aside contingencies, its councils of continuity are unceasing. Without it, man would be a dispersed being. It maintains him through the storms of the heavens and through those of life. It is body and soul. It is the

human being's first world. Before he is "cast into the world," as claimed by certain hasty metaphysics, man is laid in the cradle of the house. And always, in our daydreams, the house is a large cradle. A concrete metaphysics cannot neglect this fact, this simple fact, all the more, since this fact is a value, an important value, to which we return in our daydreaming. Being is already a value. Life begins well, it begins enclosed, protected, all warm in the bosom of the house.[26]

In brief, Bachelard argues for the centrality of the house in anyone's life or daydreams. How much more so, then, for the home-encompassed Dickinson! But even more, Bachelard's insistence that the home image as image is a "value," perhaps coalescing all of one's values, and becoming the supreme one, strengthens the importance of examining Dickinson's use of it. Poetic testimony is, in fact, what Bachelard leans upon to support his thesis, because, for him, the poet has the consummate gift of daydream, imagination, and creativity combined. Bachelard's poetic sources are mostly French, but he also refers to Thoreau, Poe, and Melville. Much better than any of these, Dickinson (whom he does not mention) illustrates his claim that the house, as an oneiric (dream-encompassing) image, allows one to explore consciousness in its depths, complexities, and logical waywardness with a scope and inclusiveness no other image provides.

For example, Bachelard devotes an entire chapter to nests in nature and to the poet's adoption of the bird's house as a metaphor for the human home at its most vital center, using "nest" to express the deepest intimacy, the gentle warmth of enclosed space. This intimacy is, as we have seen, the positive root of Webster's definition of home, "to inclose, to cover and to make fast." Bird-like Dickinson, who told Thomas Wentworth Higginson, "I am small, like the Wren . . ."[27] and whose handwriting, for Higginson, resembled bird tracks (though the analogy should not be pressed too far!) seems to speak in a poem of nest as just such a refinement of home: "For every Bird a Nest – / Wherefore in timid quest / Some little Wren goes seeking round."[28]

Before Bachelard, of course, Freud observed that the house in dreams often represents the human body, and by extension, the mind as well.[29] This suggestion has weathered successive critical storms directed against his entire system and become a psychological commonplace. And Freud himself illustrated the power of this unconscious tendency to picture man or his psyche in architectural language by using the figure of a floor plan to describe his outline of the mind's several parts: unconscious, preconscious, and conscious.[30] Dickinson's poetry, like any poetry, so akin to dreaming and daydreaming,[31] seems to confirm his observations. She follows a human bent toward setting herself forth in house imagery all the more accentuated by her progressively withdrawn existence. "Remembrance has a Rear and Front" succinctly suggests the different strata of the poet's psyche, unconscious and conscious, probably quite unknown to Emily herself.

Erik Erikson has refined Freud's theories in his well known essay, "Womanhood and the Inner Space," in which he analyzes the importance of house and home, especially their interiors, as natural feminine symbols of a woman's morphology, that is, of the precious inner space of the womb. In discussions to come, Erikson's views will be scrutinized against the background of the sociology of the nineteenth-century American family and in comparison to male views of interior space. Here they suggest that one reason for Dickinson's sense of smallness (a fact to be explored in the next few pages) may be related to her self-image as woman, that is, in possession of a womb, as confused as that identity might have been with her continuing pose as a child. Erikson argues that the womb, though small, becomes a woman's most significant "place" as creative center of life itself.[32]

Emily Dickinson shunned any obvious expression of her anatomy; doctors had to observe her as she passed by a doorway in another room, and Lavinia sometimes served as her sister's stand-in at a dressmaker's fitting, so apparently withdrawn from impersonal touch the poet became.[33] She is direct only by describing herself in dream language in the poem "In Winter in my Room," to be discussed in chapter 3. But in another, "Her breast is fit for pearls," Emily describes the ideal home, in which "her" refers to Mrs. Samuel Bowles, wife of a man whom Emily adored, thus probably the poet's vision of her *own* most valued place:

> Her breast is fit for pearls,
> But I was not a "Diver" –
> Her brow is fit for thrones
> But I have not a crest.

> Her heart is fit for *home* –
> I – a Sparrow – build there
> Sweet of twigs and twine
> My perennial nest.   (84)

Though the ostensible point of the poem is Dickinson's esteem for Mrs. Bowles, the undercurrent of a desire for Mrs. Bowles's home, especially since the word "home" is underlined, rather than for its mistress's pleasure, comes to the surface in the last line with the possessive *My*. Probably Dickinson wanted both: a place in Mary Bowles's heart and some intimacy of the sort Mary shared with her husband. In any event, Emily seems to echo, in part, Erikson's observations, for she progresses from home to nest, which suggests the womb, the unspoken inner space of the physically fulfilled woman, an implication which practical and poetic etiquette of the nineteenth century would not allow to become explicit.

The phrase which ends the poem, "My perennial nest," shows how several of the poet's levels of being (physical and psychic) may be expressed by her peculiar consciousness of space, in a more particular way this time than in "Remembrance has a Rear and Front." In this case, it is not fear and loneliness which dominate but a hope of a home, despite the deprivation of a legal nest and the emptiness of the womb. Once again we see a singular instance of the way in which the house-home poetry and prose reflect the major concerns which shift through Dickinson's spatial inscape (although no one poem holds all at once). Like Emily herself, who experienced the range of her themes within the four walls of her house, her image of home draws into itself a spectrum of varying subjects which affect her at once.

In *Attitudes toward History*, Kenneth Burke speaks about this synthesizing effect of the synecdochic figure:

> A symbol may transcendentally fuse an author's attitude towards his parents, his friends, his State, his political party, his metier, his memories of childhood, his hopes for the future, etc. If you try to consider these various components analytically, there is no "logical order" by which to progress. You should talk about them all at once. You are really engaging yourself to make a dictionary without having the organizational convenience of the alphabet. . . .

. . . since the work of art is a synthesis, summing up a myriad of social and personal factors at once, an analysis of it necessarily radiates in all directions at once.[34]

By equal necessity, some measure of order is necessary to explore Dickinson's image of home, but the associational nature of it cannot be (does not allow itself to be) forgotten as a primary given. Burke elaborates this point in the *Philosophy of Literary Form*:

> Now, the work of every writer contains a set of implicit equations. He uses "associational clusters". And you may, by examining his work, find "what goes with what" in these clusters – what kind of acts and images and personalities and situations go with his notions of heroism, villainy, consolation, despair, etc. And though he be perfectly conscious of the act of writing, conscious of selecting a certain kind of imagery to reinforce a certain kind of mood, etc., he cannot possibly be conscious of the interrelationships among all these equations. Afterwards, by inspecting his work "statistically," we or he may disclose by objective citation the structure of motivation operating here. There is no need to "supply" motives. The interrelationships themselves *are* his motives. For they are his *situation;* and *situation* is but another word for *motives.* . . .
>   . . . And as regards our speculations upon the nature of "clusters" or "equations," would it not follow that if there are, let us say, seven ingredients composing a cluster, any one of them could be treated as "representing" the rest? *It is in this way that such an image as a "house" in a poem can become a "house plus," as it does proxy for the other ingredients that cluster about it (e.g., for the beloved that lives in the house, and is thus "identified" with it).* Usually, several of these other ingredients will appear surrounding the one temporarily featured. [italics mine][35]

Dickinson's image of house and home operates just so, as illustrated in the poems above. And since it does perform this fusing of multiple attitudes, "attitude" may include physical as well as psychic expressions of the self. Again, Burke notes a possible intimate correlation between mind and body. He calls the symbolic act

the dancing of an attitude. . . . In this attitudinizing of the
poem, the whole body may finally become involved, in ways
suggested by the doctrines of behaviorism. . . .
    The accumulating lore on the nature of "psychosomatic ill-
nesses" has revealed that something so "practical" as a bodily
ailment may be a "symbolic" act on the part of the body which,
in this materialization, *dances* a corresponding state of mind,
reordering the glandular and neural behavior of the organism
in obedience to mind-body correspondences, quite as the formal dancer reorders his externally observable gesturing to
match his attitudes.[36]

In Coleridge's verse, for example, Burke finds evidence of the
poet's known physical idiosyncracies. His odd habit of crisscrossing
a footpath as if indecisive about which side to take is, for Burke,
a tangible counterpart to his "labyrinthine mind."[37]
    Burke may be too sure that anatomy determines expression; his
correspondences between bodily and verbal postures seem too pat
and certain. Although he does not use these samples, one could ask
in what way in their writings is Milton blind, George Eliot grossly
featured, or Faulkner short? Yet if a literal, one-to-one identification is not convincing, perhaps Burke's suggestion may have rela-
vance to Dickinson's "situation," that is, *her* estimate about her
body and its relative size, whether that feeling corresponded to fact
or not, or to the actual proportions of her room in the homestead.
The following poem illustrates how she could twist measurable,
empirical evidence of architecture or of her physique to suit her
self-image:

> I was the slightest in the House –
> I took the smallest Room –
> At night, my little Lamp, and Book –
> And one Geranium –   (486)

Emily's placement of a sense of smallness in the first line emphasizes its singular importance to her. Since this facet of her mind, as
it relates to her physical size, has been ignored until now, the subject deserves a few pages of discussion, incorporating facts from her
life and evidence from her poetry. Emily probably wrote this poem
in the Mansion sometime in the early 1860s, not in the Pleasant
Street house, which is now razed and whose measurements were not

recorded. In her homestead bedroom, contrary to Emily's testimony, space was ample, equal, in fact, to the room of her sister, Lavinia. Both rooms were fifteen feet square and ten feet high. Apparently the poet *felt* herself to be small and, by projection, her bedroom became small as well.

If Emily's poetic room did not represent her actual one, then all the more reason we might suspect that her physical assertion of being slight and small was not strictly accurate and that the poetic *I* is not true to the flesh-and-blood Emily. So the known facts seem to suggest. Physically, Emily was a slight child and young woman, even though her sister, Lavinia, once reported she was "getting fat" (in proportion to her thinness, Vinnie's comment seems facetious). Though thin, as her daguerreotype confirms, Emily was not short, but rather of medium height, according to her niece, Martha Dickinson Bianchi.[38] A dress which probably dates from the last decade of her life also indicates her height to be about 5 feet 5 inches, average to tall for a woman of her day. Emily herself in a nonpoetic moment reported to a school friend in 1846, two years before her daguerreotype was taken, "I am now very tall & wear long dresses near[l]y."[39]

Yet not long afterward Dickinson began to think of herself as small, as indicated by the poem above, and by a letter to Higginson in which she admitted, "My size felt small – to me."[40] In context, she signifies that she means her stature as a poet, her situation as an artist vis à vis the larger world of accepted culture. Believing herself to be small in this light, Dickinson identified with the little and inconspicuous in nature: the sparrow, daisy, mouse, or even "a hay." This self-image, pervasive beyond actual fact, appears to have so conditioned her consciousness that the "transitional object" not only of her room but of herself, as a physical presence, took on the qualities of her perceptions rather than the true dimensions of the empirical world. In short, from the evidence of this poem, her chamber and her person reflected her spatial inscape, losing their real dimensions to the poet's evaluation of herself.

Well into her forties (she died at fifty-five), Dickinson referred to herself as "little," as she was when a child. This physical sense of limited size, combined with a life lived exclusively at home with her parents, probably contributed to Emily's childlike attitude. A frequent pose among several, she retained it until her parents' deaths finally imposed an alteration in her role at home. "Small-

ness," then, supported both a prolonged sense of childhood as well
as of insignificance, despite her assumption of regal titles. These, in
fact, seem almost desperate efforts to achieve status.

A good example is the poem "I'm wife – I've finished that – /
That other state – / I'm Czar – I'm 'Woman' now – / It's safer so."[41]
The "other state" is girlhood, Emily makes clear in the second
stanza, and she boasts that it was pain compared to the comfort of
maturity. But that claim seems empty. If she is wife, she does not
specify that Christ is the bridegroom, and if not he, then who in
actuality? Herself perhaps? She ends, "I'm 'Wife'! Stop there!" but
the shout seems small. *Small* and its comparatives are, in fact, among
her most frequently used words. And she uses its synonym, *little,*
equally often.[42] Finally, even when she omits specific references to
size, she worries about inconsequence, as in "I'm nobody! Who are
you?" even though this query doubtless had its element of irony.

Dickinson's sense of physical littleness appears transformed but
recognizable in the succinctness of her expression and typical shortness of her poems. The longest one, "I cannot live with You," a
"flood subject" for the poet, as she said of her most overflowing
concerns, is only forty-nine lines.[43] Perhaps one can say that smallness, compactness and concision *may* express the poet as she looked
within to her situation or *motivation* (in part, unknown to her),
as Burke puts it. Every important aspect of her poetry, and increasingly of her letters as well (the later ones read like telegrams compared to the prolix early ones), seems to "represent" Emily's view
of her body and of related personality patterns as well.

The critics Bachelard and Burke have reinforced my own sense
of the encompassing nature of the house image, and Burke has suggested the somatic source of Dickinson's frequent use of *small* and
little. In the same way that they point to parallels between the
physical self and literary expression, the psychologists Freud and
Erikson indicate correspondences between the body and psychology. Doing so, they require further attention, while Bachelard and
Burke, perhaps echoed in later pages, will not be treated again. As
helpful as all four theorists have been, none determines my approach, and that is the subject to which I now return.

If home as a symbol synthesizes a miscellany of perceptions,
from personal items as idiosyncratic as height and room size to
social factors as general as Webster's definitions and God's mansions, where does one begin to comprehend their interconnection?

Given the levels of reality intermeshing in the image, an analysis of Dickinson's homes and houses would rightly "radiate in all directions at once," as Burke says.

Unlike the plastic arts, criticism enjoys and labors under more confinement. Not the slave of logic, it nonetheless must follow some sequential order even while it argues that that order is arbitrary. Such is the nature of the categories given below which start, as Dickinson's poems often do, with the concrete. These four areas of interest have been my general plan for pursuing Emily Dickinson's spatial inscape:

1. House *per se*: the architecture of Dickinson's two houses, attending to special areas of value to the poet

2. Home: the meaning of Dickinson's designated places and of the whole house within the dynamics of familial relationships

3. The poet's use of spatial motifs, especially domestic architecture and household objects, to represent her femininity

4. The poet's use of spatial poetry to suggest or illustrate her position as a woman and artist, a position which also involves her principal concerns.

All these elements were once intermingling in the poet's mind and together comprised her inscape of home. Yet some separation of treatment is necessary in order to discover how and why she assembled them so idiosyncratically. Thus within any single chapter some of the four items above may be interwoven, although facts of building design and biography, psychology and literary analysis will be treated in a stated order as I shall outline early in each chapter and not, strictly speaking, simultaneously. It is true that such elements as house and home are so intimately related that they beg first for description, then, quickly following, interpretation. Categories 3 and 4 may be equally intimately related to the other two but they are best separated to some degree, even though they may appear within a chapter which begins with architecture.

In reference to category 3, I should explain my use of Freud and Erikson to suggest the way in which Dickinson's imagery may speak of her sexuality. Recently, psychologists have joined literary critics in decrying the use of psychoanalysis by overly zealous biographers of artists as too often reductionistic or ignorant of Freud's own sense of limit in probing the center of creativity.[44] Such criticism may come too late (one thinks of John Cody's book about Emily Dickinson), but it would be a loss if its effect where to prohibit all use of psychological insights. Such insights, with their roots in literary interpretation, may still be helpful, if approached with skepticism and restraint. In the same manner that Karen Horney and others are respected revisionist Freudians, so also should there be a place for the literary critic or biographer who scrutinizes psychology with a tentative, judging eye or, in my case, finds Horney, on a particular tangent from Freud, quite convincing (see note 82, chapter 3).

I first align Dickinson's attitudes with certain concepts of Freud and Erikson, since they all touch basic realities, the givens of biology and the experience of neurotic feeling or behavior. In life itself or in literature and history, their sources converge. More specifically, with consideration to feminist objections, I find that Freud's observations on house symbolism and Erikson's on female physiology impinge on one of my principal points, namely, that Emily Dickinson's body was her most private house, home, or chamber. Since her consciousness of space directly relates to her self-evaluation as a physical being, this material contributes to a primary part of the poet's spatial inscape.

Second, I consider the analyses of Freud and Erikson to be as imaginative in their hypothetical forms as Dickinson's poems, allowing for differences in purpose and style. The three are fellow artists. Thus when the scientists' statements appear to complement the poet's meanings, I shall intend them merely as amplifying suggestions, not as the truth. Further, I am not uncritical of their theories and extensions of them, especially in Freud's case, and of course, I hardly exhaust the possibilities they suggest. But my study is not principally a psychological investigation in depth; thus this sort of data figures only briefly and at selected places.

In brief, the psychologists enter this study in a minor way on a major point, Emily Dickinson's conscious or unconscious view of herself. My continuing assumption is that while both writers may enlarge and enliven Dickinson, nonetheless her poetry, like their theories, is unique, and her symbols are extraordinarily personal, probing beyond biology, psychology, or anyone's "explanations," not excepting my own.

If my approach of employing four areas of interest may be made to work, then the unity of Emily's outer and inner worlds, coalescing in her inscape, should be kept before the reader as he holds a number of ideas available while only one may be under discussion. In this manner, I hope to parallel the organic nature of the poet's mind. I cannot critically duplicate how myriad impressions, step-by-step, merged into poetic image. That synthesizing occurred in the mystery of the poet's insight, the links between multiple perceptions doubtless unknown to herself. Yet I can enumerate the angles reflected by the image, posit her inscape as a sieve of consciousness (both of perceiving and conceiving), and show, at last, that the image of home, though seemingly insignificant or "small," is heavily freighted with her most vital thoughts and feelings. In its richness, it is much like Emily Dickinson's valuation of her literal place at home, "Area – no test of depth."

FIGURE 1. *The Dickinson children, painted by O. S. Bullard in 1840. Emily, age nine, is at left; Austin was ten and a half and Lavinia six. Courtesy of Harvard College Library.*

Chapter 2
The house on Pleasant Street

How we delight to build our recollections upon some basis
of reality – a place, a country, a local habitation!
WASHINGTON IRVING

Emily Dickinson owes her views of home to the two houses referred to in chapter 1, the Pleasant Street place and the Main
Street Mansion. The former, though the subject of Millicent Todd
Bingham's *Emily Dickinson's Home,* has been overshadowed, like
a faded sepia print, by the Mansion, whose imposingly handsome
brick facade, reproduced in an 1858 lithograph, has dominated
the popular view of Emily's lifetime home from her day to ours.
The razing of the house on Pleasant Street about twenty years ago,
the notoriety given Dickinson's withdrawal at the homestead, and
the composition of almost all her extant poetry there have helped
to obscure the importance of a place which housed Emily for fifteen years, 1840 to 1855.

Yet it is indispensable for understanding the poet's inscape to
recall that the Pleasant Street house was Emily's environment during her later childhood, adolescence, and young adulthood. It appears that her more positive attitudes about home developed here.
She once called this house, "my palace in the dew,"[1] while the
Mansion was not only "father's house," but "this old castle," the
epithet she gave it in 1851, four years before the family's return.
It was "haunted" as well.[2] Still the poet suffered deeply troubled
moments during her Pleasant Street years, so that her forms of behavior which began at this period, her set of responses to the world,
were only grooved and solidified in later years at the Mansion.
These responses, Dickinson's habit of existence, will be explored
in this chapter. They involve a complex of formalized family relationships, a sense of Emily's own superiority – however insecure
and wavering it might be – and a preference for solitude.

Though the Pleasant Street house is crucial in the development
of the poet's image of home, Emily's earliest years in the Mansion,

from birth to age nine, first deserve attention in order to examine the origins of her attitudes and behavior. These only become overt and personally verified when Emily, at eleven, speaks in her own voice in letters written from Pleasant Street. But the evidence of her parents' and relatives' reports gives an exceptionally vivid picture of the poet as a young child and of her parents both as models of their sex and as disciplinarians.

I.

At the time of Emily's birth, December 10, 1830, the Mansion was shared by Edward Dickinson and his father, Samuel Fowler Dickinson, who had originally built the house about 1813. Edward Dickinson had moved his little family only eight months before from a duplex arrangement elsewhere in Amherst with the Widow Jemima Montague.[3] Doubling up was nothing new to them, then, and they were accustomed to such sharing as the 1830 deed stipulated. The property line ran right down the middle of the front hall and was vertically inclusive, from garret to cellar.[4] When the elder Dickinson was forced to sell his share in 1833 and accept a post at Lane Seminary in Cincinnati, the David Mack family bought his half of the homestead, and thus the Mansion continued as the dual family dwelling it remained until 1840, when Emily's family moved to Pleasant Street and David Mack became sole owner of the homestead. With her grandfather's family and then the Macks under the same roof during her earliest years, no wonder Emily might refer to "pretty perpendicular times" in the old manse. Her memory was doubtless filled with the fact that beyond the central hallway to the east that part of the house was not her home.[5]

One definition of home, Webster's reminds us, is "the present state of existence." For the young Emily that existence was clearly dominated by her parents. In the same way that the house, roughly divided in half, probably gave Emily two ways of looking at the Mansion, "ours" and "theirs," so, too, she had two very different models of adulthood in her mother and father. Whichever traits of theirs she adopted for her own cannot be measured quantitatively – that is, one cannot say she was more like her mother than her father or vice versa – but there appear to be aspects of each parent which Emily identified with or, on the contrary, found alien to her tastes. And the evidence certainly contradicts the thesis of John Cody, who argues in *After Great Pain: The Inner Life of Emily Dickinson* (1971) that the poet did not identify with her mother nor even feel any deep feeling for her until Mrs. Dickinson became an invalid following a stroke in 1875.

Cody raises Emily's mother to attention to eclipse her in his own way once again, unfortunately a treatment typical of his whole approach and final evaluation of the Dickinson family. He exclusively relies upon the adequacy of psychology to interpret art and the artist with a confidence foreign to Freud's own sense of its limitations.[6] Thus he commits errors of method (rigidity and contextual blindness), generalization (inferences become facts), and tone (insistently narrow). Mr. and Mrs. Dickinson are the first to suffer at Cody's belabored and repetitive hand, emerging from his treatment caricatured. Edward Dickinson's capacity for natural affection and warmth, which tempered his unbending public self, is effectively submerged by Cody's insistence that inner ambitions made him a manipulative, uncommunicative, and fearful figure. And Cody ignores Mrs. Dickinson's efforts toward concerned mothering, reducing her attentions to Emily to cold indifference and snivelling servitude within the family. His chapter about them, "Earth's Confiding Time," closes with a rude, inadequate dismissal:

> Though Edward Dickinson propelled and deflected the many tormented currents of his daughter's development, the original imbalance began with the mother. The peculiar strength and bias of Edward Dickinson's personality then perpetuated and reproportioned, after its own characteristics, the existing disequilibrium. Finally, Emily Dickinson relinquished all hope of easing her sense of affectional deprivation or establishing her sexual identity through her parents.[7]

Since Edward Dickinson has been the focus of attention as the dominant parent in Emily's life, Cody has done a service in shifting that focus to his wife, Emily Norcross Dickinson. But his kind of scrutiny is both more and less than she deserves, for it is almost wholly negative. A great deal of evidence exists to show that Cody's views are too strongly put and that Mrs. Dickinson was not solely the painful nonentity he argues that Emily found her to be. Most of his argument hinges upon two statements Emily made to Thomas

FIGURE 2. *Emily Norcross Dickinson at age thirty-six, painted by O. S. Bullard in 1840. Courtesy of Harvard College Library.*

Wentworth Higginson in the 1870s: (1) "I never had a mother," and (2) "I always ran Home to Awe when a child, if anything befell me. He was an awful mother, but I liked him better than none."[8]

If a mother may be defined as the person most closely associated with her child's nurture, physical and personal, at least under normal circumstances, then Emily Dickinson's statements lose at least some of their force. Or rather, they gain force, but only as a disavowal of *certain aspects* of Mrs. Dickinson's personality. For it would appear that Emily adopted notable traits of her mother's while remaining significantly different in other ways.

In what manner was Mrs. Dickinson very much Emily's mother, that is, her dominant model of womanhood? Most strikingly, Mrs. Dickinson preferred to be at home; she was not in the least a public figure, though she doubtless did her part in the entertaining of political or educational friends which Edward Dickinson became known to be scrupulously careful not to neglect. She infrequently left Amherst except for visits to her home in Monson and occasional trips to Boston, despite Edward's wishes to have her travel and to miss nothing when she did.[9] Public notice of Mrs. Dickinson was limited to references of her services in the Cattle Show or mention of the choice samples of figs and apples she grew.[10] To act almost solely within the arena of home was as true for Mrs. Dickinson's mother as it was for her. Betsy Norcross's obituary in September 1829 could have been written equally well for her daughter:

> When individuals who are pious, amiable and useful are removed by death we may justly lament the event. . . . Few have sustained with greater fidelity and propriety the duties of her station than Mrs. Norcross, humble and retiring in her disposition. It was in the bosom of her family and among those who observed her in domestic life, that her prudence, and affection, regard to the happiness of all around her, appeared most conspicuous.[11]

Emily Dickinson, the poet, thus had two generations of kinswomen who lived happily well within the nest of home. But beyond this behavior, which would have been typical of many women of the era, Mrs. Dickinson's dominant social attitudes appear to have been inherited by her older daughter. From the letters Edward and Emily Dickinson exchanged during their early married years, while he attended sessions of the state legislature in Boston, it is clear that Emily, the mother, was naturally timid, inclined to be nervous, and at times, overcome with anxiety.[12] Relying upon her husband because of these traits, she suffered spells of acute loneliness which she nevertheless professed to be able to conquer.[13] In a word, there was frankness in her description of life at home, but a perserverance in face of the necessity to lead the small family virtually alone for several weeks at a time. Intermittently, there were boarders or young girls who gave a hand, but they were extra mouths to feed, and in one instance, a mother's helper turned out to be questionably sane.[14]

Other preferences of Mrs. Dickinson prefigured Emily's own. She was inclined to be homesick, in fact was so, for her Monson folk, even *before* her marriage and departure for Amherst.[15] In the same period, the few weeks before they were wed, Emily Norcross wrote to Edward, "I think it best that we stand up alone as I do not wish for company."[16] Further, despite the popular view that Mrs. Dickinson enjoyed spending all her energies housekeeping for her family, one must consider the comment of Lavinia Norcross, who wrote her sister after she had settled in Amherst, reporting on the appearance of the house and flowers in Monson: ". . . the chambers and lower rooms look as neat as when you was at home – if not *a little* neater."[17] Allowances for sisterly playfulness aside, which suggests that Emily Norcross had no special interest or expertise in housekeeping, it does appear that the maidenly Mrs. Dickinson had made time for thought, or else her brother's wedding gift, three volumes of Cowper's *Poems*, would have been strangely inappropriate.[18] Most especially, Mrs. Dickinson's love of plants was an avocation clearly bequeathed her daughter. Edward assured his wife, "Your plants are all safe and flourishing – the roses in the door-yard are in blossom – and the garden vegetables are coming on very fast . . ." when Emily was visiting in Monson in late spring, 1829.[19]

These attitudes and activities appear repeated in Emily Dickinson, the daughter. Her former teacher at the Amherst Academy, Daniel T. Fiske, reminisced in 1894: "I remember her as a very bright, but rather delicate and frail looking girl; an excellent scholar, of exemplary deportment, faithful in all school duties; but somewhat shy and nervous."[20] And the fifteen-year-old Emily admitted to her close friend Abiah Root, "You were always dignified, e'en when a little girl, and *I* used, now and then, to cut a timid caper."[21] The caper, though a step away from her mother's habitual gait, was still "timid." Emily's withdrawal is more than evidence that Mrs. Dickinson's "I do not wish for company" suited her perfectly. And her own, "[Pestilence] is more classic and less fell than [housecleaning],"[22] would have made any chamber for which she was responsible probably beyond report of her Aunt Lavinia.

~ Mrs. Dickinson's interest in poetry may have led her to read verse to her three children and thus early stimulated Emily's talent. She had a few anthologies of verse to which she might have introduced them, but none for children. The *Sabbath School Visitor*, which Edward sent to Austin and Emily in 1837 – "I tho't it would please them, so I subscribed for it"[23] – was not the place for valuable verse. Nonetheless, Mrs. Dickinson was doubtless as earnest about the education of her brood as was her husband. Her interest in Austin's examinations at the Easthampton school in 1842 was such that, despite her husband's suddenly taking ill, she attended, for as Aunt Elisabeth wrote Austin, " – your Mother especially, has looked forward to the time with *uncommon* anticipations."[24]

Besides the natural encouragement to learning which a devout Congregationalist mother would have provided for her children, Mrs. Dickinson seems to have been an affectionate mother as well. The first words of the infant Emily, age 2½, reported by her Aunt Lavinia, were, "Do take me to my mother," a request brought about by a frightful lightning storm which suddenly arose as the two travelled from Amherst to Monson, little Emily protected on her aunt's horse only by the lady's cloak.[25] She might have asked simply to be taken home, but not have mentioned her mother. And even though Lavinia reports that "She speaks of her father and mother occasionaly [*sic*] & *little Austin* but does not express a wish to see you," that could have meant Emily felt so secure about her place at home that she was not anxious about a loss of affection, and thus did not need to have it confirmed. Rather, Lavinia's continuing profile, "She is very affectionate & we all love her very much," suggests that her parents had succeeded in giving her the security which only familial love may provide, the well-known requisite for loving others. Even Lavinia's "She dont appear at all as she does at home – & she does not make but very little trouble –" could easily allude not to a basic dislocation of sympathies between mother and daughter at home, but rather to the usual competitiveness and normal bickering common in any family with children who are close in age.[26]

One of Mrs. Dickinson's letters to Emily, though written in 1844 from Pleasant Street, assumes a long-term warm and happy relationship with her daughter. Since the mother's voice has so rarely been heard, it is worth quoting her letter extensively (Emily was visiting the Norcross family in Boston):

> As I know you will be glad to hear from us, I will improve this favourable opportunity, in saying how we are at home. Lavinia was quite feeble the morning you left us, but you will be happy to learn that she has improved quite fast. She is now able to assist me considerable, she is very kind and gets along better without you, than I thought. . . . We are lonely without, but we hope you are enjoying yourself, and that it will be a benefit to you to be away from home a little while. . . . I understand the Monson Friends start for Boston this week, Aunt Lavinia will really have quite a family. I trust you will lend a helping hand. Some of your young friends are often in to make enquiries for you.[27]

The formalisms which enable a family to remain together, the polite manners bequeathed by culture which prevent the eruption of antagonisms which inevitably arise in the most intimate of relations, *may* have dictated the tone of this letter of Mrs. Dickinson's. Doubtless they disguised irritations which any child entering his teens (Emily was $13\frac{1}{2}$ at this time) usually causes his parents as he tests his nascent independence. And they probably hid disaffections of a deeper sort as well. But those supposed disaffections, one feels, reading this relatively simply phrased note, seem more likely to have been felt by Emily for one reason or another than by Mrs. Dickinson. Her beginning, "As I know you will be glad to hear from us," her middle, "We are lonely without you, but we hope you are enjoying yourself, and that it will be a benefit to you to be away from home a little while," and her end, "Some of your young friends are often in to make enquiries for you," are the comments of a concerned, pleasant and affectionate mother. The single admonition is a mild one: lend a hand when it is needed.

If some measure of truth does lie at the core of what the poet says, despite her hyperbole, then in what way may her two statements about her mother be accurate? I began this discussion saying that Emily may have been rejecting certain aspects of Mrs. Dickinson's personality, characteristics, I now suggest, over which she had a choice, while adopting others, over which she may have had little or no control. If one's mother is timid, shy, and inclined to be nervous, one's own unconscious conditioning is likely to be similarly molded, as Emily's apparently was. But if a child, like Emily, is intelligent, curious, and spirited, then despite involuntarily inheriting his – or in this case her – mother's habits, she may be critical of them and others and thereby strive toward a certain autonomy no matter how pervasive the parental personality may be. Such seems to have been the case with Emily Dickinson and her mother.

Almost all of the poet's denigrating references to Mrs. Dickinson have to do with her mental capacities, even the one, "I always ran Home to Awe when a child. . . ." And in scrutinizing them, it is essential to note the date of Emily's remarks. None are available until she has reached her legal majority, that is, a position at home in which she was beginning to lead a rather anomalous role, not yet a spinster, yet far from being betrothed. Such a position would have encouraged any tendency toward independence which she felt during adolescence, a bent amply illustrated by her lively letters during this period. In one, written at fourteen, her jesting poorly disguises a certain degree of self-esteem; she writes Abiah Root, "If you will [come for a visit], I will entertain you to the best of my abilities, which you know are neither few nor small."[28] In February 1852, Emily, barely two months past her twenty-first birthday, reports to Austin that their mother had blamed her "unobstrusive faculties" for the fact that the lecture her husband took her to the evening before had been "too high."[29] It is not clear if Mrs. Dickinson so labelled her own talents, or if the words are Emily's. But the daughter's later opinion, written to Higginson ten years after in April 1862, has become bluntly assertive: "My mother does not care for thought."[30]

Mrs. Dickinson did care for *some* thought, as her brother's wedding gift of Cowper's poetry suggested, but by the time Emily was old enough to know her as a person she had become largely encapsulated in wifely obligations and domestic chores, an occasional lecture or book breaking her routine. Naturally, then, Emily, whose love of literature and writing were well established by the time she attended Amherst Academy, would have regarded her mother as intellectually deprived, even though she had received an adequate amount of maternal attention and care during her crucially formative childhood years.

What do Emily's statements to Higginson in the 1870s then signify? They are, it seems, a final estimate which had cruelly progressed through the years, increasingly distorting the real Mrs. Dickinson. Reminiscing, the poet sought causes for her peculiar life, commonly enough, at the expense of her parents, in order to elicit sympathy from her esteemed correspondent, who represented the ultimate in culture, as one critic has observed.

In short, it appears that as Emily advanced in age her judgment about her mother (until Mrs. Dickinson suffered a stroke in 1875) became harsher, probably, as Thomas Johnson suggests, a consequence of her acute, though voluntarily induced, withdrawal and loneliness. For if Dickinson refers to love and affection when she says, "I never had a mother," the evidence of her parents' and relatives' correspondence contradicts her complaint. If, on the other hand, she refers to intellectual company, then this comment and the one of 1874, "I always ran Home to Awe when a child, if anything befell me. He was an awful Mother, but I liked him better than none," express Emily's keen sense of lacking a mother who could match her own sensibility and be adequate to her spiritual and emotional trials. If Mrs. Dickinson's mental abilities were scorned, despite her probable willingness to comfort her daughter, would Emily seek her out in a time of trouble? And trouble, recalled when the poet was over forty, would more than likely not have remained in her memory as an inconsequential, merely childish sort of problem.

Until now Mrs. Dickinson has been deprived of the highly significant influence she had upon her daughter, well beyond giving her the same name. To summarize, that role was essentially the one which may be traced to Grandmother Norcross, the mild, self-effacing woman who served her family and friends with wisdom and affection. She was the familiar prototype of the ostensibly contented nineteenth-century woman at home. That this type was quintessentially female hardly needs arguing, and to the extent that this role was the norm, even the ideal, for a woman of the period – both as wife and as mother – Cody's insistence that Mrs. Dickinson failed to provide Emily with a model of loving femininity with which her daughter might achieve a healthy sexual identity seems not only misleading but maligning. Yet if Dickinson adopted her mother's *public* role as the shy, retiring lady at home, her *private* position, the product of her intelligence and independence, made her disdain Mrs. Dickinson's apparently meek acceptance of her domesticity, the lot nineteenth-century society dictated for the average woman, unalleviated by mental exercise.[31] She could, therefore, be tersely dismissive in retrospect, feeling that she had been deprived of a complete mother, a guide and companion in thought.

To Mrs. Dickinson, then, one may look for the source of a number of Emily's overt habits: her reserve, her love of solitude and home, her domestic dependency, and her nervousness. Mrs. Dickinson also bequeathed her daughter a delicate constitution doubtless made all the more susceptible by their mutual tendency to be overly anxious. Interestingly, Edward Dickinson tended to reinforce these outward behavioral patterns and physical traits. But his special contribution to his older daughter was to her private self, the inner woman whose desire for independence reached the same heights as her father's, if it did not exceed his. My point is that if Emily Dickinson did not fully adopt her mother's life style, it was not for lack of dedicated mothering, which she clearly received. Rather, the idiosyncrasy of her spinsterhood, markedly more severe than that of other maiden ladies of her town and time, lies more obviously in her adoption of the two conflicting behavior patterns represented by her parents. These she struggled to unite in a tense, uneasy combination of public and private images within her own personality. She could therefore be disdainful of housekeeping and wary of men on the one hand, while she served as an extreme example of the "woman at home" dedicated to the comforts of the men in her family on the other.

The most obvious item about Edward Dickinson, previously ignored, is his constant devotion to home, a devotion which matched, and perhaps in its own way exceeded, his wife's. Even observers outside the family noted his dedication to home, family, and Amherst. The Reverend Jonathan Jenkins chose Edward's loyalty to home as the theme for his funeral sermon in 1874, in which Mr. Dickinson's attachment to his native soil earned him a comparison with a parallel Old Testament figure, Samuel.[32]

In the same way that Emily Norcross Dickinson seems to have adopted her own mother's external patterns, so Edward Dickin-

FIGURE 3. *Edward Dickinson at age thirty-seven, painted by O. S. Bullard in 1840. Courtesy of Harvard College Library.*

son's love of his home probably derived from his father's deep affection for the homestead. Samuel Fowler Dickinson longed to
return to Amherst and the Mansion after his departure in 1833.
One of his daughters, Catherine, wrote to her brother Edward
from Cincinnati in 1835:

> You probably know that Samuel [another brother] has offered
> to purchase our old mansion for father, provided he can ob-
> tain it. It is his wish to have some place which we can call
> home & where we can spend our summers if we choose . . . he
> thinks that he can not be happy in purchasing any other situa-
> tion, but the one where we all were ushered into this beauti-
> ful world. Samuel . . . will go to Amherst & see what can be
> done.[33]

Yet, as Catherine continued, it was evident that the elder Dickinson would not truly be content upon his return:

> [Father] says that if he should get it – & we all go home again –
> there would be nothing for him to do in Amherst – he would
> find his place occupied by others – & if he had nothing to do –
> he would be *unhappy* as ever. . . . His spirits are completely
> broken down & probably will never rise again. . . .[34]

Further, Catherine provided a glimpse of Mrs. Samuel Dickinson
(Lucretia Gunn), which reinforced in Edward's family any Norcross tendencies to remain aloof from company:

> Mother is not willing to stay here & I wonder not . . . she had
> no other very particular friends here of course – because she is
> not apt to form acquaintances or attachments. . . .[35]

After Samuel's death in 1838, Catherine and her sister Mary
both quickly wrote their mother, again mentioning their father's
desire to return to Amherst, despite the ambivalence noted in the
report above. Catherine bemoaned her negligence and that of all
the Dickinson children of her generation:

> I am grieved that we have done so little for his comfort while
> we had it in our power & this is the only sting. It seems as if
> his depression of spirits caused his sickness which terminated
> his life – & I cannot but think that if we children had com-
> plied with his wishes & given him a comfortable home in his
> old age – he might have been spared longer. . . .[36]

And her sister Mary added:

> Ever since I can remember his life has been one of anxiety
> & care & disappointment. Now we trust his trials are ended.
> He has done much for his children – they nothing for him.
> I am grieved that he could not have had a *home* for his last
> years. . . .[37]

Mary then continued in a curiously mixed tone of assurance and
admonition about financial matters:

> As to a home for you & Elisabeth [the youngest of their chil-
> dren] you need have no anxiety. You will of course come East
> as soon as your affairs are settled, & not of course until every-
> thing *is* settled & *paid*. We shall hear from other members of
> the family & consult with them upon the best plans for you &
> write you.[38]

Lucretia Gunn Dickinson might have been forewarned about
her children's lack of interest from their neglect of her husband.
Removing first to North Sunderland, only a few miles north of
Amherst, she reassured Edward about living with him, but in a
rambling and confused way:

> I know not what to do your Aunt & Mary seem to have
> enough to do without waiting on me I have been hoping to
> get along without troubling you with my situation but have
> at last made up my mind it would be best I do not ask to go
> to your house for I know it is not convenient. . . . I know my
> complaints trouble you but what can I do I have no one to
> look to *but* my Children.[39]

A few months later in the same year, 1839, Mrs. Dickinson, now in
Enfield, wrote Edward again, this time more plaintively:

> . . . at best I am a frail tenement, when I have turns which I
> frequently do that my life is in iminent [*sic*] danger although
> it would not prolong my life a moment, yet it would be a satis-
> faction to be with some of my Children when these seasons
> occur.
>   Catherine wrote me not long since the reason why she does
> not make me a Home. it is because her Husband does not like
> *Old Folks* it is likely the same reason operates throughout the
> family.[40]

A short period later, Mrs. Dickinson, still in Enfield, and far from home, died.[41]

Edward's behavior vis à vis his parents in their desire to return to the homestead invites speculation because it bears upon his own attitude toward the place and, indirectly, Emily's as well. It appears that Edward did as little as any of Samuel and Lucretia's children in helping their depressed and even dying "Old Folks," as harsh and unfeeling as that statement sounds.

But if they did next to nothing for them in reference to the Mansion, Edward, at least, seems to have inherited the desire of his parents, especially of his father, to own the homestead outright, independently of any arrangement with David Mack or his family. Fifteen years after he removed his family to the Pleasant Street house, he had determinedly earned enough money to purchase the entire property and Mansion which his father had once owned.[42] Perhaps a guilty conscience about neglecting his parents worked together with his own ambition to reestablish the reliability of the family name, his own in particular. In any case, by 1855 the homestead was his. When his daughter referred to "my father's house," a great deal of grief, ambition, and perhaps even greed on Edward's part, possibly known to Emily, lay behind her comment.[43] When she remarked to Samuel Bowles that friends were her sole "estate," she may have been inadvertently contrasting this extraordinary sort of personal property with her father's real estate investments.

Even before the Mansion returned to the Dickinsons, Edward affirmed his devotion to home and family. He adjusted slowly to Washington while serving his term as congressman (1853–55), obviously homesick and ill at ease with the capital's etiquette.[44] Vinnie first reported her father's malaise in a letter to Austin in December 1853:

> We've had four letters from Father since he went away, two since he reached Washington. He dont seem to be very happy, speaks of the *attractions of home* with quite a relish, he will never consent to be there more than two years, I think.[45]

Edward seems to have adjusted during his remaining time in Congress, but this evidence of his disquiet away from Amherst repeated an earlier pattern begun during his first years as representative to the General Court in Boston. Despite probable mixed feelings about his family, he appears to have genuinely regretted his frequent absences for the consequent hardships suffered by his wife and lack of fatherly attention given his children. The ring of heartfelt longing seems too strong in the following note from Edward to his wife, written in 1838, to be dismissed entirely, as Cody has done, as overcompensation for a pressing sense of guilt for neglect:

> . . . it is indeed a happiness, pure as can be enjoyed on earth, to know that we have, each, one friend, that is mindful of us — that our separation increases the affection which has ever existed between us. The expression of your regard produces no ordinary emotion in me, towards my family — who are so thoughtful of me, in my absence. . . . Home is the place for me — & the place of all others to which I am attached — and I need not tell you what constitutes its chief attraction — or what makes it so desirable.[46]

Even earlier, in 1830, though a full two years after his marriage, when any honeymoon aura would surely have worn off their relationship, Edward wrote his wife from Boston:

> I like travelling, but *home* has charms for me, which I do not find abroad, and I am happy to acknowledge that, whether at home or abroad, my family are the first object of my thought, & care; and the constant endeavor of myself & my best powers to render them happy, is the greatest pleasure of my life.[47]

Similar comments recur in Edward's letters home. Again and again, he sends commonplace messages, untainted by anxiousness, to his children, admonishing them to be good and mind their mother.[48] In a cheerful note to Emily, age seven, he ends with a natural ambition for his older daughter, "I want to have you one of the best little girls in town." In response, Mrs. Dickinson informs her husband of their children's health and their interest in him: "they all send their love."[49] Emily's special messages are also reported: "Emily sais [sic] she wishes I would write to you that she should be glad to see you but she hope [sic] it is all for the best that you are away."[50] And again, "[Emily] speaks of her Father with much affection. She sais she is tired of living without a father. . . ."[51] Without these childhood references to the esteem Mr. Dickinson enjoyed from his three children, it would be difficult to understand the affection they undeniably felt for him despite the sober, distant, reserved, and highly disciplined exterior for which he has become so rightly remembered.

Edward was, then, capable of a profound devotion to home untouched by personal ambition, though surely at times one desire conflicted with the other. If so, and the evidence just presented supports the claim, then Emily's comment about home as a holy thing apparently took its strength from paternal ambition, pride, and affection as well as maternal pattern. In short, father and mother, despite conflicting roles which coalesced in the poet's consciousness, but which she kept separate as her "private" and "public" selves, seem equally responsible for the parental attitudes and feelings which gathered in the poet's image of house and home.[52]

II.

That emotional food first came at the Mansion, even though I have brought comments from Emily's later years in the second house and her adult ones at the homestead to shed light on this earliest period. At this time, Emily was exposed not only to the unconscious conditioning imposed by the personalities of her parents but also to a conscious childrearing philosophy. That cultural advice came, to a significant degree, from a small volume Edward gave his wife in 1833, when Emily was in her third year and he was frequently absent from home. *The Mother at Home* was its title and its author was the Reverend John S.C. Abbott, an evangelical Congregationalist minister.

One of the most striking features of Abbott's book is his repetition of a cultural theme: the importance, or rather the absolute centrality, of home. In his preface, he clearly states the Puritan purpose of his work: "We have proceeded upon the principle that here [in one's earthly home] is the commencement of eternal existence, and that the great object of education is to prepare the child for its heavenly home."[53] This grand plan could be fulfilled, Abbott believed, if the home could be made as idyllic as possible: "Every effort should be made to make home the most desirable place; to gather around it associations of delight, and thus to form, in the mind of your child, an attachment for peaceful and purifying enjoyments."[54] If this goal were accomplished, then the wayward child, the prodigal son, would always carry with him "thoughts of the holiness of home" and thus the seeds for salvation and probable return to "the peace he has forsaken."[55]

Mother should be the instrument of this conditioning, Abbott repeats throughout his manual, saying in one place, "In a most peculiar sense God has constituted you [Oh mothers!] the guardians and the controllers of the human family!" and in another, "Your fidelity may elevate them to the mansions of heaven."[56]

It is impossible to say how much Mrs. Dickinson took Abbott's advice to heart, or further, attempted to follow his suggestions closely or loosely. Looking at the book physically, however, may provide one clue. Its most worn pages begin with a chapter entitled "Faults and Errors," two flowers having been pressed between the first and second pages of the chapter. It deals with the common mistakes parents may make with their children and begins with strictures concerning the growth of vanity in either the average or gifted child. Doubtless Austin and Emily, energetic and probably precocious, led Mrs. Dickinson to consult this section of Abbott more than once, or more than the rest of the book, as its handling shows. Besides advice on minimizing the achievements of one's children, especially in public, Mrs. Dickinson was cautioned not to be continually finding fault, an admonition balancing the restraint suggested earlier and elsewhere in the book. "Be even more careful to express your approbation of good conduct, than your disapprobation of bad," Abbott encouraged.[57]

This emphasis upon guiding children in a firm manner but with predominant sweetness and light was stated even more directly in an earlier section and must have appealed to Mrs. Dickinson's passive temperament:

> Guard against too much severity. By pursuing a steady
> · course of efficient government, severity will very seldom be
> found necessary. If when punishment is inflicted, it is done
> with composure and with solemnity, occasions for punishment
> will be very infrequent. Let a mother ever be affectionate and
> mild with her children. Let her sympathize with them in their
> little sports. Let her gain their confidence, by her assiduous
> efforts to make them happy. And let her feel, when they have
> done wrong, not irritated but sad, and punish them in sorrow,
> but not in anger.[58]

This passage may have been remembered by Mrs. Dickinson when she came, or returned, to the chapter on "Faults and Errors," where Abbott specifies, "Never punish by exciting imaginary fears."[59] His example of "very reprehensible" discipline is of a child conditioned to associate darkness with fear by being shut up in a cellar or windowless closet. Such children, he states, may then be unable to sleep without a light, or in some instances, may literally die of fright in the dark, and he cites real cases of such misfortune.[60]

One cannot imagine the Dickinson parents left untouched by Abbott's examples, although there is indirect evidence that Emily knew such punishment. A poem begins, "They shut me up in Prose – / As when a little Girl / They put me in the Closet – / Because they liked me 'still'."[61] And once she alluded to this treatment when she told her niece, similarly disciplined, although this time in a guest bedroom, "Matty, child, no one could ever punish a Dickinson by shutting her up alone."[62]

Actually, tests of the Dickinsons' severity beyond these are difficult to document; that is, actual instances of their punishments do not figure in Emily's letters or those of other Dickinson children or relatives. A prose fragment of Emily's, written after her mother's death, testifies, if anything, to a mildness of manner when she reprimanded her elder daughter. One of the things the poet remembers relinquishing with "Childhood" besides losing her shoe in the mud, returning home barefoot, and wading for cardinal flowers is "the mothers reproof which was more for my sake than her weary own for she frowned with a smile."[63]

Of all the reasons for the suffering which Dickinson reports, guilt does not appear to be a major one in reference to her mother, father, or even to God. "Sin," she once said, "is a distinguished Precipice / Others must resist," but not she herself.[64] And in a poem of two years before she died, she reaffirms this independence from Christian orthodoxy as if to state her lifelong position:

> Of God we ask one favor,
> That we may be forgiven –
> For what, he is presumed to know –
> The Crime, from us, is hidden –
> . . . .

(1601)

Forgiveness, of course, is not the question; indeed, it is superfluous since life is magic, as the poem goes on to say, even in the body's cage. In fact, the ecstasy of life is almost too much to bear. Within such a prison, there is no room for sin. Again, Dickinson's spatial inscape appears to define her size vis à vis traditional theology, and in this instance, her satisfaction with that position.

Edward's ability to evoke an uneasy conscience probably had less to do with discipline *per se* than with possible erotic feelings Emily may have felt for him or vice versa. The nearest episode of a potential physical encounter between them bears overtones of just such a tension, hardly uncommon between any father and daughter, but perhaps heightened by Edward's sense of propriety. Emily in her twenty-first year reports to Austin, ". . . arrived home at 9 — found Father in great agitation at my protracted stay — and mother and Vinnie in tears, for fear that he would kill me."[65] Fatherly wrath might have evoked fright but not necessarily guilt.

The single instance of Edward Dickinson whipping anyone or anything is reported by Lavinia, who in writing Austin, tells of a poor horse so harshly beaten by their father that Emily screamed.[66] That the "head" of the house, as Lavinia called him, exercised corporal punishment on his children is probable, yet how severe it was cannot be known, and then, doubtless daughters were less vulnerable to the paternal hand than sons. The distance which divided the Dickinson children from their parents, amply recorded and often reported, cannot be laid simply to the philosophy of childcare followed by the parents, as helpful as Abbott may have been either to the Dickinsons' practice or to the speculations of latter-day students of their home life. Separation within affectionate but formal relationships was the pattern of life among the Dickinsons, as is shown by evidence from later years, after their move to the Pleasant Street house in April 1840. And the cause of that mutual independence (which, in Emily's case, does appear to have led to moments of severe imbalance) may have been temperamental differences rather than the effects of the parents' childrearing regime.

III.

The poetry Dickinson wrote during her fifteen years at the Pleasant Street house is now represented by only five poems. None of them reveal her affinities for and vexations about this "holy" ground. Photographs and descriptions of its appearance remain, however, giving substantial material to appreciate Emily's prose comments about it. In the glow of her rosier views, the house emerges as a place of essential simplicity and assuring warmth, her dominant memory of it in later years. Certain areas of this place clearly evoked her most positive associations. These she might transfer from Pleasant Street to the Mansion, from earlier "objects" to newer ones when she changed houses. The objects became meaningful because of their intimate relation to subjects, namely her family, who will be treated hand in hand with the architecture. But at this moment, attention should be given to the setting of the Pleasant Street house, in particular, its proximity to the town cemetery, before returning to an analysis of the values Emily assigned to special places within and without this house.

Dickinson's personal and poetic preoccupation with death cannot be attributed simply to the frequent deaths of friends and relatives during her youth, however significant those facts may be in themselves. Her fascination with the end of life came not merely from its familiarity but from its literal proximity. The Amherst town cemetery was adjacent to her father's property and funeral cortèges passed by the back or north side of the house in full view from indoors. One of Emily's earliest references to death, in 1846, is to that of someone whom she did not know, a Negro infant, whose funeral procession she observed and then referred to as a cause for her "dark ideas."[67] Of course, relatives' deaths were more affecting and led her to muse on her theological inheritance. Two months after the black baby's death, she wrote:

> Yesterday as I sat by the north window the funeral train entered the open gate of the church yard, following the remains of Judge Dickinson's wife to her long home. His wife has borne a long sickness of two or three years without a murmur. She relyed [sic] wholly upon the arm of God & he did not forsake her. She is now with the redeemed in heaven & with the savior she has so long loved according to all human probability.[68]

But doubtless the even earlier death in 1844 of a friend near her own age, Sophia Holland, darkened Emily's views of subsequent funerals. She was only thirteen when she sat at vigil in Sophia's sickroom, dismissed only when the dying child's "Reason fled," as Emily put it. This death so depressed her that only after a month's vacation with Aunt Lavinia in Boston did her spirits revive.[69] Afterward, she had distinctively mixed emotions about death, attractive for its promise of a heavenly eternity, awesome in its lack of assurance of that haven. Fortunately, at least in 1846, Emily felt distant from that final time, though life's end was a continuing, "buzzing" problem:

> I don't know why it is but it does not seem to me that I shall ever cease to live on earth – I cannot imagine with the farthest stretch of my imagination my own death scene – It does not seem to me that I shall ever close my eyes in death. I cannot realize that the grave will be my last home –[70]

Perhaps the remoteness of that actuality was a function of the poet's great pleasure in life at the Pleasant Street house, despite recurring bouts of illness which kept her from school and friends. Perhaps such necessary seclusions adapted her preferences to solitude and her own schedule. In any event, she found particular enjoyment in named areas of this beloved house, the kitchen and its hearth, the front door, her room, and chosen places outdoors.

The Pleasant Street house, a typical clapboard rectangle with adjacent buildings set at right angles to the street, was a remarkable one even during the Dickinson's residency, before a gable, French windows, and porch altered the front façade. Its floor boards were extra wide, and they, as well as the beams, were of extraordinarily hard wood.[71] While the Dickinsons lived there (1840–55), the whole structure was dominated by a great central chimney, removed in later years to make a larger hall.[72] This giant flue served kitchen, sitting room, parlor, and dining room hearths.

Emily's fondest memories focused on the kitchen and its fireplace, as consecrated a place for her as the sacred hearth, the home altar of the Greeks. She wrote Austin in 1853, "I miss the long talks most, upon the *kitchen stone hearth*" (her italics).[73] And the next year, in another letter to her brother, she was more specific, perhaps because she had assumed Austin's usual job of starting the fires before the rest of the family awoke: "I rose at my usual hour, kindled the 'fires of Smithfield,' and missed you very much in the lower part of the house – you constituting my principal society, at that hour of the day."[74]

FIGURE 4. *The house on North Pleasant Street where the Dickinsons lived from 1840 to 1855. Photograph by J. L. Lovell, ca. 1870. Courtesy of the Jones Library, Amherst.*

Apparently, the kitchen sometimes served as a family conference center. Emily once complained that she objected to her father's opening Austin's letters before coming home, heedless of the addressee, adding, "I hope we shall all be spared to have one *kitchen meeting,* and express our . . . minds."[75] Here also was the table near a north window with a view of the cemetery and the hills northwest of town,[76] where Emily may have been sitting when she saw the funeral of Judge Dickinson's wife. Austin once described this table burdened with books, including Webster's *Dictionary,* pens, and ink paper.[77] Emily, the family letter-writer, often used this table; occasionally Lavinia and Austin did, too; less frequently Mrs. Dickinson hastily penned a note; and perhaps Edward composed his terse messages here, if writing materials were always handy.[78] But whether the kitchen were a place of family parley or of composition, its chief emotional importance for Emily, as the quotation above suggests, was its easy evocation of Austin. And the specific detail which linked him to this room was the stone hearth's fire.

When Emily herself had been away at Mt. Holyoke in 1848, she had written Austin, ". . . I think of the blazing fire, & the cheerful meal & the chair empty now I am gone."[79] The same cherished props appear in a letter to him in Boston in 1853, "You wonder if we think of you as much as you of us – I guess so, Austin – it's a great deal anyhow, and to look at the empty nails, and the empty chairs in the kitchen almost obscures my sight, if I were used to tears."[80] Exchanging the suggestion of her presence for his, Emily implies a loneliness and desired reunion with Austin, transparent in a letter written the same year on an unseasonably cold day for late June: "It is cold here today, Austin, and the west wind blows – the windows are shut at home, and the fire burns in the kitchen. How we should love to see you, how pleasant it would be to walk to the grove together. We will walk there, when you get home."[81]

This language of loneliness, incessantly repeated to Austin, in which sisterly devotion slides into a lover's concern, suggests the degree to which Emily wished to be one with a brother who, only eighteen months older, was so much her twin in temperament and taste. Only Austin could be included in Emily's innermost circle at this age; "Why are *we* so different . . . ?" (my italics). And the degree of ardency with which she spoke in the passage just quoted emerges with a bright intensity, equal to the kitchen fire, if one juxtaposes these remarks with a poem Emily wrote some years later in the Mansion:

> To my small Hearth His fire came –
> And all my House aglow
> Did fan and rock, with sudden light –
> 'Twas Sunrise – 'twas the Sky –
>
> Impanelled from no Summer brief –
> With limit of Decay –
> 'Twas Noon – without the News of Night –
> Nay, Nature, it was Day –   (638)

I am not suggesting that Austin is the unknown "He," the supposed lover of many of Emily's poems. Rather, the avowed affection –deep, immutable, and inextricably interwoven with self-love— repeatedly offered Austin seems to reappear in the poem above, especially with the support of a familiar setting. The hearth and house (heart and self, or body) are there; and the time – summer – is the crucial one when, in the mystery of love, time expands to eternity and, in this instance, eternal day.

Not surprisingly, Austin felt the same way about home and hearth as Emily did. An acquaintance remembered that he used to say his happiest years were spent at Pleasant Street.[82] In a letter to his fiancée, Susan Huntington Gilbert, he enlarges his love of home by enhancing it with the power of a hallowed past as he muses on the meaning of New England's greatest holiday, Thanksgiving. Austin, like Emily, begins with the family hearth:

> Around our own private hearth then we sit for an hour and talk over the day & evening and other like days & evenings – both past & to come – and family changes that have been & will be, and the two hundredth anniversary of the great puritan holyday . . . had come & gone forever –
> I love this Thanksgiving day – Sue – it is so truly New England in its spirit – I love New England & New England customs & New England institutions for I remember our fathers loved them and that it was they who founded & gave them to us –[83]

Austin's words become Emily's when she writes in 1858, ". . . the fires never burned low on the hearth stone of remembrance."[84]

The kitchen with its warmth (from a wood stove as well as a stone hearth) was a natural place for intimate encounters with Austin, when Emily and he could say "just what we're a mind to."[85] But other places also absorbed into themselves a highly affective value as Emily associated them with particular people. Such a potent spot was the front door and its "broad stone step," where Emily first "mingled" her life with Sue Gilbert's, as she reminds Sue in a letter of 1852.[86] Writing again to Sue in the following year, she underlines the significance of the front door at the same time she describes its design (before alterations which appear in the 1868 photograph):

Dear Susie, I dont forget you a moment of the hour, and
when my work is finished, and I have got the tea, I slip thro'
the little entry, and out at the front door, and stand and watch
the West, . . . and the great, silent Eternity, for ever folded
there, and bye and bye it will open it's everlasting arms,
and gather us all – all. . . .[87]

The cemetery on the northeast side of the house is suggested in
this scene, though the front door faced south with a prospect looking west. This entrance, then, where Emily's love for Sue "first
began, on the step at the front door,"[88] set her imagination to fusing earthly with eternal lives. At the same time, as entry, it con-
noted new and timeless beginnings in love.

One of Emily's poems, "I Years had been from Home," written
in the Mansion in the 1860s, shows evidence of referring to the
Pleasant Street house. Its explication will come in the next chapter,
but it may be noted in passing that the home in question may well
be this Pleasant Street house, since the drama enacted there takes
place throughout before a front door, the auspicious place in
Emily's mind of Sue and eternity.[89]

A third area of presentiment and potency, largely associated with
the poet alone, was her room on the second floor. Once Emily referred to it as "our room," suggesting she shared it with Lavinia,
but most often it was "my room," and at least twice, "my own little
chamber,"[90] indicating either that this room actually was small or
that the habit of attributing her self-image to her room, evident at
the Mansion, first began here. This proportional attribution she
imputed to her writing table as well (known, in fact, to be small).
The bent to cherish littleness appeared early: at age fifteen, writing
Abiah Root, she described herself, "alone before my little writing
desk."[91] Upon it, she had her "apparatus," an inkstand with pens.
Accustomed as she was to facing this stand, she indicated her dependency upon it alone despite the whimsy which substituted it
for the Bible as she vowed to Austin, ". . . as my inkstand liveth
you shall have no peace until all is fulfilled," promising a barrage
of complaints if he didn't write soon.[92]

Looking up from her desk, Emily faced west, which she again
associated with Sue.[93] (Perhaps this prospect, intimate and potent
with affection, now and always, made Emily choose the room she did
in the Mansion, a room with views also facing south and west.) If

she wrote at the kitchen table occasionally, this "study" was a more private place and useful for writing late at night.[94] Its privacy assured a satisfying coziness in a world which Emily often found "hollow," and this fulfillment she enjoyed as a regal privilege, or so she put it to Sue one Sunday morning when a snowfall gave her an excuse to stay home from church: ". . . as I sit here Susie, alone with the winds and you, I have the old *king feeling* even more than before, for I know not even the cracker man will invade *this* solitude, this sweet Sabbath of our's."[95]

A final area of special value at the house on Pleasant Street was the garden. It extended north from the house and included not only an apple orchard but also a grove of white pines which Austin planted and to which Emily often referred.[96] She had been given, or assumed, the job of caring for this grove in Austin's absence, much as she had acquired his chore of lighting the morning fires. It was here that, in the excerpt quoted, she suggested their walking together when he returned home. And as she also told him, "We all go down to the grove often. Father and mother together walked down there yesterday morning. I think they [the newly planted pines] will all live."[97]

But several years before this grove was planted, other produce thrived. Peaches, purple grapes, apples, and vegetables Emily once described so extravagantly as to make a reader's mouth water a century later; certainly Austin's must have, too.[98] So used was she to reporting the state of the garden to her brother that even as it faded a few weeks later, her desire to entice him home surpassed the season and she offered him a prose poem: "*here* is a little forest whose leaf is ever green, here is a *brighter* garden, where not a frost has been, in its unfading flowers I hear the bright bee hum, prithee my Brother, into *my* garden come!" (her italics).[99] The underlined *my* emphasizes the fantasy she envisioned; she assumes Eve's role, gives Austin Adam's and turns Amherst, even in mid-October, into an Eden of perpetual summer.

If Austin and the garden were inseparably joined in Emily's inscape, then Sue also had a special place outdoors, related to the front door. Emily began one letter in a Whitman-like vein, describing the grass about the two girls' favorite trysting place:

I am going out on the doorstep, to get you some new – green grass – I shall pick it down in the corner, where you and I used

to sit, and have long fancies. And perhaps the dear little
grasses were growing all the while – and perhaps they heard
what we said, but they cant *tell!*[100]

And although Emily only mentioned it once, "the Old Oak
Tree,"[101] where she and Sue talked a long while of Austin, may
have been a natural marker to designate a rendezvous with either
her brother or future sister-in-law. The barn figured a single time,
too, when Emily bluntly admitted wanting to see Austin and
added, ". . . my interviews with you at the *Barn* are frought with a
saddened interest."[102]

Inside and out, concrete areas bespoke particular affections of
Emily's and all became a part of that heavily valenced word *home.*
At one moment, that process seemed to reach a peak when Emily's
relentless memory and insistent desire to keep her brother near,
kept him near. She confessed to Austin, ". . . your whole soul is
here, and tho' apparently absent, yet present in the highest, and
the truest sense."[103] Similarly, Emily planted Sue within the family's gate by promising "my home will be your home,"[104] in the
biblical tones of Ruth, and this affirmation came well before Sue
had become engaged to Austin. A year later, she wrote Austin that
"it seems much more like *home* to have her with us *always,* than to
have her away,"[105] a statement revealing Emily's eagerness equal to
Austin's in desiring Sue to become a Dickinson and join their elite
circle of two.

But of what importance to the poet and her work were the special values Emily assigned these choice areas? As places, they were
insignificant though necessary: the kitchen hearth, the front doorstep, the bedroom, and certain areas outdoors. Perhaps it is their
very insignificance and yet their indispensability, *their veiled importance,* which provides a clue to the overtones of meaning they
embodied. For Emily, like these humble areas of the home, thought
herself inconsequential before the world while vital and even superior by her own standards. Physically, her "slender constitution"
tended to generate thoughts of slightness in a broader sense, even
though she described herself as growing tall.[106] She wrote in 1950,
"We are very small, Abiah – I think we grow still smaller – this
tiny, insect life the portal to another [eternity]; it seems strange –
strange indeed."[107] And she acknowledged that flowers, which she
sometimes chose to send a friend rather than making a call herself,

were "small, but *so* full of meaning."[108] Just such weight of identity and affection she gave the homely places she valued at Pleasant Street. They thereby became idealized beyond actuality and spoke not only of others and herself but of her preference for a life of solitude at home.

IV.

That preference will be discussed in the last part of the chapter. This section will explore the probability that Emily selected the hearth, front doorstep, her room, and the garden as indirect expressions of her identity. On this point, certain insights of Freud may be illuminating, although his interpretations will not be taken to delimit the extent of Emily's attachments to these areas of her house. As I said in chapter 1, the perspectives of psychology and psychosociology seem to be suggestive, sometimes highly so, as in this case, but not as final explanations. Qualified use is a necessity in light of my own and others' criticisms of Freudian conclusions about women, criticisms having to do with penis envy or Freud's apparent belief that women are intellectually inferior to men.

Inner space is the common subject which logically brings together Dickinson, Freud, and Erikson. The Pleasant Street places Emily emphasizes are interior ones. The front doorstep led immediately to enclosure, and even the garden was enclosed by a gate. Freud and Erikson have explored the nature of inner space in literary and psychological symbolism as an analogue to feminine anatomy, specifically, the womb. Perhaps Dickinson's place references allude to her sexuality – to her literal or psychic inner space. In the following discussion, I will deal only with Freud, leaving Erikson to a more relevant place in chapter 3.[109]

Emily's select places appear to have absorbed her own body image, her femininity as well as her self-estimate, because they were small, a quality she so often attributed to herself that it may have dominated her self-consciousness. The front doorstep led to a "little entry." Her room was "my own little chamber." Even the forest into which Emily invited Austin was "little." Only the hearth – except in a poem of the 1860s, when it had become "small" – had no specific size in her Pleasant Street testimony. The poet made these particular places her own by scaling them to fit her supposed dimensions. Since she repeatedly attached smallness to these special spots, often linked them to Austin or Sue, and may have unconsciously equated them, as enclosed spaces, with the womb, it appears that she made them surrogates for her affection, or even her erotic desires, for her brother and future sister-in-law. In a word, Emily's choice areas appear to exhibit the focus of her libidinal demands. Raising the issue of eroticism only suggests the sexual locus of the poet's feelings. It is not meant to imply incest or lesbianism, for erotic feeling in even an average sensibility commonly extends to both sexes. One of such intense and possessive affection as Emily merely dramatizes a bisexuality which all may feel, though few carry that feeling to fulfillment.

Freud's theories about the symbolization of female physiology, applicable to Emily Dickinson, the woman, are complemented by a second area of his thought which illuminates Emily Dickinson, the child, a role seen earlier to be one she maintained even into adulthood. This other area is Freud's description of identity or character formation in general. His treatment of crucial objects in the process of identity growth, as well as his interpretation of certain key symbols, contributes to an understanding of the depth of the poet's attachment to her chosen places at the Pleasant Street house. His objects may be equated with these preferred spots precisely because they became substitutes for Emily's attachment to loved ones. In short, they represented "people," a complex of the poet's own identity and those aspects of personality or character in others most prized by her.

In *The Ego and the Id,* Freud speaks of the form the ego assumes as a result of the workings of object cathexes and of identification. He argues that in a person's earliest, oral phase of life, object cathexis and identification may be indistinguishable from each other. Only later, he remarks, does the id appear to generate object desires while the still weak ego either attempts to control them by repression or acquiesces in their acceptance. Freud continues:

> When it happens that a person has to give up a sexual object, there quite often ensues an alteration of his ego which can only be described as a setting up of the object inside the ego, as it occurs in melancholia; the exact nature of this substitution is as yet unknown to us. It may be that by this introjection, which is a kind of regression to the mechanism of the

oral phase, the ego makes it easier for the object to be given up or renders that process possible. It may be that this identification is the sole condition under which the id can give up its objects. At any rate the process, especially in the early phases of development, is a very frequent one, and it makes it possible to suppose that the character of the ego is a precipitate of abandoned object-cathexes and that it contains the history of those object choices.[110]

At this moment, it is well to note that Freud probably refers to an individual at a much earlier stage of life than Emily during her puberty and young womanhood. Further, the "objects" which Freud refers to are persons, which, as he makes clear in the following pages, are most commonly the individual's parents. Nonetheless, his discussion still seems relevant to the poet. I have noted her persistent pose as a child well into her adulthood, and, of course, childlike ways remain even in the most mature of us. Thus the interplay of object cathexis, identification, and ego-formation which Freud discusses might apply to Dickinson past her infancy or early childhood. Her identity and ego still appear flexible during her Pleasant Street years and she was, after all, only nine when she moved there.

On the question of objects and what might be called a "sexual object," perhaps the previous discussion of hearthstone and door, room and garden, as places which denote people and connote Emily's affection for them, indicates they are justifiably considered "sexual objects." In light of Freud's symbolic suppositions and the poet's apparent identification with these objects, Dickinson may have done what Freud describes in the passage just quoted. As compensation for an object's loss, she seems to have absorbed it into herself, or in this case, she essentially did the same thing by projecting her identity upon the object.

In the same discussion of ego or character growth, Freud further comments upon the appearance of two voices within the individual which recall the "me" and "my spirit" of Dickinson's inner dialogue:

. . . it may be said that this transformation of an erotic object-choice into an alteration of the ego is also a method by which the ego can obtain control over the id and deepen its relations with it—at the cost, it is true, of acquiescing to a large extent in the id's experiences. When the ego assumes the features of the object, it is forcing itself, so to speak, upon the id as a love-object and is trying to make good the id's loss by saying: 'Look, you can love me too – I am so like the object.' [111]

Despite the fact that the id is unconscious, its voice may be heard obliquely (imperfectly controlled by a still shifting ego?). At least the last quoted passage from Freud sounds a note which seems echoed in two poems of Emily's previously discussed. (Although both poems were evidently written at the Mansion, the Pleasant Street period had a determining influence upon Dickinson's later years.) These two poems may both speak of the poet's separate selves. "The Soul selects her own Society – / Then – shuts the Door –" gives Emily away by its possessive adjective, "her," in the first line; and, as noted earlier, "Society" could well have been Emily's second self. In "I was the slightest in the House – / I took the smallest room," the first person pronoun may show the poet expressing a moment of compensatory unity between her two selves. In her "own little chamber," though that room was probably now "the smallest room" in the Mansion, "me" and "my spirit" could be speaking as one. The tone of remorse emphasized by the last line of the poem – "How noteless I could die" – might hint of the ultimate tenuousness of such possible ego-object identifications.

To summarize, Freud's analyses open the possibility of new depth for understanding Dickinson's repeated personal associations with parts of her house. Her letters alone show that not only did she match loved ones with these places but that she in part *became* such areas. Freud's interpretation of feminine symbols and of character growth presses the meaning of these facts further to suggest that they may reveal the erotic nature of Emily's love for her brother and sister-in-law, and that moreover, her object cathexes, the "sex objects" of Austin and Sue, represented eventually by the physical places with which Emily most closely associated them, may have become part of the psychic concentrate of Emily's ego. If this latter process took place, then the times of disagreement between the poet's two voices may have alternated with other, less divisive moments when the ego, "my spirit," may have been a love object to the id, "me." This conciliation, even narcissism, one may suppose, would be disguised by the self-transcending pronoun, "I."

Even if the poet's effusions about special places at Pleasant Street may be associated with her sexuality or with erotic desires, her idyllic sketches sometimes faded to sadder impressions colored by sorrow, frustration, and anger. Lavinia told Austin of such a moment, "Emilie is pensive just now recollections of 'by gones' you know, 'Old un' etc."[112] Possibly "Old un" refers to Benjamin Newton, a student in her father's law office when Emily was in her teens, who was eleven years her senior. Newton had tutored Emily, they had become friends, perhaps they were in love, but the facts about the nature of their relationship are few. Emily's memory of him, at least, was loyal, continuing throughout her life. At the time of Lavinia's comment above (December 1851), Newton had been gone from Amherst for two years, yet his gift of Emerson's *Poems* in 1849, one of Emily's most cherished momentos, no doubt kept his words alive, as the poet quoted them to Higginson years later: "My dying Tutor told me that he would like to live till I had been a poet."[113]

Depression and sadness, then, were no strangers to Emily even in this beloved home. The anguish of erupting memory may underlie Emily's complaints of early April 1852; she may have known that Newton was dying of tuberculosis, even though he had two more years to live. Yet the cause of her particular grief is unstated:

Will you be kind to me, Susie? I am naughty and cross, this morning, and nobody loves me here; nor would *you* love me, if you should see me frown, and hear how loud the door bangs whenever I go through; and yet it is'nt anger—I dont believe it is, for when nobody sees, I brush away . . . tears, Susie so hot that they burn my cheeks, and almost schorch [*sic*] my eyeballs, but *you* have wept much, and you know they are less of anger than *sorrow*.[114]

A year later, Emily's mournfulness has not abated. When she writes Austin her mood is one step beyond what she reported to Sue; resignation seems to have set in:

"Strikes me" just so, dear Austin, but somehow I have to work a good deal more than I used to, and harder, and I feel so tired when night comes, that I'm afraid if I write you, 'twill be something rather bluer than you'll be glad to see—so I sew with all my might, and hope when work is done to be with you much oftener than I have lately been.

> Somehow I am lonely lately – I feel very old every day, and when morning comes and the birds sing, they don't seem to make me so happy as they used to. I guess it's because you are gone, and there are not so many of us as God gave for each other. I wish you were at home. I feel very sure lately that the years we have had together are more than we shall have. . . .[115]

Still, Emily had one sure consolation with which she shifts her tone, " – yes, Austin, home is faithful, none other is so true."[116]

The Pleasant Street house, overseeing moments of painful nostalgia, fatigue, or loneliness, nonetheless remained sacred to Emily. Her references to the kitchen hearth, the front doorstep, her own room, and the garden suggest that its architecture and grounds apparently served, in inchoate form, as props for her psychic condition. Emily's other descriptions of the interior – scant, few, scattered, and wholly in prose at this period – invariably led to a longer treatment of her emotions or reactions to family and friends. "House" is "home" by the grace of relationships, and so their dynamics, which contributed to the poet's first steps toward withdrawal, will be seen in even more detail than before. Setting and the sentiments evoked within it together exhibit the home image's affective sources in Dickinson's younger self.

V.

I have said that in many ways Edward Dickinson shaped Emily's private, often strikingly masculine self, a crisp and cryptic individuality poised between towering independence and debilitating insecurity (Edward's initial uneasiness in Washington comes to mind). The latter side of Edward was carefully hidden under a formidable formality, relieved only occasionally, his capacity for extreme emotion suggested merely by fiery passionate eyes, as seen in his well-known portrait of 1853. Mrs. Dickinson's reticence, and even her helplessness, provided a model for Emily's public life, a culturally acceptable, utterly dutiful role. This was consistent with the social expectations of the wife of a prominent town citizen and dedicated mother who rarely left home. With no decisive adult feminine example from which her own need for autonomy might find inspiration, and with a male adult model whose natural role kept Emily always dependent, perhaps increasingly so as she grew older, the child in Emily remained a strong voice. As far as her mental life was concerned, she was a half-orphan and compensated by enjoying the protection and intellectual stimulation of her father, although Mrs. Dickinson, as we have seen, did not lack either curiosity or culture. But perhaps her dominant passivity led Emily to admire women of singular character, social poise, and public presence, such as Sue, and Emily's friend from childhood, the novelist, Helen Hunt Jackson.

If distance separated Emily from her parents, largely because of personality differences and questions of literary taste, I am arguing, rather than coldness and severity, then the gap was bridged by a fine hairline of profound loyalty. Emily's description of the day before her father's death measures the depth of her attachment and suggests his return affection with a directness which is yet subtle, its nuances hinting of more than she speaks, in the same manner as in her poems:

> The last Afternoon that my Father lived, though with no premonition – I preferred to be with him, and invented an absence for Mother, Vinnie being asleep. He seemed peculiarly pleased as I oftenest stayed with myself, and remarked as the Afternoon withdrew, he "would like it to not end."
>
> His pleasure almost embarrassed me and my Brother coming – I suggested they walk. Next morning I woke him for the train – and saw him no more.
>
> His heart was pure and terrible and I think no other like it exists.
>
> I am glad there is Immortality – but would have tested it myself – before entrusting him.[117]

Emily's final two sentences, better than any others, whether in letters or poems, illustrate the awe, fear, disdain, pity, and love all incorporated in profoundly sacrificial devotion which she simultaneously felt for her father. The bond was immutable as it was also overtly restrained.

Lavinia and Austin were Emily's closest friends within the family. At this moment in their lives, Austin was the preferred one for his quick wit, vivaciousness, love of literature and nature, closeness of age, and possibly for his sex. Lavinia, three years younger than Emily, was capable of writing a good letter, but was more often a

reporter of purely practical affairs. A journal she kept during 1851,
though sometimes entertaining and informative, reads almost like
a date book, and her later efforts to write poetry are adolescent
attempts never approaching the quality of her sister's poems.[118]
Even though Lavinia's sense of fun paralleled Emily's, her humor
as a mimic was broader than Emily's transcending sort.[119]

Emily's imperial demand for Austin's presence has been traced
before, but it should be emphasized that she haunted the house
with his ghost, on one occasion imagining, "spectres sit in your
chair and now and then nudge father with their long, bony
elbows."[120] The major theme of her letters, perhaps repeated several times in one writing, was always the desire to have him home
again as soon as possible. Some critics, of whom Cody is the latest,
have argued that her father's awesome exterior and emotional
reserve may have conditioned Emily to be afraid of men. If so,
then Austin's personality was at least a partial antidote. As previously noted, Emily could speak to Austin in a lover's language.
Her affection for him, full and warm, was sacrificial and unstinting
in the same measure that it was possessive.

With her favorite companion often absent, Emily felt that silent
miles separated the remaining four Dickinsons. The following
description of the atmosphere at home probably dates from a
period after 1855, yet one imagines the poet could have written
essentially the same character studies of her family were she doing
so from the Pleasant Street place. The trio of Father, Vinnie, and
herself were the focus; mother was almost ignored, as if she were
forever closeted in the pantry of her daughter's mind. But despite
the distances pictured here as separating each Dickinson from the
others, Emily tried to compensate for it. Her final tone was more
of selected position than of pathetic deprivation. She ended with a
voice that was nearly triumphant:

> My father seems to me often the oldest and the oddest sort of
> a foreigner. Sometimes I say something and he stares in a curi-
> ous sort of bewilderment though I speak a thought quite as
> old as his daughter. And Vinnie . . . it is so weird and so vastly
> mysterious, she sleeps by my side, her care is in some sort
> motherly, for you may not remember that our amiable mother
> never taught us tayloring and I am amused to remember those

clothes, or rather those apologies made up from dry goods with which she covered us in nursery times; so Vinnie is in the matter of raiment greatly necessary to me; and the tie is quite vital; yet if we had come up the first time from two wells where we had hitherto been bred her astonishment would not be greater at some things I say.

Father says in fugitive moments when he forgets the barrister & lapses into the man, says that his life has been passed in a wilderness or on an island – of late he says on an island. And so it is, for in the morning I hear his voice and methinks it comes from afar & has a sea tone & there is a hum of hoarseness about [it] & a suggestion of remoteness as far as the isle of Juan Fernandez.

So I conclude that space & time are things of the body & have little or nothing to do with our selves. My Country is Truth. Vinnie lives much of the time in the State of Regret. I like Truth – it is a free Democracy.[121]

Without Austin, Emily had no one at home with whom she could really speak. The distillations of her mind doubtless came out as enigmatic abstractions which even the writing down might not have clarified. But ultimately, inspired in part by Emerson's essays, Emily left wistfulness and regret behind. In "Literary Ethics," a page corner is turned up, marking Emerson's advice to the young scholar:

> Truth shall be policy enough for him.
> Let him not grieve too much on account of unfit associates. When he sees how much thought he owes to the disagreeable antagonism of various persons who pass and cross him, he can easily think that in a society of perfect sympathy, no word, no act, no record would be.[122]

Emily was in another country at home which helped her to brush aside discontent. In fact, the family circle allowed her to live for the truth even if she had to do so alone.

Attempting to reach this "Country," tenuous as it was, Emily passed through oppressive levels of community constraint, psychic divisions, disappointment in love, as well as family incomprehension. In descriptions of later episodes in her life, Emily appears in the throes of battling these forces which shaped her singular personality. During her late adolescence she experienced an identity crisis whose resolution was never quite complete.

The first and superficially most disturbing episode concerned her reaction to the three semesters she spent at Mount Holyoke Seminary, from September 1847 to August 1848. This period was the longest time she ever spent away from home, although mentally and emotionally she never left it. Her letters overflow with plaintive, sometimes urgent, cries of homesickness, even when it is determinedly denied. She wrote Austin about the excitement of adjustment, then admitted: "I had a great mind to be homesick after you went home, but I concluded not to & therefore gave up all homesick feelings. Was not that a wise determination?"[123] That the effort was actually a brave bluff is evident in her description of a dream in the same letter, which she asks Austin to explain:

> Father had failed and mother said that "our rye field which she and I planted, was mortgaged to Seth Nims." I hope it is not true but do write soon and tell me for you know "I should expire with mortification" to have our rye field mortgaged, to say nothing of it's falling into the merciless hands of a loco!!!![124]

Seth Nims, the postmaster in Amherst, was a triple threat in this imagined tragedy of Emily's. Not only was her father's position shattered on a simple economic level, but her mother and herself were injured – or violated – in the mortgaging of the rye field, for they planted it. Worse, Nims as a "loco," a Democrat, was an arch enemy for the staunchly Whig Dickinsons. Despite the playful element of mock concern about the dream, a genuine fear of separation from her family belies the humor.

Succeeding letters repeated her desire to adjust. She admired, even loved, some of her teachers. She found friends and the food was good.[125] But heartfelt longings about Amherst were never far from the surface. The feeling may have been encouraged by her recurring ill health or even by the motto saturating the sentiment of her day, embodied in the song, "Home, Sweet Home!"[126]

But Emily's malaise was much more profound. At Holyoke, she was rebelling against the gentle but constant attempts of the seminary, led by Mary Lyon, to recruit religiously uncommitted young ladies into the ranks of the "hopeful." Simply, in an atmosphere

FIGURE 5. *Emily E. Dickinson at age seventeen, a daguerreotype made at South Hadley in 1848. Courtesy of Amherst College Library.*

of rigorous evangelizing, she did not have a conversion experience. Her roommate and older cousin, Emily L. Norcross, reported.

> Emily Dickinson appears no different. I hoped I might have good news to write with regard to her. She says she has no particular objection to becoming a Christian and she says she feels bad when she hears of one and another of her friends who are expressing a hope but still she feels no more interest.[127]

Emily Dickinson put the reason for her hesitation more directly, ". . . it is hard for me to give up the world."[128] Perhaps this problem was a familiar one within the family, for at this time, only Mrs. Dickinson was a church member, although her husband and children regularly attended services at the First Congregational Church.[129] Mr. Dickinson's scruples, probably based on a legal sense of the binding nature of contract and the potential hypocrisy of spirit constrained by the rule of letter, may have supported Emily's doubts about doctrine though they did not dull her religious questings. But Emily broke with her father's example when, in 1850, he joined the church, a pledge he would restate in 1873, on the reverse of his business card: "I hereby give myself to God."[130] She was never able to make such a public commitment, nor firmly state it privately.

Emily's frequent trips home from South Hadley during her year at the seminary allowed her to contrast the demands of life in society with Dickinson independence. She chose the latter, and her father's decision not to send her back for a second year, because of her poor health, seconded her feelings.[131] Restored to familiar and beloved surroundings, Emily nonetheless found that she brought the conflict with conventional belief with her. It was internalized and exacerbated by the tireless, omnipresent voices of competing selves. This struggle demanded the privacy of home to mask her confusion and disorientation.

In the loneliness ensuing from leaving the seminary, Emily often evoked spectres of friends to keep her company.[132] In the same way, searching inward, she found "my spirit" and "me" easily conjured up as companions, and sometimes also "God." Once when her parents were away, she wrote her friend Abiah that they thought they had left her alone but not so: her "curious trio" was there. Both selves she described as part earthly and part spiritual. But in orthodox Puritan form, God was totally Other, all heaven and no earth. He was bright, glorious, even blinding. Sitting as he did in judgment, even on her thoughts, he was awesome, and Emily recalled the Old Testament taboo: "I don't dare to look directly at him for fear I shall die."[133] The problem of keeping her separate selves and God in order was a monumental job, and Emily did not hide her frustration and impatience over the heritage which made her struggle so: "The trinity winds up with me, as you may have surmised, and I certainly would'nt be at the fag end but for civility to you. This self-sacrificing spirit will be the ruin of me!"[134]

The closer parts of herself, however, were too near not to spat. She confided to her school friend Emily Fowler: "I wanted to write, and just tell you that *me,* and *my spirit* were fighting this morning. It is'nt known generally, and you must'nt tell anybody."[135] When the two, like siblings, warred at such moments, Emily's mood determined which one was the victor. More often "me" dominated. Though called spiritual as well as earthly, this self appears to have expressed her most urgent, undisciplined, basic wants.[136] In moments when loneliness was especially acute and when she could escape housework, she wrote how she felt with all the bitterness and sarcasm "me" could mobilize. Her "spirit" was more civilized and sought a cultivated, approved good of some sort.[137]

Sometimes the pair united and stood together in revolt against God, especially when they suffered from what appeared to be his passive injustice. Her use of the plural to explain herself is probably not editorial. Near the end of the letter above she wrote: "*Shall* we be strong – wont suffering make weaker this human [?] – it makes stronger not us – but what God gave, and what he will take – mourn our bodies ever so loudly. We do not know that he is God – and *will* try to be still – tho' we really had rather complain."[138]

This self-revelation of Emily's interior life not only indicates the pattern of recurring personal and religious upheaval and not only suggests Freudian parallels to her analysis (God, "my spirit," and "me" play the roles of superego, ego, and id). More significantly, the poet's description of the architecture of her psyche in terms of the Trinity indicates the inescapable lingering of the orthodox Calvinist mind as well as the conscious awareness of the darker aspects of the soul which the Transcendentalists either generally discarded, ignored, or acknowledged, as Emerson, but left unprobed. Living at the moment of decisive fracture of the Puritan mind, Emily was not able to find a new focus but suffered a succession of fleeting revelations. Her mental inquietude matched her religious indecision. With this double tension at work, the complexity of her mind, as one critic has written, was not the complexity "of harmony but that of dissonance."[139] Such cacophony of inner voices developed from family tradition and grew within its privacy, enslaving Emily at home by its discord.

In the spring of 1850, a third, perhaps simultaneous experience began whose proportions for Emily in late adolescence were doubtless tremendous, the development and dissolution of a romance. At this time, her sense of splintered identity seems to have been temporarily suppressed, or so at least it would appear from a letter written to a close friend, Jane Humphrey. Emily contrasted her own election with that of friends, including Vinnie, who had recently joyfully felt themselves sanctified. A spiritual emptiness still haunted her; but she remained puzzled about the precious something which they had sought and found and which so eluded her. Meanwhile, a desire for Christ as catalyst in a problem of conscience was not part of the cryptic ecstasy she confided to Jane. Presumably, it concerned an experience of deep encounter with a special friend. No other sort would explain her words:

> I have dared to do strange things – bold things, and have asked no advice from any – I have heeded beautiful tempters, yet do not think I am wrong. Oh I have needed my trusty Jane . . . it would relieve me to tell you all, to sit down at your feet, and look in your eyes, and confess . . . , an experience bitter, and sweet, but the sweet did so beguile me – and life has had an aim, and the world has been too precious for your poor – and striving sister! The winter was all one dream, and the spring has not yet waked me, I would always sleep, and dream, and it never should turn to morning, so long as night is so blessed.[140]

Her tone was buoyant with expectation, even though she hinted of a degree of hesitation and guilt. She felt a need to confess, not out of a pressing sense of wrong, but from a desire to tell and discuss a precious secret. Nonetheless, the setting was a dream world, in fact so much so that one wonders if the bitter-sweet experience actually happened. That it did and that she recognized the extent of her fantasies seems clear from the wish following, a few lines later: "I hope human nature has truth in it – Oh I pray it may not deceive."[141]

Later the next month, during her mother's illness, Emily vividly contrasted her sense of duty with a surging, youthful desire to be free to run off for an afternoon with a young man. In a letter to Abiah, she did this with no little flair, perhaps to illustrate her own maturity. Nevertheless, the deprivation was poignantly real, and her resignation was typically announced in the words of triumph:

> While I washed the dishes at noon . . . , I heard a well-known rap, and a friend I love *so* dearly came and asked me to ride in the woods, the sweet-still woods, and I wanted to exceedingly – I told him I could not go, and he said he was disappointed – he wanted me very much – then the tears came into my eyes, tho' I tried to choke them back, and he said I *could,* and *should* go, and it seemed to me unjust. Oh I struggled with great temptation and it cost me much of denial, but I think in the end I conquered, not a glorious victory Abiah, where you hear the rolling drum, but a kind of helpless victory, where triumph would come of itself, faintest music, weary soldiers, nor a waving flag, nor a long-loud shout.[142]

That the affair probably ended in requiring just this sort of response from Emily, but for reasons other than denial, is suggested by her admission in October 1851 that home appeared to be "a bit of Eden which not the sin of *any* can utterly destroy."[143]

Still a fourth factor, whose duration has been largely ignored, forcefully shaped Emily's attitude to home. In May 1850, Mrs. Dickinson was suddenly seized with acute neuralgia, forcing her to give up all work, temporarily but recurringly.[144] Lavinia was at Wheaton Seminary, Ipswich, so Emily at nineteen had to fill her mother's role alone. Her description of the crippled household was initially more dramatic than grief-stricken, probably because she thought it would end soon, but the self-sacrifice defined a new, more limited role for her then, and ultimately for the rest of her life. Her mother's intermittent illness has been overlooked in understanding Emily's seclusion. To her devotion to the family and dependency on its protection, Mrs. Dickinson's helplessness added an imposed responsibility, a predictable depressant.

Yet, as some compensation, this crisis satisfied two aspects of Emily's fantasy life, probably at its purest height in her early twenties. First, she could envision herself as the martyr queen, elevating herself to victory and mastery, revealing a decided pleasure in her deprivation. Now she used the title facetiously, but later, in the Mansion, she loaded it with solemn symbolism. The identification may have been partially inspired by the popular sentimental novels of her day, especially the book *Reveries of a Bachelor*, by "Ik Marvel," D. G. Mitchell, published in 1850. Harmless enough on the surface, though wantonly pious, the reveries thinly cover a basic fear of, or repugnance toward, sex, and a morbid, even erotic pleasure in the idea of death. Mitchell's last sketch extols the recluse-nursemaid daughter who renounces any adventure in the world to care for a sick father.[145] Whatever the direct source might have been, the contemporary culture idealizing the noble act certainly fed Emily's amused self-portrait when she wrote to Abiah in May 1850 about her new charges at home:

> I am yet the Queen of the court, if regalia be dust, and dirt, have three loyal subjects, whom I'd rather releive [sic] from service. Mother is still an invalid tho' a partially restored one – Father and Austin still clamor for food, and I, like a martyr am feeding them. Wouldn't you love to see me in these bonds of great despair, looking around my kitchen, and praying for kind deliverance, and declaring by "Omar's beard" I never was in such plight. *My* kitchen I think I called it, God forbid that it was, or shall be my own – God keep me from what they call *households*, except that bright one of "faith"![146]

A second assuagement, despite plaguing housekeeping duties, was the chance to continue playing the often-preferred role of little girl, even if only part-time. "I love so to be a child," she wrote Abiah.[147] And even though that innocent vision was foreshortened by the realities of life with father, especially when her emerging adulthood challenged him, still Emily's fancy had room for play. She wrote Austin in 1851: ". . . we do not have much poetry, father having made up his mind that its pretty much all *real life*. Fathers real life and *mine* sometimes come into collision, but as yet, escape unhurt!"[148]

A fifth aspect of Emily at home was her ability to tolerate solemnity and boredom, especially when Austin was away, at the same time that she wished very much to escape it. A parlor scenario comes alive as she described it to Austin in June 1851. The family was surprised by an unseasonal northeast storm. Mr. Dickinson found it "amazin' raw," Mrs. Dickinson was warming her feet and said they were "just as cold as ice"–clichés which evoked Emily's chiding–and Vinnie was plucking out a tune about "a young lady who thought she was 'almost there.' " The parents' talk of Austin, of his spiritual and moral character, was the only item of interest to Emily. In brief, she reported, "unless something new 'turns up' I cannot see anything to prevent a *quiet season*."[149] The complaint of the last two words sounded the whole letter's theme. Emily admitted to her brother: "I miss you very much. I put on my bonnet tonight, opened the gate very desperately, and for a little while, the suspense was terrible–I think I was held in check by some invisible agent, for I returned to the house without having done any harm!"[150]

Emily in a semicomic, "harum scarum" mood, mock murderer or thief, was driven from the house for excitement, anything, it seems, to shatter the tedium and discipline which vexed her. What made her stop? Perhaps it was the night. One recalls her comment of later years, "We are children still and you know that children fear the dark."[151] She needed the family hearth for affectionate concern, for identity, and even for light.

In sum, life in this house for Emily fluctuated between familial demands and private pleasures. At moments, she might protest being a drudge, but she was free and safe. No pressing public decisions kept her from reading, corresponding, or from experimenting with poetry, which she probably began composing at this time. A trip to Boston would reinforce her "opinion of the hollowness and awfulness of the world," as Austin reported.[152] She was increasingly reluctant to accept invitations to visit away, because of concern for her parents and also because she guarded her own schedule and selected friends.[153] She did not want to go to Washington even with the rest of the family in the spring of 1854. And when she finally went a year later, her observations about the capital's whirl and her affirmation about the locus of her affections were quite typical: "My thoughts are far from idle, concerning e'en the *trifles* of the world at home."[154] A letter to Austin, noted earlier, shows that the house on Pleasant Street, at least at a certain moment of solace, was her one sure object of worship:

> Home is a holy thing – nothing of doubt or distrust can enter its blessed portals. I feel it more and more as the great world goes on and one and another forsake, in whom you place your trust – here seems indeed to be a bit of Eden which not the sin of *any* can utterly destroy – smaller it is indeed, and it may be less fair, but fairer it is and *brighter* than all the world beside.[155]

This comment surely surpasses the saying "Home Sweet Home!" although it is not entirely free of the pieties of her day. Better than any other statement at this time, however, it confirms that Emily's well-being, by both circumstances and choice, depended on this island of retreat. Here was a way out of cultural conformity and a screen for the struggles of the psyche and the sufferings of affection thrown back. Emily had faced community constraint not only at Mount Holyoke but again at home. Writing to Jane the year after her return, she announced: "I dont attend [the Sewing Society] – notwithstanding my high approbation – which must puzzle the public exceedingly. I am already set down as one of those brands almost consumed – and my hardheartedness gets me many prayers."[156]

Another factor, tender feelings, she offered as a reason for preferring solitude. In a letter to Abiah in 1852, she complained that her friend had failed to see her before leaving Amherst, doted upon her unhappiness about this rebuff, then prescribed its cure:

> How very sad it is to have a confiding nature, one's hopes and feelings are quite at the mercy of all who come along; and how very desirable to be a stolid individual, whose hopes and aspirations are safe in one's waistcoat pocket, and *that* a pocket indeed, and one not to be picked![157]

Beyond public opprobrium or the remissness of friends, Emily's complex role as a child and as an idealized martyr gave her positive reasons to enjoy the protection of home. Also, her favorite places immediately evoked memories of and communion with

Austin and Sue. Finally, the latitude of time and thought she had here were perfect conditions for writing poetry. As she remarked in 1852, as if to encompass all the experiences conditioning her withdrawal, "I find I need more veil."[158]

At this age was Emily a romantic escapee from reality?[159] If "reality" is measured by relations and commitments to others, on the surface Emily followed general custom: she continued churchgoing, visiting friends (sometimes to parade new clothes or jewels), and going to parties. For her own reality, the preference for privacy was less an escape than a tactic of strategic retreat. Intermittently needed as housekeeper, in spare moments she could indulge her interests and talents as she wished. Further, she compared her family with neighbors, even relatives, as earlier mentioned, and found it both separate and special. In the early 1850s, despite moments of intense self-doubt and interior strife, she felt superior: "I don't think folks are much."[160] Mentally, she was in another country from most of Amherst, and she viewed a sufficient world from the secure citadel of home.

The conflicts which haunted Emily all her life had their origins in the Pleasant Street period. Misunderstanding, isolation, psychic and religious confusions, family duties, a thwarted love, as well as the attempts to overcome these difficulties, a queenship won as costly prize and the fantasy of childhood, including an idyllic relationship with Austin and Sue – all reappear in later years. But there were major differences in emphasis and intent. The early royalty was a pretended role tried on in play. And childhood was not a return but at least a partially legitimate continuation of family relationships. By her early thirties, however, both poses under pressure of pain reemerged in sharper form. Emily increasingly recognized that the pattern she had known would not be changed.

Like a monarch butterfly after metamorphosis, she had become the Empress of Calvary, a mature yet childish adoption of status to compensate for circumscription in the Mansion; the simultaneous self-image of an old-fashioned little girl allowed her this imaginative election as escape. As child, she could still dwell in "Possibility." Perhaps the truly constant factor linking the young and the adult Emily was the necessity to be within the family's door, as if to confirm her concentration on the inner life.

Only one surviving poem might refer to the Pleasant Street house, "I Years had been from Home," to be discussed in the next chapter. Others like it were either lost in 1855, the year of the move, or later destroyed. If still extant, no doubt they would have reflected the same combination of affection and loss as the poet's letters of this period, accentuated perhaps by her awareness that one era in her life was closing, another and more ominous one commencing. That such a change was imminent she remarked twice to Austin in 1853, the second time expressing a fervent wish, "Oh for the pleasant years when we were young together, and this was *home – home!*"[161] Yet once uprooted from Pleasant Street, the poet seems to have sharpened the meanings coalescent in the house figure. Predictably, her ever-present apprehension of the house of death seems to have led all the rest. One month before the family's move, she slid easily from concrete fact to a world elsewhere as she wrote Jane, "We shall be in our new house soon; they are papering now, and – Jennie, we have *other* home – 'house not made with hands.' "[162]

Chapter 3
The Dickinson homestead on Main Street

Each Life Converges to some Centre –
Expressed – or still –
Exists in every Human Nature
A Goal –
EMILY DICKINSON

The home is the centre and circumference, the start and the
finish, of most of our lives. We love it with a love older than
the human race. We reverence it with the blind obeisance
of those crouching centuries when its cult began. We cling
to it with the tenacity of every inmost, oldest instinct of
our animal natures, and with the enthusiasm of every
latest word in the unbroken chant of adoration which we
have sung to it since first we learned to praise.
CHARLOTTE PERKINS GILMAN

One of Andrew Wyeth's now classic paintings, *Christina's World*
(1948), shows a partially crippled woman, back to the viewer,
seated in a field of long grass in the lower left foreground. Her
head turns diagonally toward the upper right background and
skyline where a stark clapboard farmhouse sits. At a distance behind it is a lean-to barn. Christina stretches out toward the buildings, grasping the grass with her gnarled, deformed fingers as she
drags her spindly, useless legs behind her. As in most of Wyeth's
paintings, the harshly realistic style does much more than illustrate. In this one, a strong sense of ambiguity emerges as clearly
as Christina's body cuts across the composition. Her position, outside and at a distance from the house, that is, temporarily independent of it, contrasts with her obvious yearning for it. The effect is
almost surrealistic, so filled with overtones are the specific, precisely painted objects Wyeth reproduces.

Dreamlike as it is actual, the picture echoes Freud's observation
that "a house is the only regularly occurring symbol of the (whole)

FIGURE 6. *The Edward Dickinson Mansion on Main Street. Lithograph, 1858. Courtesy of the Jones Library, Amherst.*

human body in dreams."[1] Is Christina looking toward the house
not only for protection, but also because of her paralysis, almost
enviously seeing it as embodying the perfect, unimpaired body she
has lost? Does she grudgingly idealize it for its structure *per se* as
well as for its service as a shelter?

Emily Dickinson might easily be substituted for Christina in
Wyeth's painting, especially if her "crippling" is considered to be
psychological rather than physical. The same ambiguous element
of desire for, yet release from, home was true of Emily. The distance between Christina and her house was, for Emily, the isolation
she felt within the family. But two houses dominated the poet's
landscape, and her ambivalence toward each was not the same. The
Pleasant Street house, though it was the scene of sadness at times,
aroused within her profound loyalties and idealistic images of
home. The Mansion evoked similar feelings about home for Edward Dickinson and further abetted his desire to reestablish family
dignity, but Emily did not appear to share these sentiments. It
seems that her preference for Pleasant Street was rooted in the fact
that, though the pattern of her life remained essentially the same
after the move, pressures upon her increased, the result, in part, of
the substitution of a strange, even semihostile environment for one
which reflected all the loves and hopes of the poet's younger self.

Leaving this well-loved home may be compared to the childhood
fear of losing one's mother. For Emily, its loss might have been
equivalent to the loss of a primary object of nurture, vital and dependable beyond questioning. In this sense, mother and home
were identical, although Mrs. Dickinson was only one element in
the many which contributed to the complex significance Emily
gave that word. The passage quoted in the last chapter, "Home is
a holy *thing*" (my italics), makes the Pleasant Street house as affecting an *object* as mother at the same time as the rest of the statement explains why.[2] Here was an atmosphere of trust which no one
could shatter. She had acutely felt this potential loss during the
year she was at Mount Holyoke. The vein of playfulness and the
easy facetious tone of Emily's letters from the Pleasant Street years
changes to a predominant seriousness and eventually to a resounding tragic note by her thirties. This fact alone, though supported
by others, suggests that the homestead remained beyond comparison to her former home.

This chapter traces Dickinson's accentuated sense of the Mansion's enclosure, as protection or limitation, past which she sometimes made poetic leaps. It tracks, too, her search for a "center," an alternative, intangible, and unstable home. All four areas of interest outlined in chapter 1 will contribute to the argument, beginning with Emily's reaction to her displacement from Pleasant Street. Afterward, a brief view of the Mansion inside and out will set the scene for reconsidering the drama of her private world. This view of Emily's intensified anxieties will pay special attention to the spatial analogies she may have derived from the actual architecture of the house, or her situation within it, to reflect her entire self, literally body and soul. Toward the end of the chapter, Emily's preoccupation with smallness will be seen in a new light. To anticipate, her attitude reveals an intimate connection between a sense of both feminine and poetic inner space and three of her most pressing concerns: her need to discover a locus, or "center," her decision to practice a "strict economy," and her search for position or "status."

In November 1855, Emily was led away from the Pleasant Street house as if she had been a captured fugitive slave. Psychologically, however, the experience was in a sense worse, because the "old castle"[3] she was returning to was as foreign to her as a new country. She tried to stifle even the memory of the move, but the change was too dramatic to erase entirely. Two months afterward, she wrote a close friend about it, her playfulness a counterpoint to but not a disguise for an undercurrent of considerable regret, suggested especially by the last paragraph:

> I cannot tell you how we moved. I had rather not remember. I believe my "effects" were brought in a bandbox, and the "deathless me," on foot, not many moments after. I took at the time a memorandum of my several senses, and also of my hat and coat, and my best shoes – but it was lost in the *melee*, and I am out with lanterns, looking for myself.
>
> Such wits as I reserved, are so badly shattered that repair is useless – and still I can't help laughing at my own catastrophe. I supposed we were going to make a "transit," as heavenly bodies did – but we came budget by budget, as our fellows do, till we fulfilled the pantomime contained in the word "moved." It is a kind of *gone-to-Kansas* feeling, and if I sat in

a long wagon, with my family tied behind, I should suppose
without doubt I was a party of emigrants!

They say that "home is where the heart is." I think it is
where the *house* is, and the adjacent buildings.[4]

The atmosphere of arrival was doubly depressing because the
recurrence of Mrs. Dickinson's illness confined her to a lounge or
easy chair while Emily and Lavinia "regulated" and "got settled."
In itself, this must have been alarming enough to Emily – "I don't
know what her sickness is, for I am but a simple child, and frightened at myself"[5] – but as a forewarning of her future role it must
have seemed ominous. Simply the shift from a smaller to a larger
house doubtless also disturbed Emily, with the additional housework required. Even pestilence seemed less "fell" than housekeeping to her, and, eventually, she arranged to keep the "Butterfly"
(that is, the lighter, more attractive), not the "Moth" part of the
house.[6]

For Edward Dickinson, the return to Main Street marked the
zenith of his career. It was a public witness of his ability to reestablish and maintain the Dickinson honor, fortune, and homestead
lost by his father, Samuel Fowler Dickinson, in the early 1830s.
By his purchase of the property from the Mack family, the interim
owners, the family seat seemed to be returned to its rightful heirs.
From it, Edward, leading lawyer, recent representative to Congress, Amherst College treasurer, active churchman, and indus-
trious pioneer in bringing the railroad and the telegraph to the
town, unequivocally established his position as one of the first, if
not the first, among the town fathers. The extensive additions and
renovations he made to the Mansion were noted by the local press
and by townspeople.[7] Edward's birthplace, so improved, confirmed
the worth of his contributions. The Greek Revival features of the
new architecture suggested how much the place was now truly his
temple.[8] In contrast, for Emily the return meant the beginning of
a special and solemn imprisonment, special because in part she
willed it, solemn because in the willing there was no escape.

The new home left Emily half-numb and immediately nostalgic
for the old. Her prose comments seem to be seconded by at least
one poem. In *Littell's Living Age* for spring 1855, in her father's
library, the bottom corner of a page is turned up, perhaps by her.
It partly covers a poem entitled "Home," by T. Westwood, re-

printed from *Frazer's Magazine*. His sentiments, gothic and ghostly as they are, parallel Emily's regrets about leaving the Pleasant Street place. She might have read his first stanza, probably after the return to the Mansion, with a sharp sense of empathy:

> Broad lands and stormy seas lie spread
>   Between me and my home,
> But still its ancient paths I tread,
>   Still round its walls I roam.
> A stranger hath my heritage,
>   But he'll ne'er be rid of me.
> I climb the stairs, I pace the floors,
> I pass unchallenged through the doors,
>   A ghost no eye can see.[9]

Westwood's verse appeared the same year as the family's change of residence. But the following poem of Emily's, which doubtless refers to the Pleasant Street house, is dated in its earliest version about seven years afterwards, in 1862. It shows her inability even then to adjust, a measure of her consistent loyalty to memories (it was written also at the height of her crisis of the early 1860s). The first version (1862) reads as follows:

> I – Years had been – from Home –
> And now – before the Door –
> I dared not open – lest a face
> I never saw before
>
> Stare vacant into mine –
> And ask my Business there –
> My Business – just a Life I left –
> Was such – still dwelling there?
>
> I fumbled at my nerve –
> I scanned the Windows o'er –
> The Silence – like an Ocean rolled –
> And broke against my Ear –
>
> I laughed a Wooden laugh –
> That I – could fear a Door –
> Who Danger – and the Dead – had faced –
> But never shook – before –

I fitted to the Latch – my Hand –
With trembling care –
Lest back the Awful Door should spring –
And leave me – in the Floor –

I moved my fingers off, as cautiously as Glass – .
And held my Ears – and like a Thief
Stole – gasping – from the House.

The second version is dated 1872:

I Years had been from Home
And now before the Door
I dared not enter, lest a Face
I never saw before

Stare stolid into mine
And ask my Business there –
"My Business but a Life I left
Was such remaining there?"

I leaned upon the Awe –
I lingered with Before –
The Second like an Ocean rolled
And broke against my ear –

I laughed a crumbling Laugh
That I could fear a Door
Who Consternation compassed
And never winced before.

I fitted to the Latch
My Hand, with trembling care
Lest back the awful Door should spring
And leave me in the Floor –

Then moved my Fingers off
As cautiously as Glass
And held my ears, and like a Thief
Fled gasping from the House –   (609)

If Thomas Johnson's dating of the poems is correct (and his most
scrupulous critic, R. W. Franklin, has not faulted the dating of

these poems)[10] then Emily's revisions indicate a continuing concern for the theme of this poem: a longing to return to the other
life she lived in the only house which she could truly call *her*
home. We have noted that the two versions are ten years apart, the
first written seven years after the return to the Mansion. Home as
a locus of safety and peace seems to have remained as a fervent
hope in Dickinson's consciousness, playing against her hard knowledge of death's house. The new environment of the homestead
could not erase the earlier inscape.

From the very first line of the poem, I assume that she refers to
the Pleasant Street house and not the Mansion. She returns to a
consistent problem or conflict which presses her, which forces her
to relive it, and thus she attempts to master it. Again and again, she
seeks to redeem her loss, even if she "escapes" a solution once more.
So the poem re-presents an opportunity for changing the past,
though only in the realm of fantasy, at the same moment that it
alleviates anguish. It performs the service that Emily admitted to
Higginson was accomplished for her by writing poetry: "I felt a
palsy, here – the Verses just relieve."[11]

This poem shows Dickinson struggling to adjust to a new self,
first in 1862, then again, to another, in 1872. She is in the act of
reexperiencing a crisis of identity, not once or twice but more
times than we may know, arriving at slightly altered, yet significantly changed, views of herself, even though her pattern of behavior remains constant.

There are small but central changes in the two versions of the
poem. The first stanza reads almost identically in each version except for alterations in punctuation. The radical decrease of dashes
in the 1872 poem suggests that a certain helplessness has been exchanged for a sense of surety, even though it is a certainty of danger or despair, when Emily "returns" to her old home. This new
tone of expectedness becomes reenforced by the capitalization of
Face in line three of the second version. The "Face" of the stranger
in the house now becomes by its move to the upper case a terrifying, larger-than-life abstraction, a general hovering Fear, all the
more because she never actually confronts it.

The sharper features of that Face, "vacant" in 1862, "stolid"
("or – horrid," as she wrote in the margin) in the 1872 manuscript,
also suggest the cementing process of Emily's terror during the in-
tervening years. The "Business" which brought her back, nothing

less than to seek the "Life I left," was by 1872 sealed off by the impassivity of that Face, and even by its horror. Could the happy time of 1840–55 in the Pleasant Street place, now nearly idealized beyond reality in retrospect, never be retrieved? By 1872, it seems, Emily had either accepted or frightened herself into adjusting to the fact that it could not.

In the third stanza of the 1862 copy, she had "fumbled" at her nerve and "scanned" the windows, still thinking she could "see" something of her former self there. But ten years later, again the abstract has replaced the concrete: "I leaned upon the Awe – / I lingered with Before." The mode is of resignation, teased by some hope, but not real anticipation. Also, the time of her actual hesitation before the door has been telescoped. Earlier, it had been an indefinite period, the "Silence" of a far distant ocean wave, not yet within "breaking" audibility, that is, decision. Later "Silence" becomes "Second," the actual moment the wave hit the beach, signifying that she was not vacillating either long or even at all this time.

The mood of self-mockery, "I laughed a Wooden laugh," also diminishes almost to nothingness as the laugh becomes "crumbling" in 1872. And the sense of the self as victor over adversity appears stronger in the revised version. In 1862, she had merely "faced" danger and death. Later she had "compassed" Consternation, once again a change to the abstract, that word bearing the weight of danger and death combined, and so she could stand unwaveringly, at least until this moment.

The fifth stanza remains virtually the same with its image of the door as a bear trap which touched even lightly would capture the trespasser and snap her to the floor. The sense of guilt underlying this stanza may well go beyond the simple sense of entering a house which is no longer one's own home. Emily seems ashamed to be trying to recapture a period she knows in part she cannot possibly claim again. Perhaps her childish wish for a simple harmony was still operative, though her more mature self knew another sort of happiness would be her only present hope.

The final stanza also remains almost intact, except, again, for the reduction of four dashes to a final one. She holds her ears, presumably to block cries from the Face ("Stop! Thief!"), as if she had managed to steal a portion of her earlier life anyway. (She flees instead of steals away in the 1872 version, suggesting a greater sense of objective reality.) But the nervous palpitation which is the rhythm of both poems is reemphasized by the flight from the house while "gasping" from fright and perhaps a touch of guilt.

Emily has not reached a completely stable self in the process of her rewriting. The act of refashioning the 1862 version has led her to substitutions suggesting a more realistic view of her impossible quest. But she is still "gasping." Her search for a true home is unsatisfied, even through the act of composition. She begins the poem speaking of her home; she ends it fleeing from the house. It is no longer hers, but an objective building or, more, a house haunted for her not only by an irrecoverable time past, but by fear itself. She is set on an endless odyssey to find a home, which the Mansion could never completely be.[12]

Emily's sense of homelessness becomes more specific in additional poems dating from her crisis or from an unknown time. The following one, also written about 1862, expresses both the frustration of the first version of "I Years had been from Home" and the qualified sense of reality of the 1872 copy. But the subject has become more focused. Sexual allusions surface sufficiently to suggest that Emily's frustration now relates to unrequited romance. Further, this inner experience is set in an exterior scene. Dickinson's inscape goes "outside," and the perspective from outside looking in (an interesting reversal of Emily's usual position, yet still an "inner" look) helps work toward the transcending observations of the final stanza, however temporary they might be.

> I had been hungry, all the Years –
> My Noon had Come – to dine –
> I trembling drew the Table near –
> And touched the Curious Wine –
>
> 'Twas this on Tables I had seen –
> When turning, hungry, Home
> I looked in Windows, for the Wealth
> I could not hope – for Mine –
>
> I did not know the ample Bread –
> 'Twas so unlike the Crumb
> The Birds and I, had often shared
> In Nature's – Dining Room –

The Plenty hurt me – 'twas so new –
Myself felt ill – and odd –
As Berry – of a Mountain Bush –
Transplanted – to the Road –

Nor was I hungry – so I found
That Hunger – was a way
Of Persons outside Windows –
The Entering – takes away –   (579)

Emily's explicit theme is a search for a true home, an earthly household where she would be mistress, privy to a "Wealth" she felt she would never have in actual fact. Her implicit theme of a desire to satisfy long-buried erotic needs seems almost equally transparent. In daydreamlike words, Emily may be expressing a hunger of the profoundest sort, a psychobiologic cry for a place to call her own home, a locus of sexual fulfillment. As any young girl might, Emily owns that for years (she was then in her early thirties), she has anticipated the food of marriage, and then "My Noon," the apex hour for Emily, signifying the meeting of a crucial want, arrives. Nervously Emily draws near the table, an object which in dreams is very often found to represent a bed.[13] Conscious or unconscious of the depth of her need, perhaps Emily reveals a normal but accentuated desire for the pleasures of the marriage bed. There is "Bread." Yet even imaginatively, the "ample Bread" is too much. It sickens rather than sustains, simply because of its novelty. "The Plenty hurt me – 'twas so new – / Myself felt ill – and odd." Disillusioned, she loses her appetite, implying that desire may be quenched by even a taste of its object. The state of want is far preferable to satiety.

This reluctance to fulfill herself is a recurring hesitancy, perhaps more than it is a resignation to fact. It reveals that part of her which forestalled losing the pleasure of anticipation by withholding the final object. In part, contentment was a state of becoming behind her father's hedge rather than an act of completion in the world outside it. The tension pleased: "Consummation is the hurry of fools . . . , but Expectation the Elixir of the Gods."[14] Almost intuitively, but also by experience, cultural and personal, she developed restraint as a supreme virtue, part of the soul's frugality.

II.

Even if the Mansion failed Emily's requirements for home, it did more than merely shelter her. Its design and the use of its rooms set the movement of her daily life, perhaps even suggested a mood, and put before her seemingly endless concrete materials for her poetic use. One student of her vocabulary, William Howard, has noted her preference for the physical symbol. Even death, he points out, absorbed her as a biological process, not only as a mysterious or mystical experience.[15] Quite naturally, she reached for available external props to support insights of her inner life. Also, this habit had intellectual roots, the Puritan appreciation of the emblematic value of natural objects as well as the Emersonian version of idealism.

But more immediately it arose from the simple fact of being a woman. For Emily as a housekeeper, the humble article of daily use, though its upkeep annoyed and postponed the ecstatic life, still pressed on her consciousness with its symbolic potential: bones, cobwebs, cups, brooms, aprons, balls of yarn, seams, baskets, but above all, windows and doors, pantries, chambers and rooms.[16] The single "thing" could be a simple object, a feature of architecture, or a whole room. (In general, girls earlier than boys have been observed to be able to do limited, detailed, and concentrated work with objects, and have a correspondingly acute and sensuous appreciation of them: seeing, touching, and hearing.)[17] In light of Emily's sensitivity to and poetic use of the plan and furnishings of her father's house, a quick tour of certain parts of it may serve as rather more than a travelogue.

The original rectangle of the Mansion was built about 1813, probably of local brick, in a country version of the elegant Federal period style.[18] Outlined on the top by an oversized cornice and on the bottom by the granite blocks of a deep cellar, a first sign of the owner's wealth, the early section was enlarged, probably by Edward in 1855. The additions included a two-story east wing with a conservatory on the south side, a rear ell with a porch to the east, and a veranda on the west. At the same time, the front entrance and portico in the Greek Revival style, and the cupola, a popular feature of mid-nineteenth century Victorian houses, may have been added.[19] No doubt in order to disguise the scars of these changes the house was painted yellow, which faded to a dull white in later

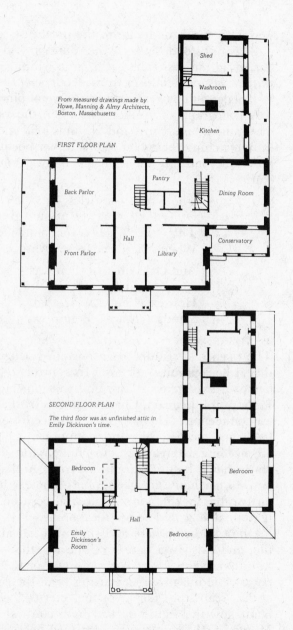

From measured drawings made by
Howe, Manning & Almy Architects,
Boston, Massachusetts

Shed

Washroom

Kitchen

FIRST FLOOR PLAN

Back Parlor

Pantry

Dining Room

Hall

Conservatory

Front Parlor

Library

SECOND FLOOR PLAN

The third floor was an unfinished attic in
Emily Dickinson's time.

Bedroom

Bedroom

Hall

*Emily
Dickinson's
Room*

Bedroom

FIGURE 7. *Floor plan of the Dickinson Mansion in 1915, before changes
made by the Hervey Parke family.*

years.[20] Behind the house to the northeast, a large barn with car-
riage wings stood between the Mansion and a grove of oak trees.
Guarding the east side was a large white oak, while on the west
was a towering hemlock. In the front, shooting tall above the hemlock hedge and picket fence, were several pine trees.[21]

A lithograph of Amherst in 1886, the year of Emily's death,
shows the house, barn, and grounds held in precise focus, graphi-
cally matching the mood of one of her poems, although the poem
points beyond any object, even natural ones, to her country of
truth.

> The Truth – is stirless –
> Other force – may be presumed to move –
> This – then – is best for confidence –
> When oldest Cedars swerve –
>
> And Oaks untwist their fists –
> And Mountains – feeble – lean –
> How excellent a Body, that
> Stands without a Bone –   (780)

. . . .

The essence of truth's power, or at least her first requirement, is
that it be constant, "stirless." Its control contrasts so sharply with
her own experience of turmoil that one understands the reason
this aspect is primary. Changeless, it is trustworthy and loyal, "best
for confidence." Then, moving to place it next to the giants of her
landscape – cedars, oaks, and mountains – she finds it surpasses them
all, needing no structure, no "Bone," for support. So powerful is
truth that it holds "without a Prop." And she, trusting it, stands
beyond her house or any support, "boldly up." Emily is momentarily calm, looking far past physical position to the "place" which,
if attainable, would be her ideal home.

One could stop here and state that her ability to surpass situation and exist in a nation of one was the central paradox of her
seclusion. "The Heart is the Capital of the Mind." But in other
poems, the image shifts, starting from the actual to Emily's views
of the "real," the "ideal," or the "eternal," changes which help explain how this figure evoked both coziness and awe in the poet.
Moreover, the subtle corners turned on this theme deserve closer
study, which will follow a description of the Mansion's interior.

Inside the house, the atmosphere largely reflected Edward Dickinson's preferences, a goal which Mrs. Dickinson abetted to the best of her abilities.[22] But it also varied with the arrangement of space and light. The dominant impression was of a Greek temple, seemingly windowless with its shutters drawn. Emily's niece noted that the house was often "sacredly closed"[23] in the winter to keep heat in and in the summer to keep the house cool. The front parlors on the west side gave some lightness with their white wallpaper, marble-topped tables, and gay Brussels carpet, but the dominant somberness of these rooms must have been nearly sepulchral.[24] Thomas W. Higginson noted in 1870 that they were "dark and cool and stiffish. . . ."[25] No wonder one winter Emily wrote a friend, ". . . in my Pearl Jail, I think of Sun and Summer as visages unknown."[26] The setting was of a Gothic romance, materials for a story which Emily's life may well have suggested to Helen Hunt Jackson.[27]

If the shadow of her father filled the air of the darkened parlors, his influence also permeated the ground floor rooms to the east which were more frequently heated and unshuttered. Across the hall in his library, floor to ceiling bookcases filled two walls.[28] And no doubt an engraved portrait of Daniel Webster, affirming Edward's Whig affiliations, was hung here.[29] Through a doorway off his study was Emily's conservatory where she grew ferns, wild flowers, and exotic plants. Here, too, her father may have been hauntingly present. He encouraged her botanical interests with the gift of a book, *Wild Flowers Drawn and Colored from Nature,* in January 1859.[30] And he had made a watering pot with an antenna-like spout to reach the plants on the topmost shelf.[31] When she used it or consulted *Wild Flowers,* she may have been distantly aware that he was supervising the conservatory specimens almost as much as she was.

The family dining room, in the eastern addition, was the one "Father loved the most," Emily recalled in 1881.[32] Its spaciousness and proximity to the kitchen just behind made it a natural sitting room as well. One feels the casualness of the spot, with Edward's law papers haphazardly filed in a soup tureen, a lounge in which Mrs. Dickinson rested near the fireplace, and a writing table for Emily in the southeast corner of the room.[33] With her view both of the conservatory and of the garden to the east, Emily doubtless enjoyed the comfort and convenience of this room as much as her father did.

FIGURE 8. *The Evergreens, Austin Dickinson's house, ca. 1900. Courtesy of Harvard College Library.*

Parts of the house can be clearly associated just with Emily and her increasing need for a "polar privacy." The "Northwest Passage" was a middle pantry and hallway whose five exits allowed her easy escape from unwanted visitors.[34] The deep cellar was in a sense a bank vault where her storage cupboard for gingerbread, as well as the family liquor supply, were locked up. Not for sampling these, but rather to escape her father's command to go to church, Emily was once reportedly locked in the cellar by Maggie, the Irish maid.[35] Perhaps this time, too, she was prepared to confront the fears she found cellar-deep in the poem "Remembrance has a Rear and Front." On the east porch running the length of the ell, she could regally sit surveying the sloping grounds, surrounded by luxuriant plants brought from the conservatory.[36] On a drop-leaf table under a west window in the kitchen, she precisely measured her ingredients for breads and desserts.[37] And in the garret, she was known to have read Shakespeare and perhaps written poetry as well.[38]

But the place to which Emily could retreat as to a special sanctuary within "father's house" was her bedroom-workroom. Located on the southwest corner of the second floor with two windows facing each exposure, Emily had views of Main Street – the world passing by – and of a garden adjoining the Mansion which was cut by a narrow path to the Evergreens, Austin's house. The campanile of the Evergreens and the windows of the east side of the house were visible from Emily's west windows, a reminder of her "beloved Household" next door, a household which increasingly became her one touch with any dwelling other than her own.

A double mahogany sleigh-style bed dominated the room, placed as it was on the east wall with advantageous, though veiled, views of Main Street and Austin's grounds (because it was set back from curtained windows).[39] Waking one morning, she doubtless conceived the poem "The Angle of a Landscape – / That every time I wake – / Between my Curtain and the Wall / Upon an ample Crack."[40] Into this crack, she fitted a bough of apples, a chimney, a hill, a weathervane, and finally a steeple. She may have piled the scene on purpose but the delight of doing so seems motivated by a more serious purpose than cataloguing the landscape. Except for the bough of apples, replaced by a snow-burdened branch in another season, all the other subjects of her view "never stir at all," as she claims in the last line of the poem. Controlled, structured, dependable, above all trustworthy objects, so much in contrast to Dickinson's own inner life, as earlier noted in discussing "The Truth is stirless." Once again, Emily seems to be seeking supports which she does not find within herself, her room, her house, but rather ones which could only be bestowed by Nature or by God, not immune to change but perhaps more stable than the poet.

Opposite her bed was a Franklin stove on one side of which was a lounge or day bed. These objects and their accessories once occasioned a bit of defensive fancy from Emily, a typical tactic to forestall fear. This particular passage also suggests the depth of a loneliness which encouraged the poet to people her room, even with inanimate objects:

I am somewhat afraid at night, but the Ghosts have been very attentive, and I have no cause to complain. Of course one

FIGURE 9. *The original Franklin stove in Emily's bedroom with 1853 photograph of Edward Dickinson above. Photograph by Lewis Mudge.*

FIGURE 10. *A painted Hitchcock-type chair and cherry writing table used by Emily Dickinson in her room at the Mansion. Photograph by Lewis Mudge. Courtesy of Harvard College Library.*

cant expect one's furniture to sit still all night, and if the Chairs do prance – and the Lounge polka a little, and the shovel give it's arm to the tongs, one dont mind such things! From fearing them at first, I've grown to quite admire them, and now we understand each other, it is most enlivening![41]

Relatively inconspicuous but all important to the poet was a lady's writing table (probably the same she had used in her room at Pleasant Street), only seventeen and a half inches square and with a single drawer. Sitting before the table in the southwest corner of her room, Emily had choice views looking south, to the activities of Main Street and the Holyoke Range beyond, or west to her brother's house and the setting sun. As she suggests in "Myself was formed – a Carpenter," the table was her "board" where she tooled her constructions. The quantity of poetry she produced here in toto, about 1775 poems, radically contrasts with the table's dimensions, an odd, illogical fact which yet parallels in physical terms Dickinson's ability to surpass her supposed smallness. (This fact has even a second parallel in the contrast between the poet's subjects, "large" beyond further choice, and the typical succinctness of her expression and the shortness of her poems.) The table provided Dickinson with a "board" where she could "plane" ideas which might occur to her by a single glance, as in "The Angle of a Landscape," by a passing circus, by a sound when someone whistled on his way down Main Street, "Heart, not so heavy as mine / Wending late home – / As it passed my window / Whistled itself a tune," or by the light rising higher on her east wall as the sun sank and the "Juggler of Day" disappeared.[42]

Her purpose, as she says in ending her carpentry poem, is to "build Temples," the architecture of *her* house, the house of poetry. But paper temples may be fitted to furniture, and Dickinson carefully did so, making small booklets of her finished poems and collecting her work sheets or semifinal drafts loosely, storing all in a large mahogany bureau. The poem, "Essential oils are wrung," to be discussed later in the chapter, hints of the bureau's use as a vault for the poet's unknown writings, protecting her treasure of insights, her "essential oils."

If scenes, interior settings, or specific objects suggested themes or images to Dickinson, the overarching importance of her room

FIGURE 11. *Emily Dickinson's cherry bureau, where she kept her letters and poems. Photograph by Lewis Mudge. Courtesy of Harvard College Library.*

was equally close to consciousness and available for poetic use. In her own chamber, she had Virginia Woolf's ideal requirements for the woman writer in *A Room of One's Own:* her own retreat and no financial worries. Only time to write might need to be bought, although Lavinia, convinced that Emily's role in the family was "to think," absorbed a large portion of her chores.[43] Also, this room gave her the privacy and liberty she could have nowhere else. Usually, she brought her letters here even before they were opened – "The way I read a Letter's this."[44] And she was protected from encounters of any sort except those which were self-imposed.[45] On one occasion she led her niece up to the room, shut the door, then took an imaginary key and pretended to lock it with the remark, "It's just a turn – and freedom, Matty!"[46]

The continuing possibility of that state, however, is seriously questioned by Emily's poetic testimony. In certain poems, one sees the irony of a spirit sometimes in acute torture in her most private, secluded, and presumably secure sanctuary. "I am afraid to own a Body – / I am afraid to own a Soul."[47] But her struggle even to acknowledge the "space" due her physically or spiritually alternated with moments of self-integration and release. These bouts with anguish and their defeat illuminate Allen Tate's generality, "Her life was one of the richest and deepest ever lived on this continent."[48] His comment should be kept in mind for its relevance to a later section of this chapter, an exploration of the recurring anxieties which challenged the poet's self-possession. Repeatedly, her contending selves divided or frightened her as did unidentified spectres, or her more general consternations, especially about death, men, and loneliness. The room that promised freedom, then, even with its door supposedly locked, had no defense against her own fears.

III.

To pursue these anxieties in depth, Erikson's psychosociology of femininity is suggestive and deserves review. As mentioned before, his essay "Womanhood and the Inner Space" supports Freud's supposition that the womb, place of creation, and by extension of safety, becomes symbolized quite naturally by a house or by home.

In structure and function, uterus and house parallel each other. They enclose a protective, nurturing space.

Erikson's empirical evidence in support of his thesis derives in part from an experiment involving the toy and block play of normal, pre-adolescent children. They were asked to build on a table "an exciting scene from an imaginary moving picture," a suggestion whose purpose was to maximize the free play of imagination and minimize a predetermination of the results whether by cultural orientation or Erikson's own direction.[49]

Boys typically arranged structures with an emphasis on the exterior. And the architectural features chosen to elaborate the roofs or walls of these buildings were protrusions like cones or cylinders, used to imitate decorations or cannons. A preferred form was the high tower, suggesting to Erikson the erect phallus. Further, this male-child world placed the scene's activities largely outside the buildings and stressed the dynamic movement normal to streets and the dramatic encounters and stops at cross sections. Accidents were a major interest, but also the controlling or arresting role of the policemen was involved. As if to reflect contrary drives another way, the high towers could be knocked down and the collapse cause pleasure, or be built for their own sake suggesting downfall and the excitement of that danger another way. Such ruins were built only by the boys.

The feminine counterworld which the girls constructed concentrated on the opposite, the interior of a house, loosely suggested only by furniture or by blocks representing enclosures. Walls were generally low, although doorways might be elaborate. Again, Erikson interprets this sign of architectural preference as a symbolization of a biological given, the womb, its entrance, and its nurturing, pacific nature. To this point, Erikson notes that people or animals placed inside this interior space were generally engaged in a peaceful activity, or were even in a static position, sitting or standing. If the scene was interrupted by either an animal or a man, the girls' reaction was mixed, involving fear, pleasure, or even amusement.

In brief, then, the differing sexual responses to space shown in this experiment tend, Erikson argues, to parallel either male or female morphology, that is, genital forms, specifically the phallus or womb, as well as social roles, whether active, even aggressive in the male or more circumspect and subdued in the female. *Erikson allows that these differences, though based upon the male and female "ground plans," are only indications of predilections and preferences.* They are not exclusive to each sex. He merely says that they "come more naturally."[50]

Women's liberationists, Kate Millett leading the rest,[51] have taken issue with Erikson as being narrowly Freudian and deterministic about women on this point. Millett may be incisive, entertaining, and sometimes brilliant in *Sexual Politics,* and I completely support her general thesis, but here her criticism seems to assume too much in Erikson's theories. He does not suggest that women have an *exclusive* interest in the home nor does he *prescribe* that they should stay there. On the contrary, he wants to make the traditional "feminine" qualities of warmth, understanding, and peace more operative in the world at large. He only suggests that women appear to have a psychological proclivity for establishing and cherishing an enclosed protected locus, a desire that lies rooted in their physiological design or ground plan. Millett's attack on the evils of a society controlled by a patriarchal mythology is sometimes faintly echoed in Dickinson, as in the poem, "Title divine – is mine!" to be discussed shortly. But Millett's generally justified thesis should not be accepted at the expense of erasing sexual differences or of losing genuinely germinal insights like Erikson's.

Obviously, one may relate Erikson's hypothesis to the first area of Dickinson's spatial inscape, her own body. In this way, her arrangements of words (analogous to Erikson's experimental blocks) in the image of house and home or their corollaries may be read as referring to her unconscious awareness of womanliness fulfilled or empty. Possibly these verbal signs reveal her response to inner structure, to the fact that she harbored an almost sanctified space. Her feeling that "Home is a holy thing" could assume an additional meaning, referring directly to herself as a female phenomenon. The close association, even identification in the case of the hearth, that she made with parts of the Pleasant Street house lends weight to this supposition.[52]

Dickinson lacked the worldly identification of "Mrs.," and one cannot know for certain whether her satiric poem on this theme masks great disappointment about her celibate state or not:

> Title divine – is mine!
> The Wife – without the Sign!

Acute degree – conferred on me
Empress of Calvary!
Royal – all but the Crown!
Betrothed – without the swoon
God sends us Women –
When you – hold – Garnet to Garnet –
Gold – to Gold –
Born – Bridalled – Shrouded –
In a Day –
"My Husband" – women say –
Stroking the Melody
Is *this* – the way?   (1072)

If a bitterness about being unmarried underlies these lines, it is
overshadowed by a certain satisfaction with femininity alone. She
asks about possession of another by having his name, "Is *this*"
truly fulfillment or, conversely, even true wifehood? What she
needed, wanted, and fantasized that she had, according to her first
line, was a self-elected status which achieved divinity. That sort of
title alone properly acknowledged her degree of suffering and
renunciation. Reaching the ultimate in resignation, she felt deserving of a regal title, nothing less than the Empress of Calvary!
Her royalty was, like Christ's, based on worldly deprivations. But
they did not make her Jesus' bride. Here, then, she displays
femininity apart from man or even God's son, cherished for itself,
despite its empty state. The womanly self is honored independent
of any human or divine addition to its identity. If there is any
marriage suggested, it is to this ideal.

Dickinson poems which directly speak of her femininity, as in
this one, or allude to it in imagery paralleling female morphology,
do further service. They indicate her current state of identity, her
self-image of the moment. Emily's position as an adult, still living
as a child at home with her parents, helped to prolong her development toward a settled, mature self. Adolescence and its crises
plagued her, a phenomenon not uncommon to creative minds.[53]
The two versions of "I Years had been from Home" strongly hint
of this arresting, cyclical pattern. The resulting instability abetted
Emily's natural antipathy toward holding firm beliefs about the
"flood subjects" of life. Her personality-in-turmoil, her advances
and regressions toward new levels of identity, help explain how

she could control the fears which haunted her and yet sound as if their submission existed primarily in the poems.

Renewed and invigorated by the press of the Mansion's size and inhospitality, the problems Emily knew at Pleasant Street appear again, but with greater intensity, duration, and effect than previously reported. Her competing selves – "me" and "my spirit" – emerge with God normally absent. At times her self-examination was done almost reverently, as if intruding on her own privacy. "As there are Apartments in our own Minds that . . . we never enter without Apology – we should respect the seals of others."[54] Respecting her seal but prepared by Erikson and by the evolving nature of the poet's identity, I would like to examine tenacious anxieties penetrating the innermost chambers of her mind: encounters with her two selves, death, sex, and the reverse side of her separateness, desperate loneliness. Each powerfully presents itself in house or home imagery.

IV.

Emily's dependence solely "On a Columnar Self," an image which she might have derived from the front portico of her house with its Ionic columns in sight from her bedroom windows,[55] may be read as the romantic embodiment of her self-reliance. But this poem and others which speak of self-sufficiency appear to do so, not from an unmitigated sense of power and release, but more from the deep shadows of uncertainty. One is reminded of Emily's admission, ". . . I sing, as the Boy does by the Burying Ground – because I am afraid."[56] In this poem her boast seems extreme, perhaps because of its insecure roots. She looks down from a height above circumstance and somewhat self-righteously finds herself with "Rectitude" and near God, that is, approaching a life independent of the "Crowd" but not outside of divine purview.

In another poem, "The Soul selects her own Society," her attitude is impressively arch. She is the "divine Majority" to whom all worldly entreaty is meaningless, even an emperor's offered while he kneels on her matted floor. One feels that though the Soul "Choose One" for companionship, that one, through distrust of all others, may well be the self. In fact, that drive toward total separateness finally leads her to eschew even architectural support, as the fifth verse of "I am alive – I guess –" illustrates:

> I am alive – because
> I do not own a House
> Entitled to myself – precise –
> And fitting no one else –   (470)

Her self-entitlement echoes the theme of independent femininity
in "Title divine – is mine!" Emily's actual house becomes inconsequential before her more central "house," which is "myself," that
is, body and soul. On this house, she continues, is marked "my
Girlhood's name – / So visitors may know / Which Door is mine –
and not mistake – / And try another Key." In these lines, Emily
Dickinson seems almost stridently married to herself.[57]

As I have been saying, however, this affirmation of superiority
appears to arise as forcefully as it does because of its base in self-
doubt. In "The Soul's Superior instants"[58] Emily saves the height
of ecstasy for total privacy, but her subject is exhilaration, not
self-reliance. In the other poems just mentioned, a note of insistent
superiority seems to be hiding a gnawing insecurity and lack of a
whole or healthy identity.[59] In brief, her tone of totality, of satisfaction with oneself for society, seems to rest on the unsure truce
between her two selves.

That this compromise could collapse and turn one's other side
and sometime companion into the opposite, an arch enemy, who
relentlessly hunts and always succeeds because he is ever-present,
is vividly evoked in the following stanzas. Again, the architecture
of the house describes not only her psyche but the scene of action
within it as well:

> One need not be a Chamber – to be Haunted –
> One need not be a House –
> The Brain has Corridors – surpassing
> Material Place –
>
> .   .   .   .
>
> Ourself behind oneself, concealed –
> Should startle most –
> Assassin hid in our Apartment
> Be Horror's least.   (670)

This is a poetic recapitulation of the same sort of encounter between "me" and "my spirit" of earlier years, only it is more sinis-

ter and desperate. "Ourself" precariously balances on the brink of reality. From meetings with that "Cooler Host," after pursuit through corridors and alleys, no escape in her room is possible despite the locked door, because the other self is "superior" to physical barrier or, more, holds final security and sanity in its hand.

Another poem, more directly on the problem of freeing herself from this persistent "me," announces the dilemma with brilliant precision. The root of the problem is that the two selves reign simultaneously as "mutual Monarch."[60] One cannot quash the other without subduing consciousness because consciousness is almost life itself, certainly the first requirement for perception. She is left with only the puzzle of how to flee the offending part of herself, which even the perspective of a third person, the artist as "objective" analyst, finds impossible to solve. A further annoyance is the capriciousness power of the self to switch from antagonist to ally, increasing anxiety by its unpredictability. This tension arises clearly in a third poem, "No Rack can torture me," on the theme of liberty. Until the last stanza, she has steadily affirmed spiritual freedom possible no matter what may be her physical torture. Then at the end she admits:

> Except Thyself may be
> Thine Enemy –
> Captivity is Consciousness –
> So's Liberty.   (384)

Obviously, herself inside herself was a danger always making her room an uncertain sanctuary. Spectral company threatened her, too. Although certain ghosts might be welcome, some could frighten by their surreptitious arrival and by the knowledge that they were never truly gone. The hold these involuntary conjurings had upon Emily, the near-paralysis they could effect, combined with other sufferings, is made clear in a letter from Emily to her cousins, Louise and Frances Norcross, explaining a delay in writing:

> The nights turned hot, when Vinnie had gone, and I must keep no window raised for fear of prowling "booger," and I must shut my door for fear front door slide open on me at the "dead of night," and I must keep "gas" burning to light the danger up, so I could distinguish it – these gave me a snarl in

the brain which don't unravel yet, and that old nail in my
breast pricked me; these, dear, were my cause.[61]

Perhaps some of her imaginings were inspired by portraits of
friends and admired literary figures hung on her walls, including
those of Elizabeth Barrett Browning, George Eliot, and Thomas
Carlyle.[62] Although she venerated Eliot and Browning, and Emily
Brontë as well, their example as successful female writers could
have contributed to her insecure "place" as an unpublished poet.
Yet the tone of the following poem is of a more threatening sort
than literary idols would have inspired. In fact, the anonymity of
the "Hosts," so vaguely drawn as to be hardly even shadows of
humanity, accentuates her fear:

> Alone, I cannot be –
> The Hosts – do visit me –
> Recordless Company –
> Who baffle Key –
>
> They have no Robes, nor Names –
> No Almanacs – nor Climes –
> But General Homes
> Like Gnomes –
>
> Their Coming, may be Known
> By Couriers within –
> Their going – is not –
> For they're never gone –   (298)

If her warring selves and unidentified spectres shattered the
security of Emily's own chamber, so did death. From its threat of
finality, it probably penetrated the furthest of any fear into her
psychic apartments. Appropriately, the apprehension it aroused
in the poet appears in poems which use a room or rooms as their
imaginative setting. Death becomes the last and quite literal inner
space. Early and superbly she wryly fitted the beloved dead "Safe
in their Alabaster Chambers."[63] In another poem, she imagines
herself dead, having died for beauty, yet able to talk to another
who died for truth "between [Their] Rooms."[64] In still a third
poem, "I heard a Fly buzz – when I died,"[65] her death slowly takes
place within her chamber. The dull buzz of the fly against her
windowpane, suggesting the fly's anticipation of her as decaying
flesh, ultimately echoes her larger theme that this world is all.

Yet death as eternity rather than brutal extinction – that "Bare-headed life" under the grass – appears in poems in which the poet looks west from her bedroom windows. The earliest one, "On this wondrous sea," was written about 1853 at Pleasant Street where, as noted before, her room also faced west. Later poems, composed at the Mansion, continue the hope of eternal life as the west's promise.[66] One poem begins by precisely placing the poet in time as well as space:

> Behind Me – dips Eternity –
> Before Me – Immortality –
> Myself – the Term between –
> Death but the Drift of Eastern Gray,
> Dissolving into Dawn away,
> Before the West begin –   (721)

Looking out rather than within, then, seemed to give the poet a more positive view of life's end. From the latter view, space seemed shrunk to the wood and stone of the grave, while the former, taking Emily beyond her house to another "not made with hands," prompted her to speculate about the extended flowering of the inmost self in limitless space.

A related but independent sense of death, a recurring reference to a deathlike life, also emerges in the language of rooms. It is as if Emily felt herself prematurely fitted to a coffin while still alive, possibly a partial reflection of the withdrawn life she led. A poem which ends with her emptiness within as a religious experience recedes illustrates her dependence upon the room figure:

> Did Our Best Moment last –
> 'Twould supersede the Heaven –
> A few – and they by Risk – procure –
> So this Sort – are not given
>
> .   .   .   .   .   .
>
> A Grant of the Divine
> That Certain as it Comes –
> Withdraws – and leaves the dazzled Soul
> In her unfurnished Rooms –   (393)

"Unfurnished" focuses upon the state of deprivation the poet feels after grace is gone. Not illuminated but dazed, the soul must deal without props in a barren room which is the self.

In the following poem, Emily plays upon the theme of the empty self, this time a room too filled with dark and suffering to accept any other "furnishings." She has been so accustomed to her loneliness that its opposite "Peace"

> Would interrupt the Dark –
> And crowd the little Room –
> Too scant – by Cubits – to contain
> The Sacrament – of Him –   (405)

Here grace has not withdrawn to leave the room unfurnished. Rather the reverse, the room is already too crowded within its meager proportions to admit any religious "objects" such as peace, or as she continues, hope as well.

Another poem of a single quatrain echoes her view of the self as a diminished chamber:

> Sweet hours have perished here –
> This is a timid room –
> Within its precincts hopes have played
> Now fallow in the tomb.   (1767)[67]

The hopes she mentions here may be religious ones, as in the two previous poems. But they might also obliquely register a further anxiety making her room "little" and "timid," Emily's problem with men.

To say baldly that Emily was a frigid woman is to presume unavailable knowledge. Further, to place her decisively in the old maid category, as a critic has done, is to be blind to her deeply passionate nature. It also ignores certain facts requiring her to remain unmarried, for example, her mother's health and her father's apparent wish to have her near. Yet a native reserve and seriousness were notable aspects of her character as a young adult. Joseph Lyman remarked in 1858, "Emily Dickinson I did like very much and do still. But she is rather morbid and unnatural."[68] At another time, he called her "platonic."[69] Later in 1858, Lyman remarked that though Emily and another young woman much like her were both "noble women — neither one of them will probably ever marry tho' both would make most true and devoted wives. . . ."[70]

Emily's natural restraint combined with an experience of unrequited affection (a probable factor in her crisis of the early 1860s) and longstanding but different attachments to her father

and to Austin no doubt helped build, at the least, hesitations about
sex and, at the most, encouraged certain inhibitions. Also, as independent as she was of custom and convention, "my spirit," the part
of her which spoke for society's restraints, was ever-present. One is
reminded of her rye field "mortgaged" to Seth Nims in the dream
she had at Mount Holyoke. Did she feel herself punished for her
planted field, her sexuality fulfilled, although only in fantasy?

Considering this evidence, it is not surprising to find in Emily's
poetry mixed terror and fascination concerning intimate relations
with a man. The theme of her poem about hunger, considered
earlier, appears to be truncated or sublimated eroticism. More
overtly, if the following discussion is acceptable, one undated
poem in particular displays the ambivalent nature of her attitudes:

> In Winter in my Room
> I came upon a Worm
> Pink lank and warm
> But as he was a worm
> And worms presume
> Not quite with him at home
> Secured him by a string
> To something neighboring
> And went along.
>
> A Trifle afterward
> A thing occurred
> I'd not believe it if I heard
> But state with creeping blood
> A snake with mottles rare
> Surveyed my chamber floor
> In feature as the worm before
> But ringed with power
> The very string with which
> I tied him – too
> When he was mean and new
> That string was there –
>
> I shrank – "How fair you are"!
> Propitiation's claw –
> "Afraid he hissed
> Of me"?

"No cordiality" –
He fathomed me –
Then to a Rhythm *Slim*
Secreted in his Form
As Patterns swim
Projected him.

That time I flew
Both eyes his way
Lest he pursue
Nor ever ceased to run
Till in a distant Town
Towns on from mine
I set me down
This was a dream –   (1670)

Freud reminds us that dreams are dangerous messages to take at face value. As bulletins from the unconscious they have had to work their way not only through several layers of the psyche in perhaps a myriad of tangled connections before "registering," even as a dream, but they have also had to push through a censorious memory before being recalled by the dreamer in a wakened, conscious state. Thirdly, Dickinson's use of such material poetically may mean a further distortion of the "truth."

Yet there are several warrants for interpretation of this poem-as-dream from the poet's experience and typical behavior.[71] First, her poetic imagination, so akin to daydreaming, can be considered "a continuation of and substitute for the play of childhood,"[72] especially because of her continuing pose as a child. Also, her attitude toward men whom she respected or loved, doubtless conditioned first by her father and Austin, was warm, even ardent, but disguised and decidedly subservient. Finally, in this dream of intense conflict, she appears to follow psychology's hypothesis in at least two ways: the unconscious shows its continuing battles with earlier crises or unfulfilled wishes stimulated by an actual experience, and further, a negative identity, her fascination with sex, characteristically arises at night to haunt her.[73] With these observations, a tentative reading of the poem follows.

The season is winter. Emily's actual house, including her room, was then often closely shuttered against the cold and thus dark. The reference to her room in wintertime when she is shut in most literally (one January she called the house "my Pearl Jail") suggests that "Room" may represent her vagina.[74] And the worm-snake hardly needs introducing as a probable phallic substitute. Commonly a dreaded creature, the snake becomes even more abhorrent to neurotics,[75] a label which underscores Emily's sensitivity rather than implying deficiency. In a letter of 1850 she made a short discourse on snakes in which she confessed to loving "the little green ones that slide around by your shoes in the grass," but she said solemnly of the striped snake, "There is an air of misanthropy about [him]."[76] Emily's apprehension of actual snakes of this sort reaches an anthropomorphic height in this imagined encounter.

The worm is introduced with adjectives which picture him as harmless or even attractive. But he is suspect. Emily is not quite "*at home*" with him (my italics). Orthodox Calvinist theology would never allow a worm to represent less than the worthlessness, that is, total depravity of man. Emily's view of him is somewhat softer.[77] Nonetheless, control is necessary, thus the string. She goes along almost casually about her usual round. But in no time, the worm has metamorphosed from only a moderately bothersome creature into an altogether threatening one. Emily's consciousness allows her to believe this terror only because she feels it "with creeping blood" (the moment of imagined entry?). The frightful worm-turned-snake, richly mottled, attracts by his very abhorrence. And he fully knows her, because he is not only physically present in her innermost sanctuary, her "chamber floor," but because he acutely studies, "surveys," her. His knowledge is complete by the third stanza where she dispassionately remarks, "He fathomed me."

Worm and snake are identical, with the same "feature," but the difference is the rare mottled coat (probably signifying both Emily's dreaded striped snake and thus her dislike of only a particular type of "snake") and surrounding aura of power which the snake possesses and the worm does not. Tumescence has occurred. Interestingly, the string Emily tied to the worm remains on the snake. Does it signify her ambivalent desire to possess this "animal" at the same time that she wants to control it and keep it at a distance? Is this her way of manipulating Him, the man (or men) in her life who had first attracted, then frustrated, threatened, or circumscribed her in some way?[78]

When conversation begins, we are again reminded by Freud that

FIGURE 12. *A winter view of the Mansion, late nineteenth or early twentieth century. Courtesy of Harvard College Library.*

"A speech heard in the dream always originates from a speech either heard or uttered in waking life."[79] The snake then takes on characteristics almost caricaturing the classic nineteenth-century villain, with curling mustachios, leer, and "line": "How fair you are!" Emily reads this as propitiation, and when he asks if she fears him she immediately goes to the root of the matter: "No cordiality," no sincerity, no heart, no warmth. The snake's cold-blooded nature, that "zero at the bone" he registered with her in another poem ("A narrow Fellow in the Grass"[80]), surfaces again. Puritanism and neurosis meet in this exaggerated fear.[81] Yet immediately he fathoms her, and she apparently is unresisting. The vision of his part in coitus (not hers) concludes the stanza as Emily "sees" the sperm ("Patterns") ejaculated. His rhythm has been "slim" perhaps both because of the snake's narrow confines and because its mean purpose repels her, preventing her climax.[82]

This encounter, imprinted on her memory with the power of double sight, so instills her with the fear of domination and potential violation that she feels compelled to run away to "Towns on from mine," as far away as possible. She wants to escape her "room" when that place offers no security against the advance of sexual abuse. Certainly, strings would not be strong enough.[83]

This poem is central because its scene is Emily's most private place and the forces at play are so basic. Also, it encompasses the multiple but overlapping concerns of this chapter and the study as a whole – spatial, biographical, psychological, and literary. And it touches on the fear which probably terrorized Emily most, the greatest deprivation she could imagine: to be lonely. Uncaring, aggressive sexuality could threaten and force escape and retreat, but Emily did not want to avoid a true lover; in fact, she blatantly pursued him, a subject to be considered in chapter 6.

Basically, the problem of loneliness was nearly opposite from the one of sexual aggression just discussed. Loneliness towered above any other anxiety. It dwarfed being embattled between opposed identities, haunted by spirits, hounded by death and despair, or pressed by importunate masculinity. These fears at least had the surprise of action and the possibility of the unknown. But to be left in involuntary solitude was to be frozen, impounded, useless. "Doom is the House without the Door" announces this anxiety as starkly as a fear arrives.[84] And the phrase "Lethargies of Loneliness" stresses the stasis she abhorred.[85]

In 1863, during the period of Emily's well-known crisis, she wrote the following poem:

> The Loneliness One dare not sound –
> And would as soon surmise
> As in it's Grave go plumbing
> To ascertain the size –
>
> The Loneliness whose worst alarm
> Is lest itself should see –
> And perish from before itself
> For just a scrutiny –
>
> The Horrors not to be surveyed –
> But skirted in the Dark –
> With Consciousness suspended –
> And Being under Lock –
>
> I fear me this – is Loneliness –
> The Maker of the soul
> It's Caverns and it's Corridors –
> Illuminate – or seal – (777)

Emily's words here recall those mentioned earlier in relation to a sense of death-in-life. Now, instead of religious unfulfillment, which is not alluded to in these lines, the poet seems to be speaking of a somatic anguish put in spatial terms.[86] Loneliness is so akin to extinction that she dares not guess its extent, much less measure it. Viewing loneliness whole is to die. Even if it is superficially observed, consciousness is numbed and existence imprisoned. Until the fourth stanza, Emily has been one with this nullity, but by naming it and thus separating herself from it, she escapes its lock. She implores God either to explain or else to block the threat in its penetration and pervasiveness ("Caverns" and "Corridors"), recalling the deep cellar and numerous hallways of the Mansion and of herself. At this moment, the throne of divinity she reached as Empress of Calvary seems collapsed below stairs.

V.

When Emily examined, analyzed and labelled her fears, as in this poem, she could temporarily overcome them and find a time that was creative and a place which was a true center. In "Conscious am I in my Chamber," the problems of both the anonymous "Hosts" and of death are met at once.[87] This time they do not overwhelm her, because of the arrival of immortality's fulfilling company. Eternity's immanent presence crowds out any horror, even the end of life. In a second poem, "To own the Art within the Soul," Emily again illustrates her ability to resolve inner strife. The soul finds it can "entertain" itself "With Silence as a Company" but without sacrificing "Festival," or joy.[88] To be performer and audience in one is an "Art," suggesting how painfully it was accomplished. Yet sometimes it was a pure gift, sheer grace, or as Emily puts it, "unfurnished Circumstance."

The emphasis on the word "unfurnished" in this poem and in one immediately below means the opposite of emptiness, its definition in "Did our Best Moment last." Here it connotes self-reliance beyond the need of any supporting objects. And in the following poem "furnishings" of a calumnious kind will not even crowd the poet's room. There is absolutely no space at all for their slanderous sort:

> Size circumscribes – it has no room
> For petty furniture –
> The Giant tolerates no Gnat
> For Ease of Gianture –
>
> Repudiates it, all the more –
> Because intrinsic size
> Ignores the possibility
> Of Calumnies – or Flies.   (641)

In these verses, Emily acquires a "size" which signifies an inviolate self-esteem; thus she eschews the inconsequential, belittling word. She has discarded smallness for "Gianture." In such moments of true independence, as opposed to the seemingly shaky affirmations of superiority of "On a Columnar Self" ànd "The Soul selects its own Society," the poet can speak about finding what was her first and continuous search: a true place, locus, or identity. Such a center is delicately elusive, yet Emily can sufficiently envision her own to make its quest a lifetime's motivation:

> Each Life Converges to some Centre –
> Expressed – or still –

> Exists in every Human Nature
> A Goal –
>
> Embodied scarcely to itself – it may be –
> Too fair
> For Credibility's presumption
> To mar –
>
> Adored with caution – as a Brittle Heaven –
> To reach
> Were hopeless, as the Rainbow's Raiment
> To touch –
>
> Yet persevered toward – surer – for the Distance –
> How high –
> Unto the Saints' slow diligence –
> The Sky –
>
> Ungained – it may be – by a Life's low Venture –
> But then –
> Eternity enable the endeavoring
> Again.   (680)

Even if her goal is left unstated in this poem, it can hardly be a secret. It is the gift of writing true, even great poetry. This, then, is Emily's "Centre." Her creative inner space becomes the place where poetry is conceived, a complement to, if not a surrogate for, a procreative biological center. Persevering toward her goal, Emily moves beyond the precarious fulfillment announced in "Title divine – is mine!" and appears to approach the comment of her last decade, "Consciousness is the only home of which we *now* know." Poetic consciousness was thus at once her goal, center, and ultimate home. "Embodied scarcely to itself," as she says in the second stanza, yet she cherishes her intuition of this quality of mind for its heights of perception, perhaps at moments touched by grace. She ends the poem hoping that in the next life there will be opportunity for further striving.

Whether or not her goal of poetry may continue beyond death, at least poems achieved in life may have a certain immortality. The following one on this theme seems to be a natural sequel to "Each Life Converges to some Centre":

> The Poets light but Lamps –
> Themselves – go out –

> The Wicks they stimulate –
> If vital Light
>
> Inhere as do the Suns –
> Each Age a Lens
> Disseminating their
> Circumference –   (883)

Emily expands poetic inner space to "Circumference," that is, the magnification of the poets' innermost sensibilities. By implication, she joins this company whose centers are lights used by posterity to refocus and relive the poets' visions of reality. In both poems, she illustrates her escape from imprisonment by circumstance within her father's house or by her multiple fears within her own room. Finding her center in creating poetry, she writes for future readers and thus, while still alive, inhabits another world which only succeeding generations will know. And that world, as she says in another poem, was "Possibility, / a fairer House than Prose."

The same theme of a center from which power, in this case an odor instead of light, emanates underlies another poem:

> Essential Oils – are wrung –
> The Attar from the Rose
> Be not expressed by Suns – alone –
> It is the gift of Screws –
>
> The General Rose – decay –
> But this – in Lady's Drawer
> Make Summer – When the Lady lie
> In Ceaseless Rosemary –   (675)

Emily envisages herself, the Attar, still perfuming the drawers of a chest after her death. Within her own bureau she collected her fascicles and packets of poems. These were her remaining scents, preserved in the protection of her chest for a second birth for generations to follow, which would liberate them at last from poet, drawer, room, and house.

Emily discovered her center to be the gift of writing poetry. How, then, does her awareness of inner space as a woman and poet relate to her insistence on the frugal life and to her desperate need to have some position in the world? Richard Chase's exploration of these two quests complements the theme of this chapter.[89] Her

desire to practice a "strict economy" derived from the awareness of
the benefits of a disciplined, defined existence. That definition was
possible, as Emily came to see it, only through crucial experiences
which led her to exclude certain aspects of living, aspects considered, for a woman, the most commonly fulfilling ones, at least in
nineteenth-century custom: love, marriage, and society. What resulted was a pyramid of renunciations reaching the apex or final
renouncement of death. As each sacrifice ensued, however, she
could advance in "status," so that the highest "estate" achiev-
able would be immortality, whether for herself or through her
poetry. In short, the progress toward Emily's queenship rested on
a series of apparent impoverishments whose other side, a pro-
founder communication with life itself or with a higher voice
within her, was the true sign of a costly superiority, justifying such
regal titles as the Empress of Calvary.

The interior dialogue issued in an original, self-generated election, privately known in the present, and only a presentiment,
though a powerful one, of the future. She plainly described the
role of the emphatic ego, transmuting Puritan dogma to what appears to be a wholly self-determined discipline. She began the
following poem with the statement, "Renunciation – is a piercing
Virtue," then analyzed the authority directing it. The key words
are "Unto itself":

> Renunciation – is the Choosing
> Against itself –
> Itself to justify
> Unto itself –
> When larger function –
> Make that appear –
> Smaller – that Covered Vision – Here –   (745)

The "Vision" which is covered in this life refers to the first "itself," whose claims are blind and incomplete because they are
limited to a view from "Here," that is, this world as opposed to
eternity. She has become "larger" by discarding her "smaller" self.

A renunciation which finally establishes status for the poet turns
on the same point of limitation as does Emily's conscious discovery
of a center and the probably unconscious perception of an interior
space. The poet's vocabulary is a touchstone. Again, the critical
word "small" is Emily's base for more various, precise self-defini-

tions or actions. She speaks of a "letting go" of life, a personal "position," and a measurable "depth." Her "banquet of abstemiousness," "abstemious Ecstasy," "sumptuous Destitution" (left by a joy that "has no home"), or "white election" arose from the same events of rationed stimuli and dimension as did her "intrinsic size" and "gift of Screws." All of these expressions merge in the remark, "Existence has a stated width / Departed, or at Home."[90]

For Emily, revelatory experience traced the eye of a needle. It was a secularized, select revelation, which sometimes might become religious and orthodox, particularly at the moment of death, of which she echoes the doctrines of predestination and election, envisioning that only a few will see paradise. Her thought moves toward a peaceful resolution of conflict, a satisfaction with coming home to a center, rooted in the ground plan of herself. "Tho' I get home how late – how late – / So I get home – 'twill compensate –"[91]

Was this satisfaction with deprivation, the frugality of subsistence, the pleasure with inverted royalty, even though sexually based in part, really a self-delusion? Self-delusion probably was not a continuing possibility for one who consciously scrutinized every facet of herself she could find, as a jeweler examines a gem. Rather, Emily's economies were generally chosen forthrightly as recompense with its own reward. Emerson's essay "Compensation" was literary support for her own experience. In a family edition of his essays, a thin line marks the first sentence of the following passage, and a vertical dash serves as a stop after "all":

> The inviolate spirit turns their spite against the wrongdoers. The martyr cannot be dishonored. Every lash inflicted is a tongue of fame; every prison, a more illustrious abode; every burned book or house enlightens the world; every suppressed or expunged word reverberates through the earth from side to side. Hours of sanity and consideration are always arriving to communities, as to individuals, when the truth is seen, and the martyrs are justified.
>
> Thus do all things preach the indifferency of circumstances. The man is all.[92]

To be known as a martyr was hardly Emily's goal, as she made clear in "A *Wounded* Deer – leaps highest."[93] She found a "compensation fair" in other ways.[94] If she sometimes wondered if the other side of life's "hill," immortality, would compensate "for climbing it alone,"[95] then she could also announce moments echoing Emerson's last lines above, as if she were justified by breath itself: "I find ecstasy in living – the mere sense of living is joy enough."[96] At such times (evanescent, to be sure), her increasing seclusion in the Mansion, the whole question of space, in fact, seems trivial.

Chapter 4
Literary antecedents of the image of house and home

Culture implies all that which gives the mind possession of its own powers; as languages to the critic, telescope to the astronomer.

RALPH WALDO EMERSON

When Emily Dickinson wrote her brother in 1851 that Hepzibah and Clifford in Hawthorne's *House of the Seven Gables* made her recall their own relationship, she not only indicated how literary models may have affected her self-image and her impression of others. Even more clearly, this reference illustrates another way in which her home-centered culture left its imprint, namely, through contemporary literature. In America, Emerson outdistanced everyone in his influence upon Dickinson, but she also read Hawthorne, Thoreau, and perhaps Melville among other native authors.[1] A fuller list of English writers engaged her, especially Charlotte and Emily Brontë, Elizabeth Barrett and Robert Browning, George Eliot, and Dickens.[2] Besides current works, the King James Bible and Shakespeare gave Emily historical sources for the house image, as did her readings of the seventeenth-century metaphysical poets and of selected eighteenth- and nineteenth-century British poets and novelists.

All such sources provided literary suggestions relating to architectural imagery, but I will treat only those which most strongly echo in Dickinson's work: the Bible, Shakespeare, both Brownings, Hawthorne, Thoreau, and Emerson. Among these select few, the home figure alone hardly exhausts material which fully exhibits each author's spatial inscape. My purpose, however, is not to be comprehensive but rather to lift up the most obvious writings of this sort which claimed Dickinson's attention and by their light to illuminate another, and this time intellectual, source for *her* inscape when she uses the home image herself.

I.

Emily's early and constant exposure to scriptural passages made it natural that the King James Bible would be her most frequently quoted reference.[3] At the First Congregational Church three times a week, at the Amherst Academy on weekdays, and at home each morning in worship led by her father, the Bible molded her childhood consciousness. In 1843, when she was twelve, her father gave her a Bible of her own.[4] From these pervasive oral and written reminders, she referred to the Scriptures almost half-consciously, their phrases easily surfacing. Some of her quotations are incorrect, suggesting that main themes and verses had become so familiar that they were ready for instant recall without the aid of direct reference. Her errors might also be read as hints of her religious heterodoxy, if her impieties about the Bible were the rule. She could certainly be vividly irreligious: "Lay up Treasures immediately – that's the best Anodyne for moth and Rust and the thief," and "Peter took the Marine Walk at the great risk." But comments like these are the exception. She affirmed her loyalty to the Bible's eschatology, if not to specific items of theology, at the age of forty-two:

> Science will not trust us with another World.
> Guess I and the Bible will move to some old fashioned spot where we'll feel at Home.[5]

Words referring to house, home, and temple all recur in the Bible so consistently that Emily would have been steeped in them, especially since they appear in the five books which she most frequently quoted, Matthew, Luke, John, Genesis, and Revelation.[6] From her reading of Genesis, supplemented by other books, Emily envisioned at least two sorts of theological houses, Eden – a primal home – and Eternity – its final successor. Eden, "the ancient Homestead," she called it, was a hallowed place, a refuge of protection and peace.[7] In a mood of momentary elation, she even found it "that old-fashioned House / We dwell in every day."[8] Paradise appeared possible here and now, with or without Adam. But in another moment, an Eden without a beloved did not suit. Her cry for "Wild Nights" ended with the expectation of "Rowing in Eden – Ah, the Sea! / Might I but moor – Tonight – / in Thee!"[9] For Emily in this sort of humor, Eden's activities remained thoroughly "old-fash-

ioned" or rather, classic. There, beyond morality, one might come
home. That may be why in another poem she spoke cautiously,
"Come slowly – Eden!"[10]

Besides a recovered, prelapsarian home, Emily saw another,
"Genesis' new house" – eternity. She made high drama of the
events to occur in this house, the reunion with her beloved. But
her constant, essentially Puritan concern with the end of life found
only momentary rest in the Christian hope of immortality. Intermittently, she returned to doubt and the cold assurance that only
the "Bareheaded life" underground followed death. In such times
she could be sneeringly bitter as in "Papa Above! / Regard a Mouse
/ . . . Reserve within thy kingdom / A 'Mansion' for the Rat!" or
" 'Many Mansions,' by 'his Father,' / I don't know him; snugly
built!"[11] Then back again she could shift to a more hopeful expectation; when referring to 2 Cor. 5:1, she stated, "We have *other*
home – 'house not made with hands.' "[12] In that house, her favorite
book, *Revelation,* assured her, she would truly be at home and
"thirst no more."[13]

Revelation also promised that "home is bright and shining, 'and
the spirit and the bride say *come,* and let him that' wandereth
come."[14] As a supplementary source on this theme, the books of
Isaac Watts, *Christian Psalmody, The Psalms, Hymns and Spiritual Songs,* and *Village Hymns* were in constant use in church, and
copies were also in her father's library at home. In these pages
were such hymns as "O God, Our Help in Ages Past," with its reminder that He was "our eternal home," and one of her favorites,
"There is a Land of Pure Delight."[15]

Emily made more of the New Testament concept of the body as
a spiritual house than the Bible does. In this revised version of
Scripture, she followed her bent of scaling the idea to her own
dimensions. Using Matt. 19:28–30 as a text, she imagined a dialogue between herself and Jesus in which her complaint, "I am
small," was answered by Christ, " 'The Least / Is esteemed in
Heaven the Chiefest – / Occupy my House."[16] She used a slightly
different version of the same idea (Matt. 11:11) when she sent a
note to congratulate a friend on the arrival of a granddaughter.
Her words applied equally to her own self-estimate as to the newborn: "She that is 'least in the kingdom of Heaven' has the Scripture Warrant for supremacy."[17] This allusion to election would be-

come more strongly stated and independent of religious orthodoxy when Dickinson used the word temple.

In reference to both Matthew and Luke, Emily identified with Christ's homelessness. Unlike the foxes and birds who have holes and nests for their respective homes, "the Son of man hath not where to lay *his* head." Emily assured her friend, Mrs. Holland, that "I, who sleep always, need no Bed. Foxes have tenements, and remember, the Speaker was a Carpenter."[18] Her intent, too oblique alone, becomes clearer juxtaposed with a poem beginning, "Myself was formed – a Carpenter," in which she assumes Christ's role, becoming her own builder, "We – Temples build – I said."[19] Emily, independent and homeless as Christ, nonetheless can remedy her own want by employing her "Art of Boards," as she says in this poem. She builds a life-sustaining temple of poetry which becomes, in effect, her own sanctified house. At the same time, her achievement, based on her own designs, also signifies self-election.

II.

From Dickinson's own testimony, Shakespeare's influence upon her equalled, if it did not exceed, the Bible's. At least, she was less critical of the bard than of God. From her first introduction as member of a Shakespeare Club at Amherst Academy, Emily insisted upon reading his works complete and unexpurgated, joining other girls in a protest against their tutor's plan to delete offensive passages.[20] Her interest in Shakespeare, perhaps stimulated by the enthusiasm of her friend Otis P. Lord, did not abate as she grew older.[21] Yet Shakespeare did not become an intimate part of her poetry, at least not in the obvious manner of the Bible. As Jack Capps, a student of her reading, states: "[Shakespeare's] works failed to provide the vast quantity of usable commonplaces she found in the Bible; furthermore, her favorite passages, though they served admirably as quotations in letters, could not be easily tailored to fit into poems."[22] According to Capps, only six poems clearly show Shakespearean sources.[23]

Yet perhaps the "commonplaces" Capps refers to as biblical staples might also have derived from Shakespeare, in this case from his references to home, especially since he may have been a source for a definition of the concept which Emily knew but which the Bible leaves undeveloped. That definition is the adverbial use of "home," most commonly meaning "to or at one's own house or home," as in "welcome home." But much more pointedly, Shakespeare uses the word to suggest the touching of one's most sensitive spot, home as heart, with an intended and usually devastating effect, as in "charge" or "strike home," or more lyrically, "snip, snap, quick and home."[24]

In plays including Emily's favorites – *Hamlet, Macbeth,* and *Othello* – Shakespeare employs a fundamental meaning of home as fulfillment: a completion of knowledge or emotion, often touching a vulnerable place, or of earnestness, effectiveness, and worthiness.[25] In similar use of the home image, Dickinson avoids Elizabethan quaintness but still incorporates Shakespeare's richly inclusive meaning. In the following Dickinson stanza, for instance, completion also includes the idea of protection:

> He was weak, and I was strong – then –
> So He let me lead him in –
> I was weak, and He was strong then –
> So I let him lead me – Home.   (190)

In a probable tribute to Mrs. Samuel Bowles, Emily sent her husband a two-stanza poem the second half of which reveals the poet's own desire for rest and fulfillment:

> Her heart is fit for *home* –
> I – a Sparrow – built there
> Sweet of twigs and twine
> My perennial nest.   (84)

As noted in chapter 1, when Emily underlines home she emphasizes its surpassing value, charging it with significance well beyond mere place. Unlike the poet, Mrs. Bowles enjoyed her own home and, in Emily's view, with a highly estimable and beloved man.

Other classic writings Emily knew were those of the metaphysical poets – especially George Herbert – and John Milton, either from volumes of their own works or from anthologies in her family.[26] Creased pages or pencilled lines (some pencil markings are strongly characteristic of Dickinson) show the influence of these writers as models of architectural imagery. The last lines of "Il Penseroso," for example, marked in the margin, may indicate how

Milton's praise of sacred seclusion spoke to Emily's situation. Burns, Keats, and Byron – in particular, "The Prisoner of Chillon" – are even probable starting points for Emily's poems.[27] But the writers who most obviously contributed to the poet's own use of the home or house image are the Brownings, Hawthorne, Thoreau, and finally, Emerson.

III.

Not unnaturally, leading women writers in England, Emily's contemporaries, were her special idols: Elizabeth Barrett Browning, George Eliot, and Emily Brontë. Portraits of the first two she had on the walls of her room. Her indebtedness to Elizabeth Browning in fact, appears to be extensive, and perhaps a few of her borrowings approach plagiarism.[28] But as T. S. Eliot observed, "Immature poets imitate; mature poets steal."[29] Aesthetically mature in this sense, Dickinson accomplished her "thefts" discriminatingly and with results quite distinct from the "taken" goods.

Emily's copy of E. B. Browning's *Aurora Leigh,* a nine-book, blank verse romance, was an edition of 1859, two years later than the copy Sue owned. Perhaps reading Sue's, which is heavily marked, had made Emily want one for her own; her copy is relatively clean. The book's themes, the sexist, philosophic, and romantic tribulations of an aspiring and eventually successful woman poet, spoke to many of Emily's professional and personal concerns, and the markings in both copies sometimes, though not always, point to them. Lines of Browning's which may have prompted Emily's imaginings are not often singled out by her pencillings.[30] Thus, when the wealth of house and home images in *Aurora Leigh* remain virtually untouched, it cannot be assumed they had no influence upon her; and neither can the opposite be argued: that Browning's houses or homes strongly affected Emily. Yet the house of Leigh, the Tuscan home of Aurora (her "first nest"), the house as the body of Aurora's cousin Romney, whole and in part (for example, Browning makes the stone-stair which remains after the family mansion has burned symbolic of Romney's life, since it too has led "to nought"), the "house of Nobody" – these references and others must have been duly noted by Emily, since she read the book at least twice and perhaps many times.

One striking example of the sort of noting Emily may have done may be illustrated by examining the last section of the poem's final book (Sue's copy is marked; Emily's is not). It is also an excellent case of Emily's probable manner of "stealing." In these lines, Aurora and Romney, united in a belated love, stand with clasped hands raised to the sun and the dawning of their life together, "the new, near Day." Romney, in particular, is absorbed in "the thought of noon." Emily's poem "To my small Hearth His fire came," it will be recalled, builds toward "Day" through the precious moment of "Noon":

> To my small Hearth His fire came –
> And all my House aglow
> Did fan and rock, with sudden light –
> 'Twas Sunrise – 'twas the Sky –
>
> Impanelled from no Summer brief –
> With limit of Decay –
> 'Twas Noon – without the News of Night –
> Nay, Nature, it was Day.   (638)[31]

Despite the use of identical words in a similar context, Emily has made her experience separate in several ways. First, the present, pulsating moment is emphasized as it is seen in retrospect, not the future. Day in this poem is the particular time, noon, expanded in illumination so that its power has the full force of many hours of sunlight. But the impression is that the relationship, as opposed to the love (begun in the hearth), does not necessarily continue for long. Immediacy and intensity are the primary effects of Emily's poem. Not so with Browning's melodramatic finale. Here Aurora and Romney stare into the sunrise and take its rays as an omen of their new history. The "I" in Emily's poem feels the intensity of a fire which may have no future, except perhaps in memory. This point seems related to a second: Emily brings this experience to just one, the female partner, although presumably the "Day" ecstasy is a shared moment. Third, Emily has set this illuminating instant, akin to a conversion experience, within a house. And though it begins in the very center of that house, her love expands beyond any walls in a total freedom of place or time. In short, if Emily borrowed from Browning in this instance, then she fused "stolen" elements with her own sensitivity and style. And the whole, it seems, was seen through her own particular inscape of space.

Robert Browning's work, too, held a strong attraction for Emily, even though his portrait was not hung in her bedroom. In 1862, Emily wrote Higginson that both Brownings, with Keats, were what she had for poetry.[32] In a review of R. Browning's *Dramatis Personae* (the *Springfield Republican,* September 14, 1864), she could have read about both his genius and his obscurity, the latter attribute limiting his audience, according to the reviewer, to "an appreciative few."[33] Emily and Sue were among this elite, for they both appear to have lined the margins of Sue's copy of *The Ring and the Book* (1869). And Emily marked certain poems in her own edition of his *Men and Women* (1856). She may have read other works of his in her father's library, so well perhaps as to recall his words without special effort.[34] For example, she incorporated a line from his poem "The Last Ride Together," without quoting it or mentioning his name, as if it involuntarily arose in her mind. In another instance, when she said that "Browning told me so," the admission is as if he spoke to her with frequent, unquestioned authority.[35]

Robert Browning's reference to house (443 times) and home (154) may have seeped into Emily's consciousness in just such a surreptitious, unconditional way as in the examples above. This is all the more likely since no firm evidence exists to show that Emily borrowed his use of the image. Rather, his similar celebration of home as a cherished shelter unite the two. Of course, he may speak of it, as she did, with the awareness that this ideal had gone awry. A sampling of a few of his lines suffices to illustrate this kin interest and also the range of other uses of the image, some of which parallel Dickinson's.

In a variety of works, beginning with *Paracelsus,* the house appears in selected lines of Browning thus:

Fancy the crickets, each one in his house. . . .

Until the Formidable House is famed. . . .

But no, your house was mute, would ope no eye

Pouring heaven unto this shut house of life

Of the munificent House that harbours me

Her house had only dreamed of anciently

Where's Door, where's Window? Needs must House have such!
I' the house of Hades have thy unsunned home!
Father and house to dust away!
Until, columnar, at the house they end
Lest I house in safety's self – a tombstone o'er my head!
Craved in your whole house a closet, out of all your means
  a comfort.
Soft sanctuary-tapers of thy house.[36]

And home, as follows:

Thick, busy human cluster, house and home
On shore, so home a feeling greeted me
Row home? must we row home? Too surely. . . .
Did Shakespeare live, he could but sit at home
"I show Opora to comment Sweet Home" –
For safe maternal home recovered thus, –
A certain refuge, solitary home
Housed she who made home heaven, in heaven's behoof
Cheer up, all safe at home! Warm inside makes amends
On still a working pretext – "Hearth and Home,"[37]

These lines are exclusive of any appearing in *The Ring and the Book*, the work in which Browning most frequently refers to house and home and the book which Emily and Sue marked. Since this lengthy poem concerns the honor within a family or house, the ubiquity of the image is not surprising. Emily read such lines as, "Home enclosed still, the rest would be the world's" and "concerns of the particular hearth and home." In "She lives, – wakes up, installed in house and home," Emily might have fleetingly thought of herself, though in context these words mean something inappropriate to her situation. Other lines which might have struck her are "On panel somewhere in the House of Fame," "To house as spectres in a sepulchre," and "But in the very house, home, nook and nest."[38]

Beyond these excerpts and others quite like them, Dickinson sharply specified certain passages with her thin pencil line. Among

them is "Oblivion gone home with her [Time's] harvesting," a
sentiment stated more conventionally at the close of Book I, and
also marked: "In those thy realms of help, that heaven thy home."
Again, the breath of death seemed to mingle with Emily's own,
especially when she noted such lines of promise as, "In patience all
of ye possess your souls! / This life is brief and troubles die with
it: / Where were the prick to soar up homeward else?"[39] But the
houses and homes of this life interested Dickinson more, it seems,
if double lines marking the following passage indicate more
emphasis than single ones elsewhere:

> Such unprofitable noise [of being cheated]
> Angers at all times: but when those who plague,
> Do it from inside your own house and home,
> Gnats which yourself have closed the curtain round,
> Noise goes too near the brain and makes you mad.[40]

Such a dramatic example instantly poses the question of a
parallel situation in Emily's life. Who might be the cause of a
similar plague? Edward Dickinson? Sue, who might be cheating
Emily's affection? One of Emily's selves? Speculation of this sort
has to give way to another. Emily's marked sections of *The Ring
and The Book* are not noteworthy sources of possible inspiration.
But the list given earlier, left untouched by Emily's pencil, includes a few lines which seem to resound in her poetry. For example, Browning's "Pouring heaven unto this shut house of life"
might have given Emily the idea for her last lines in "I dwell in
Possibility," namely, "The spreading wide my narrow Hands / To
gather Paradise." Or his "Where's Door, where's Window? Needs
must House have such!" has a certain affinity with Emily's "Doom
is the House without the Door," or finally, "A certain refuge,
solitary home" may have been readily at hand in her consciousness
when she wrote "The Soul selects its own Society." The assumption is that Browning, almost like the Bible, could cut a memora-
ble notch in Emily's mind and thus perhaps be "used" inadvertently, without the poet's conscious knowledge of borrowing.

Before turning to the Americans, it should be briefly noted that
Dickinson's tastes in contemporary English novelists, as well as in
poets, leaned toward female writers, with Robert Browning and
Dickens the notable exceptions. Although she read several others,
her favorites were Emily and Charlotte Brontë and George Eliot,

and she knew well the masterpieces of these three, *Wuthering Heights, Jane Eyre,* and *Middlemarch.*[41] Original and dissimilar though their works may be, a striking similarity of approach and perspective is common to them all: a feminine narrator tells each story and develops the effect of interior atmosphere upon their heroines' (and others') inner lives, and thence upon their outer fortunes. The focus of attention is within doors. This concentration most sharply appears in *Wuthering Heights,* where the dusky-chambered, ancestral house almost assumes the role of an independent character, so determining is its presence (past, present, or future) upon those who dwell within it.

No markings in any of these books reveal special passages which interested Dickinson, but as the Brownings' works suggest, she did not always note in her books particulars she would nevertheless remember. It may be enough to point to the similar situation shared by Emily and her admired English heroines: each was living in someone else's house and each self-image and fate was conditioned by that fact.

IV.

Among the American writers Dickinson preferred, Hawthorne, Thoreau, and Emerson stand out as those attracted to the house as object or image. In order to appreciate fully their prominent position in the use of house imagery, a sketch of the national scene and general literary landscape precedes a discussion of each author.

A wealth of sources referring to house and home appear in the works of Dickinson's literary peers. The stimulus to such abundance lies in the theme not only as idea but as *project*. Home-building was a necessity in a country expanding westward or in communities, like Amherst, growing with each generation. Between 1796 and 1862, Congress passed a series of public land acts enticing settlers to take advantage of considerable acreage offered at extremely low rates. For example, the Harrison Land Act of 1800 established prices ranging from $1 to $2 per acre with tracts varying from 80 to 320 acres. And squatters could become legal settlers after two Preemption Acts in 1830 and 1841 allowed them title to 160 acres of public land at $1.25 per acre. By 1862, the Homestead Act served both settlers and squatters by providing

160-acre tracts on liberal terms.[42] These inducements opened up migration to the west, part of which movement Austin Dickinson would have joined had his father not persuaded him to remain in Amherst to become his law partner.

The national focus on new houses and homes must have fed the sentiment of the era in a practical way, so that leading nineteenth-century writers – Hawthorne, Melville, Poe, Thoreau, and Emerson – would have been hard-pressed to escape its effects. In fact, they magnify the country's focus on home. Both insight and technique make them a collective lens, for their romantic leanings upon allegory, emblem, symbol and metaphor return us to the penetrating significance of the house image. Not that its associative potential was absent from the English writers just considered. Yet the Americans seem to press and squeeze the image to its utmost with a vengeance which may be in direct proportion to their insecurity as writers.

The concentration one finds upon house and home in nineteenth-century America thus appears to be not just a reflection of growth or a universal longing to find shelter from worldly cares in a fantasized equivalent of the womb. The concept of home enticed the American author also because of his inchoate identity as American, as writer. This lack of identity, a primary, often-noted fact, left him operating as a postcolonial British author, his national place not yet truly independent. And the imaginative writer still suffered from the hangover of an intemperate Puritan; his head could throb, as Hawthorne's appeared to do, with the question whether he served Pan or God; or he might deny such spirits at work, as Melville and Poe, and yet indirectly reveal that, in fact, his malady had similar causes. In any case, the early nineteenth-century native writer was, in essence, a nowhere man. His "place" was indeterminate culturally, professionally, and, as in Dickinson's case, sometimes personally.

What then could obsess him more? Nothing, according to Richard Poirier, who in *A World Elsewhere* explores the stylistic tools by which selected nineteenth-century American writers built "new houses," that is, patterns of structure for the mind and its expressions.[43] Poirier thus points to the expanding depths reached by the psychological and literary search for a home in America, a search which Norman Mailer and others continue today.

An archetypically mythic short story by the now-forgotten William Austin, "Peter Rugg, the Missing Man" (1824), illustrates this anomalous position of homelessness at home. The hero, abroad for several years, has lost his way and seeks to return home to Boston, but his efforts are continually thwarted despite his combined vow and self-curse, "I will see home tonight . . . or may I never see home!" At last he does reach Boston but only to see his house in ruins and its remaining goods being auctioned. When he protests, a voice from the crowd puts him down:

> Time, which destroys and renews all things, has dilapidated your house and placed us here . . . You were cut off from the last age, and you can never be fitted to the present. Your home is gone, and you can never have another home in this world.[44]

Rugg's experience of aimless journeying followed by a return to a radically altered home is a prototypical story for those American writers who saw their lives in the new country much more ambiguously than did their brethren. Living with but above the materialism about them, they were gripped by the power of darkness they saw shadowing the American dream, perverting the pursuit of happiness to a mad scramble for possession of property or of power in all its guises. In *The Power of Darkness*, Harry Levin argues this thesis emphasizing that our best writers, Hawthorne, Melville, and Poe, were not alone in possessing or being possessed by this consciousness.[45] Even such robust adventurers as Whitman and Twain, Levin suggests, suffered severe, not atypical moments of similar anxiety. And this anxiety was all the more accentuated since it did not obliterate hope.

In spatial terms, darkness worked as a sense of limitation, even in a country of vast territory unclaimed at least by Europeans and bordered by open seas. Or one could argue that an environment of wilderness and threatening oceans served to enforce rather than mitigate an awareness of limit. This psychic awareness of boundary, the sensitivity to enclosed or closed space, appears repeatedly in the symbol of the house or of the ship, the house at sea: the Pyncheon-Maule house, the *Pequod,* the Usher mansion, Prince Prospero's palace in "The Masque of the Red Death," Billy Budd's ship, the *Indomitable,* and after two years of experiment, even the hut at Walden. In these terms, Dickinson easily joins her nineteenth-century contemporaries, for she also employs the ship image so often that she is an archetypal example of its use in American literature.

Dickinson, then, shares an acquaintance with the dark and circumscribed with Hawthorne, Melville, Poe, and Thoreau. Even Emerson, predominantly positive, acknowledged in "Fate" (1860) and elsewhere an amoral, universal force at work. At present, however, Hawthorne and Thoreau are the focus. Melville and Poe are excluded because, of the former, Dickinson's knowledge is almost wholly conjectural and, of the latter, she admitted to Higginson, "I know too little to think."[46] Quite possibly her affinity with these writers in a common consciousness of enclosure is a function of period and particular circumstance more than of any mutuality of influence. Relative weights of influence are diffi-cult to determine, but on the question of Dickinson's readings – as with her borrowings — her degree of apparent familiarity may be belied by the paucity of her direct references. Some of them hint of a wider knowledge than they overtly show.

On the basis of her extant letters, Hawthorne came closer to Dickinson's conscious artistry as an influence than did Thoreau. She mentioned Hawthorne in five letters, more than she did any other writer, twice noting his death in 1864, and speaking famil-iarly of him elsewhere.[47] And her appreciation-as-identification in the case of Hepzibah indicates how his seemingly equivocal appeal – "[He] appals, entices" – penetrated her sensitivity.[48] Besides *The House of the Seven Gables* (1851), in her father's library there were copies of *The Blithedale Romance* (1852) and *The Marble Faun* (1860).[49]

It would seem strange if Dickinson did not know Hawthorne's *Twice-Told Tales* (1837, enlarged 1842). In both editions appear two stories which reveal his peculiar spiritual pilgrimage toward home, "The Gentle Boy" and "My Kinsman, Major Molineux." In "Gentle Boy," he made a point of emphasizing home when, in preparing for the 1837 edition, he made a number of changes in the text. Originally, soon after the beginning of the story where Tobias is introduced, Hawthorne wrote, "a gloomy extent of nearly four miles lay between him and his house." Hawthorne changed the last word to home. Seymour L. Gross speculates that this substitution was made because of the "richer" and "warmer" overtones of the word "home."[50] Possibly Hawthorne also wished to imply subtly that Tobias is a sympathetic, homelike man, preparing the reader for his roles as benefactor to the orphan Ilbrahim and as tragic hero.

Hawthorne's concern with home overtly arises when Tobias learns that Ilbrahim's only home is nothing less than his father's grave, again an adumbration of action to come. When Tobias later indicates to the child where his home is, "a thrill passed through [Ilbrahim's] frame." And, at last, the boy adjusts momentarily to his adoptive parents when he feels their house to be his home.[51]

Less obviously, the theme of the entire tale searches the possibilities of a religious, philosophic, and above all, humanitarian home in this life. Hawthorne juxtaposes two absolutisms, the Quakers' sweet but fanatical suffering and martyrdom and the Puritans' relentless psychological and physical containment of heresy. Between these poles, he asks, where lies home? By his tragic ending, Hawthorne implies that a solution which avoids these extremes, eschewing all doctrine, and which places human empathy and concern foremost is the surest route to reaching that coveted place.

As with "The Gentle Boy" so in "My Kinsman, Major Molineux" Hawthorne reveals the central role of time in his quest for the nature of a true home. The past, in danger of being used largely to celebrate the sunny aspects of American nationalism, was Hawthorne's chosen province for a special purpose. Probing the roots of the country's heart, he could at once reach the individual and communal center of America's spiritual house. From "Boy" and Boston's first generation of colonists, he moved to prerevolutionary New England in "Kinsman," as if to suggest chronological if not moral development.

In fact, Robin is as homeless in this life as Ilbrahim, although not to the point of death. As "a shrewd youth," he has defenses of age denied Ilbrahim. Still his confusions, externally represented by his meanderings through twisting streets and simultaneous encounters with ambiguously friendly or downright suspicious strangers, are so great that they culminate in the larger confusion of reality when not even the reader, much less Robin, is sure whether his perceptions record actuality or dreams. More subtly, Hawthorne points to the complexity of human perplexity when he suggests that its ultimate source is hidden, unpredictable, idiosyncratic, in short, one's own. Robin is the surprising stranger to

us and to himself when upon encouragement from the crowd, he
reacts to his kinsman's barbaric ignominy in tar and feathers by
laughing the loudest of all. A man at home with his principles
would risk the same plight himself rather than abet the forces of
betrayal. Robin's nowhereness, then, is as much a function of his
own ambitions (he came to the city to seek Major Molineux's aid,
but his downfall renders him useless) as it is of outer circumstance.
In contrast, Ilbrahim's innocence left him totally impotent against
such forces. Robin's journey toward home, we are led to assume,
thus depends upon his self-possession, in turn related to his loyalty
to human ties of blood or to traditional values.

Turning to *The House of the Seven Gables,* Dickinson's full
statement about Hepzibah and Clifford gives clues to her own life
plan as she saw it in 1851, and also indicates the affinity of mind
between author and reader. Writing to Austin on a bleak day in
early November, she set a semi-Gothic scene:

> How lonely it was last night when the chilly wind went
> down, and the clear, cold moon was shining – it seemed to me
> I could pack this little earthly bundle, and bidding the world
> goodbye, fly away and away, and never come back again to be
> so lonely here, and then I thought of "Hepzibah" how sorrow-
> ful *she* was, and how she longed to sleep, because the grave
> was peaceful, yet for affection's sake, and for the sake of
> "Clifford" she wearied on, and bye and bye, kind angels took
> both of them home, and it seemed almost a lesson, given us to
> learn. I don't mean that you are *him,* or that Hepzibah's *me*
> except in a relative sense, only I was reminded.[52]

Again, Emily's double view of home appears at once, the everlasting and the earthly, the last winning out temporarily, despite
the appeal of the former, in the name of affection and duty. Further, the home in this life is to be dedicated to "Clifford," at
least in large part, and the final reward for this care, "almost a
lesson, given us to learn," is an angel-led procession homeward.
Hepzibah, as the provider for, and thereby unmistakably the
possessor of, Clifford, bears "burdens" Emily could understand as
the basic reasons for living! Such analogic thinking comes as no
surprise after the poet's endless admissions of affection for Austin,
especially as they were focused in the most active hearthstone of
the house, namely, the kitchen.[53]

Dickinson may have read Hawthorne's preface to *Mosses from an Old Manse* (1846) and his sketch "The Haunted Mind" in *Twice-Told Tales*. Both provide a richer view of his sensitivity to enclosure, a much more positive one than suggested by the depriving aspect and atmosphere of the Pyncheon-Maule house. In "The Old Manse" preface, Hawthorne pictures the life he enjoyed for four years in Concord in the quiet seclusion of a residence once belonging to Ezra Ripley, clergyman and relative. In fact, the holiness of that house immediately settles upon Hawthorne's imagination as he muses that only men of the cloth have resided there before his arrival. And though a flicker of guilt arises when he compares his "idle stories" to the wisdom of his predecessors, he gains spirit by envisaging "a novel that should evolve some deep lesson and . . . stand alone."[54] He is further inspired by the delightful coziness of a small study facing north and west with "the sunshine glimmering through the willow branches while [he] wrote."[55] And Hawthorne carefully notes that Emerson used this room while he was engaged in writing "Nature."[56]

Touring the house, first outside, then within, Hawthorne focuses upon the garret, large, dimly lit, roughly finished and swathed in dust and cobwebs. It is a perfect place to meet a ghost, and there one is! Hawthorne identifies the spectre of a deceased divine who has previously appeared in the house by finding his likeness on a century-old canvas. And yet, perhaps because he does not want to edit the ghost's quantities of dusty manuscripts, Hawthorne minimizes the occurrence with, "Houses of any antiquity in New England are so invariably possessed with spirits that the matter seems hardly worth alluding to."[57] Spectral company in the Mansion was as easily accepted by Dickinson, so she would have half-seriously agreed with Hawthorne.

Moving on to a fishing trip with Ellery Channing, Hawthorne dwells upon the pleasures of the outdoors once more and compares the cooking, the fare, and the smell of the fire very favorably to the same duty done indoors. In fact, in this woodland kitchen and banquet hall, Hawthorne has a fleeting experience of complete communion with nature, a penetrating sense of the oneness of creation. Perhaps Emerson's or Thoreau's ghosts lurked there: "Our fire, red gleaming among the trees, and we beside it, busied with culinary rites and spreading out our meal on a moss-grown log, all seemed in unison with the river gliding by and the foliage rustling over us."[58]

Yet this idyllic place and others like it (where trees whispered "Be free! be free!") were still, Hawthorne admits, "less sacred in my remembrance than the hearth of a household fire."[59] Reminded of the manse once again, Hawthorne offers a paean to it, especially for a wisdom which he implies Nature does not know:

> [The old Manse] had grown sacred in connection with the artificial life against which we inveighed; it had been a home for many years in spite of all; it was my home too; and, with these thoughts, it seemed to me that all the artifice and conventionalism of life was but an impalpable thinness upon its surface, and that the depth below was none the worse for it. Once, as we turned our boat to the bank, there was a cloud, in the shape of an immensely gigantic figure of a hound, crouched above the house, as if keeping guard over it. Gazing at this symbol, I prayed that the upper influences might long protect the institutions that had grown out of the heart of mankind.[60]

Hawthorne echoes Emily's "Home is a holy thing . . ." in this passage, only he invokes greater protection for it, by the hound of heaven, because he enshrines the domestic house as one of mankind's highest institutional achievements. Writing five years before *The House of the Seven Gables,* composed in the wake of his dismissal from the Salem Customs House, Hawthorne is much more sanguine about the virtues of the old manse than he was to be later about the Pyncheon-Maule house. And his references to hound and to heart in connection with home bear a certain similarity to one of Emily's poems, "What shall I do – it whimpers so – / This little Hound within the Heart," in which the message implied is that the whimpering arises from lack of a master and home.[61]

Another, even shorter autobiographical piece of Hawthorne's, "The Haunted Mind," has its physical setting entirely inside a room and, in large part, a bed. Yet, in fact, the psyche is the true scene with the midnight, moonlit hour turning on its imagination to optimum power. Again, Hawthorne writes with the ambiguous

awareness of space which makes him unwittingly appear to be
Dickinson's preceptor:

> You speculate on the luxury of wearing out a whole existence
> in bed, like an oyster in its shell, content with the sluggish
> ecstasy of inaction, and drowsily conscious of nothing but de-
> licious warmth, such as you now feel again. Ah! that idea has
> brought a hideous one in its train. You think how the dead
> are lying in their cold shrouds and narrow coffins, through the
> drear winter of the grave, and cannot persuade your fancy
> that they neither shrink nor shiver, when the snow is drifting
> over their little hillocks, and the bitter blast howls against the
> door of the tomb.[62]

Then Hawthorne adopts allegory to enumerate those forces
which flee, as he puts it, the "tomb" and "dungeon" of the self, the
deepest self, recalling Emily's dread of the passions packed into her
deep cellar of remembrance. His list of Sorrow, Disappointment,
Fatality, Shame, and Remorse would be supplemented by her Fear
and Despair. But just as he could turn to happier thoughts of the
sunniness of nature, from a rainbow at Niagara Falls to the radiant
hearth of newlyweds, so Dickinson's haunted chamber of the mind
could shift to the signs of nature's "Inn," to its glory and beauty.
Finally, Hawthorne's midnight musings push him past the confus-
ing flux of disjunctive polar thoughts to the last mystery. And he
compares the return to sleep which eliminates these vicissitudes to
one's final rest. For still another time, his words strike a popular
sentiment increasingly favorable to Emily's mind, especially as she
grew older:

> Your spirit has departed, and strays, like a free citizen, among
> the people of a shadowy world, beholding strange sights, yet
> without wonder or dismay. So calm, perhaps, will be the final
> change; so undisturbed, as if among familiar things the en-
> trance of the soul to its Eternal home![63]

That Dickinson knew Thoreau's work, and perhaps rather well,
appears in her casual question to Sue, vacationing at the shore in
1886: "Was the Sea cordial? Kiss him for Thoreau."[64] Perhaps she
had read *Cape Cod* and Thoreau's unsparingly detailed descriptions of the bodies of Irish immigrants washed ashore after a ship-

wreck. Sue's copy of *Walden* (1862) has some corners turned down, possibly by Emily. And several years later Emily would have read Lowell's essay on Thoreau in *My Study Windows* (1872) and Higginson's 1879 sketch. Then in 1881, by an offhand reference, she again hinted of the degree of her familiarity with Thoreau: after describing a fire which devastated the Amherst business district, she wrote her cousins, "The fire-bells are oftener now, almost, than the church-bells. Thoreau would wonder which did the most harm."[65]

Even superficially, the facts of Thoreau's life would have made him a spiritual brother to Dickinson. He was home-centered and emotionally dependent on his family. Alone among his literary peers, he never left New England and disdained English and European tastes and manners. But more profoundly, Thoreau lived the same sorts of paradoxes Emily attempted: society in seclusion and solitude, communication either by silence or the slanted, succinct word, and far-flung voyages of the mind at home.

More particularly, Thoreau's harangue in *Walden* against elaborate houses probably reawakened Emily's own sense of the contrast between her preferred simple life and the grandeur of her father's Federal-style Mansion (refurbished in 1855; Sue's copy of *Walden* was the 1862 edition). With little doubt she would have assented to Thoreau's observation that "We have built for this world a family mansion and for the next a family tomb,"[66] feeling buried at times by even her reduced load of housework. And her father's image might have arisen as she read:

Who bolsters you? Are you one of the ninety-seven who fail, or the three who succeed? Answer me these questions, and then perhaps I may look at your baubles and find them ornamental. The cart before the horse is neither beautiful nor useful. Before we can adorn our houses with beautiful objects the walls must be stripped, and our lives must be stripped, and beautiful housekeeping and beautiful living be laid for a foundation: now, a taste for the beautiful is most cultivated out of doors, where there is no house and no housekeeper.[67]

Thoreau qualifies himself a bit further on:

Not that all architectural ornament is to be neglected even in the rudest periods; but let our houses first be lined with beauty, where they come in contact with our lives, like the tenement of the shell-fish, and not overlaid with it.[68]

Thoreau's description of his own house-building may have aroused in Emily great empathy, perhaps even envy. It would have been sufficient that he calls his readers to life through simplicity rather than to work. But he also speaks about the poetic mind in avian language in the same way Emily frequently describes herself:

It would be worth the while to build still more deliberately than I did, considering, for instance, what foundation a door, a window, a cellar, a garret, have in the nature of man, and perchance never raising any super-structure until we found a better reason for it than our temporal necessities even. There is some of the same fitness in a man's building his own house that there is in a bird's building its own nest. Who knows but if men constructed their dwellings with their own hands, and provided food for themselves and families simply and honestly enough, the poetic faculty would be universally developed, as birds universally sing when they are so engaged.[69]

Possibly Emily could have been reading this passage or remembering it at the time she wrote, "Her breast is fit for pearls," the poem about Mrs. Bowles which ends with a reference to home as "My perennial nest."[70]

Prepared by Thoreau's reference to poetry, Emily may have read his question, "What does architecture amount to in the experience of the mass of men?" with some curiosity. It should, argues Thoreau, count for a great deal, but a society dependent upon division of labor and trained architects leaves houses encumbered with meaningless decoration, thus untrue to the men who inhabit them. Immodestly, he announces that only the man who has literally built his own house can be hopeful it will genuinely reflect him. And insofar as he lives "unconscious truthfulness and nobleness" his dwelling will be beautiful. Aesthetic success is most often found, Thoreau then argues, in "the most unpretending, humble log huts and cottages of the poor. . . ."[71] Since Dickinson also located genuine beauty in the inner life and often mocked conventional standards of the beautiful (maybe because she felt herself unattractive: "Myself the only kangaroo among the Beauty . . ."), she might have thought of the Pleasant Street house as a cottage in comparison to the Mansion. Her poems about cottages speak of or imply a combination of coziness and awe which, as earlier noted, she reserved for encomiums about home.[72]

Several other sections in *Walden* speaking of architecture, house, or home doubtless drew Emily's attention,[73] a guess made surer by the fact that corners are turned down marking the first few pages of his chapter 13, "House-warming." Here Emily's special interest could easily have been Thoreau's comments about the dimensions of his hut. Her "own little chamber" seems described in his words:

> My dwelling was small, and I could hardly entertain an echo in it; but it seemed larger for being a single apartment and remote from neighbors. All the attractions of a house were concentrated in one room; it was kitchen, chamber, parlor, and keeping-room; and whatever satisfaction parent or child, master or servant, derive from living in a house, I enjoyed it all.[74]

With a fireplace and lounge as well as a writing table and chair, Dickinson's bedroom in the Mansion was akin to this one-room hut, except for kitchen functions. Serving as a parlor, it "received" the spectres of friends or the presence of the poet's second self and was as well the place where Emily retreated to read her letters. Emily's solitary and social selves, not unlike Thoreau's parent, child, master, or servant, thus lived in passing contentment in a room which might be called a second Walden.

Emerson may have been the route through which Thoreau reached Emily, that is, his profile of Thoreau in *The Atlantic Monthly* in August 1862, shortly after Thoreau's death.[75] Any word of Emerson's would have been closely attended to by Dickinson. His work had been introduced by her "gentle, yet grave Preceptor," Benjamin Newton, who had given her Emerson's *Poems* (1847) as a memento after his departure from Edward Dickinson's law office for his home in Worcester in 1849. Subsequent writings of Emerson, associated with this well-loved tutor, would claim Emily's intense interest. Sue's copies of his *Miscellanies* (1860), *The Conduct of Life* (1861 and 1879 editions), and *Essays,* first and second series (1861 and 1862 respectively), were readily at hand and Emily probably turned in corners and pencilled sentences in these volumes. She also knew his *Representative Men,* a copy of which she gave to Mrs. Higginson for

Christmas 1876, with the inscription, "a little Granite Book you can lean upon."[76]

That Emily leaned heavily upon Emerson for certain modes of thought, subjects, aesthetic concepts, and at least a few elements of her style is now an elementary fact in Dickinson scholarship.[77] The relationship, however, was one of adoption-in-part or adaptation. Emily depended on Emerson to the degree that she might not have become a poet of stature without him, but at the same time, she preserved her own identity and reached independent solutions. She might accept and practice, or alter but little, his principles of perception and his poetic method, but yet she stopped short of his Transcendentalism. In brief, she followed his advice, "Do your work and I shall know you," so well that she was finally free of him.[78]

Emerson's epistemological method, from the eye and heart of the viewer, was open, exuberant, at times ecstatic, especially in his earlier writings, matching Emily's individualistic and sensuous approach to reality.[79] This similarity of method led both to positions forever avoiding stasis, typically reaching for broader horizons. But Emerson's findings were much more constantly expectant, idealistic, and sanguine than the recurring melancholy and resignation of Emily's expressions. Their conclusions (if this word accurately describes ideas tentatively held) could be at almost polar extremes.[80]

Yet Emerson's words encouraged Emily to assume seriously the "business" of poet at the same time that he described her solitary situation at home as quite perfect for the scholar-writer. Perhaps she read his *Miscellanies* and *Essays* during the period in which she attempted to surmount her crisis of the early 1860s. Such pieces as "Compensation," "Self-Reliance," and "Friendship" would have been immensely helpful in redirecting her attention from personal tragedy in unrequited affection to a mature friendship. "The Poet" would have set before her a congenial plan of life, the vocation of poet, in terms suited to her temperament and location, while "Nature" recalled the bounty of material available for the sensitive, poetic eye, helping her to look anew upon the largely unspoiled landscape of Amherst.

Markings in "Literary Ethics" indicate that this essay was just such a timely inspiration. It spoke of confidence and opportunity and prescribed a discipline for the young scholar in America. A page in which Emerson dealt with the writer's regime is folded over and this passage marked:

> Let him know that the world is his, but he must possess it by putting himself into harmony with the constitution of things. He must be a solitary, laborious, modest, and charitable soul.[81]

The following paragraph, unmarked, is on the same page and must have been impressive reinforcement to the above:

> He must embrace solitude as a bride. He must have his glees and his glooms alone. His own estimate must be measure enough, his own praise reward enough for him. And why must the student be solitary and silent? That he may become acquainted with his thoughts.[82]

On the strength of her agreement with this essay, Emily may have adopted the habit of signing her letters to Higginson, "your Scholar," which she began to do by July 1862, presumably after he had agreed to become her "Preceptor."[83]

Whatever general Emersonian insights inspired Emily, his house imagery, a favored, even belabored, figure, must have worked its permeating influence upon her. In "Nature," Emerson sees the whole universe as a house abundantly filled with objects to serve men, especially its most perceptive residents. Its furnishings provide human sense not only with commodity, beauty, and language, almost unconsciously used, but also manifest the undergirding idealism and spirit which are the creative and unifying source of visible phenomena. Though total comprehension of nature is beyond expectation, though it always remains a sea with some unknown currents, nonetheless, with all humility, Emerson argues that man may become a "creator in the finite" and explore the world as deeply and as far as his energy and intellect allow. He – or she – does not stop with the exercise of understanding alone, like the scientist, but may push further into nature's mystery with "Reason," a sensitivity infused with affection and "soul," or spirit. With the same, fundamentally religious intention of Paul's message that the world is yours, Emerson calls anyone imbued with this soul, specifically the poet, to build a universe or house of his own, typically restating the same point from "Literary Ethics." The power promised must have charged any reader with high purpose, and Emily all the more because of Emerson's phraseology:

Every spirit builds itself a house, and beyond its house a world, and beyond its world a heaven. Know then that the world exists for you. For you is the phenomenon perfect. What we are, that only can we see. All that Adam had, all that Caesar could, you have and can do. Adam called his house, heaven and earth; Caesar called his house, Rome; you perhaps call yours, a cobbler's trade; a hundred acres of ploughed land; or a scholar's garret. Yet line for line and point for point your dominion is as great as theirs, though without fine names. Build therefore your own world. As fast as you conform your life to the pure idea in your mind, that will unfold its great proportions.[84]

In "The Poet," Emerson elaborates his argument about nature's vast potentialities and the poet's central role in uncovering, ordering, and enunciating them in his own voice. Emphasizing the concrete object, he sees it as the basis of the poet's creation of his own idiosyncratic house from nature's. Each generation, he argues, needs fresh observations in fresh forms. The acute study of the thing-in-itself is the primary requirement for this new creation. The object alone awakens a "living power" within the eye or heart of the beholder, that is, a suggestive, symbolic meaning inherent within the thing and linking it to the world of ideas or spirit. This innate, emblematic quality of the object confirms the oneness of all creation. Unity is further perfected by the poet's gift not only to grasp its inner meaning but to tie it temporarily to his own thoughts. Natural phenomena or events either in their essence or in their appearance, then, become the poet's tools, but at the same time always remain themselves.

This divination of the concrete and specific, even of the meanest, lowest, or even obscene object must have appealed both to Emily's inherited Christian concern with all of God's handiwork, including the mouse and the dandelion, and to her simple enjoyment of nature bare of theology, from the leopardlike sunset to the pink, small, and punctual arbutus. And for Emily, as housekeeper, Emerson's suggestions would have been carried indoors. His stress upon the obvious objects at hand must have seemed easily applicable to herself, all the more because she had already symbolized certain areas of the house on Pleasant Street. Emily marked this passage in his essay:

Why covet a knowledge of new facts? Day and night, house and garden, a few books, a few actions, serve us as well as would all trades and all spectacles. We are far from having exhausted the significance of the few symbols we use. We can come to use them yet with a terrible simplicity.[85]

In Emerson's concluding comments, perhaps an apology for his own quiet life, Emily would have found romantic suggestions seconding his words in "Literary Ethics" and justifying her own sense of separateness and sovereignty. He asks the poet to persevere in his self-revelation of a creative gift. To do so, he recommends isolation from the marketplaces of life, exchanging them for an existence close to nature. Here the world's objects and events may be "owned" without actual possession, but with insight and imagination which knows no boundaries:

The world is full of renunciations and apprenticeships, and this is thine; thou must pass for a fool and a churl for a long season. This is the screen and sheath in which Pan has protected his well-beloved flower, and thou shalt be known only to thine own, and they shall console thee with tenderest love. . . . And this is the reward; that the ideal shall be real to thee, and the impressions of the actual world shall fall like summer rain, copious, but not troublesome to thy invulnerable essence.[86]

It is no surprise that Emerson, who favored his own study and, as Hawthorne reveals, also the small one at the old manse, should dwell upon the house with an affection and an implied need that only Hawthorne approaches among the American writers just considered. In "Nature," he makes the whole cosmos a house in a figure of enclosure which matches his vast hopes for the compassing potentialities of the human enterprise. Quite strikingly, he speaks of the house of *this* world, not the next, departing from Biblical and contemporary theological tradition in yet another way. Most centrally, it is the house of intellect which is his special focus. When Dickinson writes, "The Brain is wider than the Sky," she speaks inebriate with the liquor of Emerson's words.

Such a line naturally poses a question: if a male writer appears to share Dickinson's focus upon home, or if she appears to push past it, as in this comment, what does that interest mean in relation to Erikson's theory of sexual morphology as the general basis for differing views of space? In some instances, Hawthorne's and Emerson's treatments of house seem quite similar to her own, and Thoreau's "Housewarming" is an encomium to enclosure. Yet I think distinctions, or preferences at least, may still be made following two points: 1) the predominant external or internal use of the house figure, and 2) the operation of a heightened bisexual imagination, enabling the writer to participate acutely in the probable psychology of the opposite sex.

In the first instance, Emerson's "Nature" exhibits the house as nothing less than the whole universe, and "Circles" treats circumference at much greater length than the voyage from one's center inward. Thoreau's *Walden* takes its name from the pond and its environs, which he observes in much greater detail than his hut or its interior. In Melville's case, Tom in *Typee* teaches Marheyo his first English words, "Home" and "Mother," yet the author's final emphasis is upon the open sea. In *Mardi,* the hero's exploration of innerness in "The Center of Many Circumferences," where he probes the retreat of a native chief, leads to no spiritual repose, and he is left at sea pursued by spectres on the last pages. A passage from *Moby Dick* contributes to understanding Melville's intent in *Mardi's* conclusion, when he says, ". . . all deep, earnest thinking is but the intrepid effort of the soul to keep the open independence of her sea," and, "in landlessness alone resides the highest truth, shoreless, indefinite as God. . . .[87]

Even Hawthorne seems to subordinate the rich details of the Pyncheon parlors to the more broadly symbolic front of his seven-gabled house and its grounds. While his autobiographical musings appear to be more appreciative of the inside of the old manse, he is oppressed by the clerical spectres of its past. His moment of true appreciation follows upon an afternoon's outing when he spies the house once more from the outside. And his praise of it derives from its value as a social and cultural institution rather than simply as a personal haven. These samples are hardly conclusive, of course, merely interesting. Moreover, one can agree that social conditioning may play as great a role as psycho-biological factors.

Nevertheless, the bisexuality inherent in any personality, accentuated by imagination, at least partly accounts for masculine sensitivity to the feminine world and helps to explain the success some men authors have with interior description used to extend their heroines' characters and moods. Such insight at times enables a man to portray a woman's view of domestic arrangements or home in general with a depth which may excel even that of gifted women. One compares James's portrait of Isabel Archer with George Eliot's Dorothea Brooke. Or it may allow him, as narrator, to be specially tuned to the nuances of a house and its objects. Again, one thinks of James's *Spoils of Poynton*.

Erikson stresses that his differentiations are proclivities rather than sure formulae, and it is in this light that I find convincing his emphasis on morphological distinctions as primary in consciousness of space. Interior house imagery may then be read as quintessentially feminine even as it is profoundly explored by men capturing the feminine "position" all the better to enhance their readers' appreciation of the woman's situation, as in the case of Hawthorne's Hepzibah. Or, in depicting Clifford's situation, Hawthorne exaggerates the virtual imprisonment of the unjustly treated or weak, making the life of Hepzibah's brother a touching parallel to the historic social role women have been given. The reverse, equally true, accounts for a woman writer's strength and subtlety in depicting the male mind, as in George Eliot's best moments with Bulstrode at his bank, Lydgate and his hospital, and Casaubon in his study in *Middlemarch*. Yet the point to keep in mind may be illustrated for a final time by returning to Dickinson. Though she may find the brain wider than the sky, probe circumference along with Emerson and Melville, and even go "beyond the Dip of Bell" to touch the universe, she does so from a sure sense of her center, the safe perspective of a circumscribed life, and the particular sense of a limited home, one's own "Brain" or consciousness. These distinctions in comparison to Emerson will become clearer in the last part of chapter 5.

The survey I have just presented of possible literary sources for Emily's use of house and home imagery has been something of a gambol through time, traditions, and genres. If it has suggested that she had a plethora of diverse materials to stimulate her, rather than exhaustively explored all possible references, then it has achieved its goal.[88]

Once again, my focus here should be fitted to the larger goal of reaching toward Emily's spatial inscape, that blend of life history, literary legacy, cultural emphasis, and poetic insight, all of which enter into her unique view of houses and homes. It is helpful to remind ourselves of this sweep of significance as we move from a chapter about the historic word to another concerned with Emily's word as act.

Chapter 5
The Conservatory

*Nature is a Haunted House – but Art – a House that tries
to be haunted.*

EMILY DICKINSON

Emily's conservatory, on the southeast corner of her father's house,
was lined on the wall side with white shelves for her ferns, flowers,
and exotic plants.[1] Access to it from the inside was only possible
through Mr. Dickinson's study. A second doorway led directly outside to the south and the Mansion's spacious grounds. In both an
actual and an aesthetic sense, this room was a halfway house for
Emily. Probably built especially for her by her father, its glass-
paned walls captured the sun for her beloved plants and for herself
alone. It was a bridge between the house, largely dominated by her
father's tastes, and Nature outdoors. Both areas alternately imprisoned or sheltered her, but the conservatory was a seemingly neutral unit for her own pleasure, perhaps more so than her bedroom.
The stifling effects of the Mansion or the indifference of an impersonal universe might be escaped either in the simple tending of
the favorite specimens she gathered here or in the more delicate,
deliberate culture of poetry. Her niece remarked that she was
known to write here, "watching with her plants lest they freeze in
zero midnight."[2] The small writing table in the dining room
"where Emily oftenest sat" was near a window looking through to
the conservatory.[3]

This room may be taken as an arbitrary but appropriate setting
for Emily's musings about theology, philosophy, and poetry. Metaphorically, it provides a perspective more accurate and apt than
the Mansion's cupola. In fact, "cupola" or equivalent words never
occur in her writings, though it was a contemporary architectural
term and a structure familiar to her at home and from the Hills'
house next door.[4] The "garret" was where she read Shakespeare
aloud, but then that was probably not the cupola. "The rafters
wept" on hearing her recite "John Talbot's parting with his son,

FIGURE 13. *Conservatory on the east wing of the Mansion facing south, where the poet grew ferns, exotic plants, and wildflowers. Photograph by Lincoln Barnes, early twentieth century. Courtesy of the Jones Library, Amherst.*

and Margaret's with Suffolk,"[5] and attics, not cupolas, have rafters. More significantly, the altitude and limited space of the cupola might suggest a sense of superiority on Emily's part above deity and creation, a position she sometimes points to but does not insist upon. She longed for unity with these forces but, unconvinced of their benevolence, she was left to stress her distinctiveness from both.

The conservatory's location on the Mansion's ground floor set a truer symbolic scene for the poet before God and Nature than did any other part of the house. It was a dual purpose workroom where she brought plants and poems to life. Her bedroom, though most private, was at times a melancholy, even terrifying, sanctuary: "Sweet hours have perished here." The conservatory, one imagines, provided a unique prism for scenes against which to measure herself, where, mood and circumstances permitting, she could be the controlling actor.

What did she "see" here when she focused on Creation, Creator, and her own center, that "imperial self" behind the poetic center discussed in chapter 3? Through the three windowed walls of the conservatory, she had a partial, subjective view of God and "Great Nature" (her term), as opposed to the nature she cared for inside. Equally partially, but more intimately, she saw herself – that "Undiscovered Continent"[6] – her center, consciousness and circumferences, large and small, by turning her gaze inward as far as she could go. Her vision then had a special doubleness other than what she reported to be hers, a simultaneous "convex" and "concave witness," the lens of either microscope or telescope.

Only by establishing the triple loci of God, Nature, and Self – in a way reminiscent of her Puritan ancestors or of Emerson, but distinctly her own – could she position herself "at home" in an uneasy but productive independence within a sense of final finiteness before these cosmic giants. In scrutinizing them, she found the form and spirit she needed to be a poet. Emerson's thoughts remained suggestions as she evolved her idiosyncratic image as artist; that is, the figure of house as a poetic tool as opposed to a felt symbol may have been suggested by him, but she made it uniquely hers. It is no slight statement, then, but one founded on the basis of circumstance and perhaps morphology, that she embedded her aesthetic theory in the language of architecture: "Nature is a Haunted House – but Art – a House that tries to be haunted."[7]

Emily's odyssey of consciousness toward this statement has shaped the structure of this chapter, a form which had to allow for close scrutiny of details, thus apparent digressions, without truly moving afield from the house or home figure. It remains as an overarching scaffolding, if the reader looks up or around for a moment from the page at hand. The poet appears to move through the chambers of her mind progressively eliminating or adjusting the theological or philosophical furniture, and finally settling for the pillows of poetics, easily arranged and rearranged.

Before exploring Emily's views of deity, nature, and self, it is important to notice her relationship to the nature she placed within the conservatory's walls. Working here, one imagines, she was led from mundane thinking about the practical care of her plants to more cosmic thoughts about her own place in the order of creation. Emily's exquisitely modest or, alternately, subtly tyrannical identification with these plants also mirrors her admiration for and even envy of them.

In addition to a wide variety of ferns, which had interested her ever since she began a herbarium at age fifteen, Emily cared for a rich range of flowers.[8] Besides primroses, heliotropes, and carnations, there were more exotic, romantic plants, her special favorites: two cape jasmines (the gardenia), a rare scarlet lily (the resurrection calla?), a giant daphne odora, and oxalis (wood sorrel) in hanging baskets. The effect of this collection made the conservatory an unmatched fairyland even in winter, perfumed with heavy scents.[9] Though the jasmine became Emily's preferred conservatory flower "next dearest to Daphne [Odora]," none outranked wild flowers.[10] But their soil requirements doubtless prevented her from growing them herself. Of these, however, she chose the Indian pipe, a sample of which still rests in her herbarium, as the first uncultivated flower with which to identify.[11]

The rose and the daisy, also probably wild varieties, were other signatures, one symbolizing royalty, the other, humility. They often accompanied poems sent to friends. A typical stanza, perhaps used often, explicitly shows Emily's unique intimacy with flowers, justified by her care of them:

> I hide myself within my flower,
> That fading from your Vase,

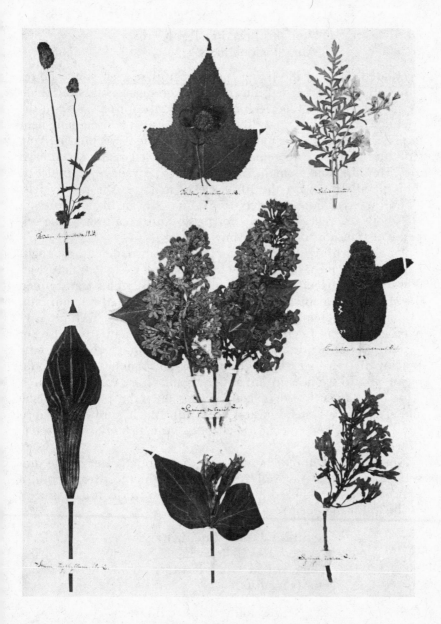

FIGURE 14. *A page from Emily Dickinson's herbarium, 1845, with Latin labels in her hand. Courtesy of Harvard College Library.*

> You, unsuspecting, feel for me –
> Almost a loneliness.   (903)[12]

Hidden there in the living specimen to last even as the flower withered, she left a faded hint of self. The suggestion is of loneliness, a description of her feeling, literally an emptiness, toward the friend, which probably prompted the gift. But it is also a statement of presence, because she moves from containment within the living structure of nature to remain within its dried remnants after it dies. Her kingdom, domain, or immanence pervades even in decay. This parallelism with the life cycle of a flower she deeply felt: "The career of flowers differs from ours only in inaudibleness. I feel more reverence as I grow for these mute creatures whose suspense or transport may surpass my own."[13]

Among such highly select companions, no wonder Emily might have felt at home. Here storms or snakes were excluded; nature-as-flowers was a friend with no qualification. Blossoms transformed life into an immediate paradise. As she commented one autumn, "We are by September and yet my flowers are bold as June. Amherst has gone to Eden."[14] Apparently, she frequently found it so; "Eden," she once said, "always eligible, is peculiarly so this noon." By this she referred to the grounds of the homestead: "It would please you to see how intimate the Meadows are with the Sun."[15] Thus the larger world of Nature, not only the part which she chose, could be beneficent and beautiful. But it also was as capricious, evasive, and unconcerned about human fate as God sometimes could be.

Not only the unpredictability but the cryptic center of the universe and of deity, as well as her own distinctness from both, a stance so well symbolized by her conservatory world, are all aspects of the following poem:

> Nature and God – I neither knew
> Yet Both so well knew me
> They startled, like Executors
> Of My identity.
>
> Yet Neither told – that I could learn –
> My Secret as secure
> As Herschel's private interest
> Or Mercury's affair –   (835)

The poem begins with commonplaces for Emily; the great abstractions were beyond comprehension. But it immediately moves to a surprise, startling because nothing should be new to God or Nature, but suggesting that their attention was now focused on a special object as executors scrutinize a will: Emily's actual nature. Yet they remain mute, probably a function of their basic impersonality. The implication is that her "affair" (an incident? a state of mind or heart?) is safe because of their unconcern. Though she is known, she is free. The tone is of delicious pleasure. A version of this poem was sent to Samuel Bowles, who doubtless shared her secret, to be discussed in the next chapter. Somehow Emily is beyond the control of God or Nature while at the same time she is dependent on both. How that could be and why it was essential to her as a poet sets the problem to be pursued for the rest of the chapter. Significantly, the separation is tellingly put in the language of house or home.

I.

Emily's affirmation that she knew neither God nor Nature stands as an apparently simple statement of the boundary of her belief and her knowledge. But applied to the orthodox Congregationalism of the Connecticut Valley, it hides Emily's wistfulness concerning a sustaining faith and a dismay issuing from God's seeming hypocrisy or bland passivity to human supplication and suffering, especially her own. Her experience at Mount Holyoke revealed how close this longing to believe lay to her final rejection of a commitment to the community confessing even a "hope" of salvation.

God's house of faith in this life or his eternal mansion continued to elude Emily's mapping, despite her ever-curious searchings and her deep need for order and structure, a necessary counterpoint for her apparently radical self-reliance. It was not so much that her imagination and intuition could not make a leap of faith, if the facts warranted. But unlike Jonathan Edwards and Edward Hitchcock, who could read divinity through nature's intricate or magnificent display, Emily's sensuous approach to nature involved first her heart before her mind and thence her faith.[16] She put it beyond doubt, "The Heart is the Capital of the Mind,"[17] and it was precisely here at her center that she felt betrayed. How then, could she surrender herself in an episode of conversion? How could one expect her to sense the conventional Puritan ecstasy of God's election?

One recent critic, William R. Sherwood, is convinced that in fact she did. For evidence, he concentrates on the poetry which Thomas Johnson dates about the year 1862. Emily's tremendous outpouring of verse in this period of the early 1860s witnesses to an enormous emotional crisis involving a profound and unfulfilled love for an unknown man, and in Sherwood's view, also to a turning toward God because of an immediate, if not a continuing, influx of divine favor or Grace.[18] As he puts it, "The contention here is that her Puritanism, far from being the stock from which she manufactures intellectual supports, was live, firm, and deeply rooted."[19] In saying this, Sherwood denies the position of other critics, led by Allen Tate, that Emily simply used the given, almost unconsciously absorbed, vocabulary of Puritanism for her own purposes and divorced it from a dead theology. Sherwood and Tate seem to represent opposite extremes of an explanation of Emily's attitude toward her inherited Christian milieu. More precisely, I would argue that she occupied a middle position between these views in which she neither totally rejected her Puritan past nor completely embraced it.[20]

Far from being infused with a conventional Puritan definition of grace in a dramatic moment of accepting election, Emily consistently witnessed to what seems a perpetually tantalizing position on the brink of, but still definitely outside, that electric encounter. Even when she pictured herself as "Convex – and Concave Witness –" at the moment of sensing imminent death, reaching a transcendent view of the relation between this world and the next, in which she looked "Back – toward Time – / And forward – / Toward the God of Him,"[21] she described a vision, not a commitment. The message was not a prescription, for herself or anyone else, but an expectation buoyed by the wish to see God in eternity. It was conventional theology, yet singularly expressed, probed rather than affirmed, the tone parallel to the theme, expressing hesitancy and contingency.

It was not a matter of confidently rejecting faith. She constantly registered the tension created by oscillating between the frontiers of belief and unbelief. She did not truly enter either "country."[22]

The situation was the simple and historic paradox; she altered orthodoxy by her probings with the intense sense of individuality which Puritanism fathered. But unlike predecessors, such as Anne Hutchinson, the self-confidence was without the sure overlay of a concerned, conversing God. In this position, Emily reworked three essential affirmations of traditional election: an admission of total depravity or original sin, a view of Christ as the word convincingly made flesh, and an orthodox understanding of grace. Exploring her views on these cardinal points of Puritanism shows how closely her theological meanderings are related to the central metaphor of home. It is a way of measuring her estrangement from God's house, the church, in this life, at the same time that she could entertain a vacillating hope of entering his home in eternity. She did remark at one moment, "Home is the definition of God."

For the Puritan heart to be pure, the doctrine of original sin had to be the first and last item of dogma to be known personally and reenforced communally. The infusion of grace into the soul required a preliminary and wracking recognition of the infinite despicability of one's very being. Only when an emptiness, a total worthlessness, was then acknowledged as the core of his character would the sinner hope to return to the restoring center of creation, God. With an eye both to psychology and poetry, the Puritans plainly expressed the effect of sin as "an old House gone to decay," with only faint suggestions of "what a famous Structure it once was, but is now nothing but Rubbish." Whereas before his fall, he was "like a fair house, new built, fit to entertain the King of Glory, fit for a Temple for the holy Ghost to dwell in."[23] To return to this state was a matter not of human determination but of divine will.

In relation to God's purpose as well as to sin, man was mere worm, as any Amherst preacher might have told Emily. However, she had a more generous, sometimes almost an opposite, estimate of this helpless creature, and herself. She wrote to Samuel Bowles in 1858, "Our Pastor says we are a 'Worm.' How is that reconciled? 'Vain – sinful Worm' is possibly of another species."[24] Still, she knew human nature to be "freckled" or "brittle." She herself might be "spotted." A "little Angle Worm," she could find her "Modesties enlarged."[25] But she was not totally black, spiderlike suspended over Jonathan Edwards's pit of the damned. Sin, after all, was the "distinguished Precipice" which "*Others* must resist" (my italics).[26]

Egocentrism saved her from this ledge, as many of the 1682 references to "I" in the poems convincingly show. More, when she asked God to grant her the favor of forgiveness, the request was ironic, "For what, he is presumed to know / The Crime, from us, is hidden."[27] Emerson's "Self-Reliance" and "Experience" were two supporting, if not wholly convincing essays. Could Grace set camp in a center repeatedly committed to one's own consciousness, even a divided consciousness? It seems unlikely.

Emily's parallel doubts about the efficacy of Jesus' mission and therefore his divinity also dispel thoughts of a far-reaching experience of grace and regeneration. Her inherited assumptions that Jesus was in fact the Son, that he was "innocent," that he was an announced avenue to the Father if one would follow his call, "Come unto me," and especially that he suffered supreme sacrifice for man, are all apparent.[28] But the question remains, did she thoroughly accept them? The evidence suggests she did not, though she wished she could. Rather, that feature of Jesus she could truly acknowledge was what she knew so well herself, his suffering.[29] In her earliest reference to Jesus, she makes the identification with his humiliation clear:

> "They have not chosen me," he said,
> "But I have chosen them!"
> Brave – Broken hearted statement –
> Uttered in Bethleem! [*sic*]   (85)

The poem was sent to Mrs. Samuel Bowles and "they" no doubt conflates to refer also to Mrs. Bowles and her husband. Emily ends the poem by addressing Jesus, "Sovereign! Know a Daisy / Thy dishonor shared!" In a second poem, she equates the denial of Jesus by Peter to one she had known, both founded on a supposed lapse of memory. The implication is that Emily's friend – "He forgot" – was as guilty as Peter in his avowal that he did not know Jesus. A further poem assumes that Jesus' crucifixion, not his position as Lord, enables him "to guess / The smaller size!" that is, estimate her worth. And, as if in self-remonstrance, she stated, "Our Lord – thought no / Extravagance / To Pay – a Cross."[30]

Emily repeatedly emphasized Jesus' humanity and function as potential solace in this world rather than as an avenue to faith either in a Father or in immortality. About 1884, her earlier position was reaffirmed, illustrating a consistent doubt: "When Jesus tells us about his Father, we distrust him. When he shows us his Home, we turn away, but when he confides to us that he is 'acquainted with Grief,' we listen, for that also is an Acquaintance of our own."[31]

Similarly, her assumptions about the meaning of grace were aberrent versions of dogma and not the all-consuming encounter with God's reconciling spirit. Although she was characteristically inconsistent on this point, the main thrust of her meaning appears to give grace a three-fold definition, of which the first element is the potency of truly living, an ecstatic moment, but not in the traditional juxtaposition in which grace follows recognition of sin. It is a blessed event, a gift, though again, not specifically acknowledged to be from God. Yet, as for the Puritans, the experience of grace in Emily's sense remained somewhat enigmatic and ineffable: "One Year ago – jots what? / Was't Grace? Not that / Was't Glory? That – will – do." The essential ingredients – immediacy and joy – are explicit in a poem in which she slowly, laboriously grasps for "Bliss," then suddenly gains it by an "instant's Grace."[32]

A second aspect of the definition, grace as election, is a more slippery item. When Emily speaks of "new Grace" as part of becoming "Baptized – this Day – A Bride," she sees it as a culmination of a process of adorning the soul and spirit to be "too proud – for Pride." Orthodoxy seems to guide her pen. Yet the whole poem expresses a wish, not a fulfillment. She yearns as a "Dowerless Girl" for one to teach her, bejewel and dress her for the event to make her "No more ashamed – / No more to hide." But the instructor, Christ or God, is absent, and beneath these lines pulses the cry of another poem, "And Jesus! Where is *Jesus* gone?" She lacks the achievement; the bridegroom is not there. In fact, the poem's basic motivation can be read not only as a religious quest but equally urgently as a search for status. She focuses on the self and its elevation beyond another because that other – whether divine or human (and "new Grace" also describes the lover's face encountered in eternity in the poem "I cannot live with You –") – never appears here. Emily's ambiguous intent is echoed, too, in "I'm ceded – I've stopped being Their's," when receipt of Grace is acknowledged, but the grantor remains unnamed. Achieved, however, is a "small Diadem," Emily's symbol of queenship, "the supremest name," elsewhere gained through struggle and suffering, a process of self-election, rather than divine choice. The point remains debatable,

but tends to illuminate Emily's independence unstably balanced
between a will-to-believe and experience's abrogation of that will.[33]
In a third facet of her understanding, Emily views grace in the
perspective of death as a premonition of immortality, an intima-
tion of its reality, immanent but not assured in this life, fully
known or not in eternity. Speaking of the silence of the dead, she
says, "Grace is still a secret."[34] Throughout poetry of this sort,
communion with God, the essential Puritan corollary to conversion as the human response to his call in anticipation of promised
salvation and assurance of it after death, is notably missing. Emily
speaks of grace as the possibility, not a promise, of an afterlife,
prefaced not by a mention or even allusion to God, but on the
contrary, by an icy affirmation of self-sufficiency, "The Soul's Superior instants / Occur to Her – alone." And the poem ends:

> Eternity's disclosure
> To favorites – a few –
> Of the colossal substance
> Of Immortality　　　　　　　　　　　　　(306)

This autonomy is underlined elsewhere by an elliptical analysis of
the projection involved in the individual's understanding of receiving conventional grace:

> 'Tis opposites – entice
> Deformed Men – ponder Grace –
>
> . . . .
>
> To lack – enamor Thee –
> Tho' the Divinity –
> Be only
> Me –　　　　　　　　　　　　　　　　(355)[35]

Emily's elusiveness about what motivated her moments of grace
makes any definite statement about a commitment to or exploration of faith finally precarious. My argument is that she did not
specify such incidents as an infusion of God's spirit into her own
consciousness. When Emily unequivocally spoke of God, she referred not to a thankfulness for grace received, nor to an ecstatic
wholeness through communion with him, but to a preconversion
apprehension of a remote deity, not unlike her usual attitude toward her own father.[36] Insofar as God was described (and of course

the Puritans constantly acknowledged his final mystery even though they studiously made mountainous attempts to define him), he appeared as a foreign potentate of a far-off country whose long arm might reach into her own sphere, but whose center was beyond her immediate horizon. In fact, she once spoke of him as an "Eclipse" whom her family, but not herself, worshipped as their "Father."[37] Far from enhancing life, knowledge of the deity was primarily an awareness that he "summons all to death." In brief, "None see God and live."[38]

Only when Emily felt herself to be confronting Truth, and those were rare moments, did she meet God. By analogy, it was when her beloved asked, "Would I be whole?" More obliquely, it was when she glimpsed the glory of sunset, again an allusion to death, and saw God in his "Royal Dress" in the "far Theatricals of Day," recalling the Puritan drama of the soul on the stage of divine purpose. However, Emily was impressed by God's wonders and strength, the impending forces of an Old Testament Yahweh or Jehovah, not the New Testament Father. It was his might and not his mercy which she felt.[39] As the Lord of Judgment, he was preeminently a power to be avoided. This plaintive poem registers how fully Emily might feel homeless either at the homestead or in heaven, that presumed place of final communion with him:

> I never felt at Home – Below –
> And in the Handsome Skies
> I shall not feel at Home – I know –
> I dont like Paradise –
>
> Because it's Sunday – all the time –
> And Recess – never comes –
> And Eden'll be so lonesome
> Bright Wednesday Afternoons –
>
> If God could make a visit
> Or ever took a Nap –
> So not to see us – but they say
> Himself – a Telescope
>
> Perennial beholds us –
> Myself would run away
> From Him – and Holy Ghost – and All –
> But there's the "Judgment Day"!   (413)

Eight years later, when Emily states that "Home is the definition of God,"[40] the intent is similar. All the best to be known of him has to be concentrated in this earthly Eden. Beyond that, definition dissolves.[41]

Nowhere does God's beneficence truly appear for Emily except perhaps at the approach of death. Her yearning for faith by clinging to prayer is fused in the following poem in the irony of Emily's final recognition of "Our Old Neighbor – God":

> It was too late for Man –
> But early, yet, for God –
> Creation – impotent to help –
> But Prayer – remained – Our Side –
>
> How excellent the Heaven –
> When Earth – cannot be had –
> How hospitable – then – the face
> Of Our Old Neighbor – God –   (623)

Her resentment is well-disguised perhaps, but may be acutely revealed by the telling adverb "then."

A longer poem of 1862 registers not only the use of prayer as a last resort, and it is finally given up, but also the staggering encounter with ultimate space or void:

> My period had come for Prayer –
> No other Art – would do –
> My Tactics missed a rudiment –
> Creator – Was it you?
>
> God grows above – so those who pray
> Horizons – must ascend –
> And so I stepped upon the North
> To see this Curious Friend –
>
> His House was not – no sign had He –
> By Chimney – nor by Door
> Could I infer his Residence –
> Vast Prairies of Air
>
> Unbroken by a Settler –
> Were all that I could see –
> Infinitude – Had'st Thou no Face
> That I might look on Thee?

> The Silence condescended –
> Creation stopped – for Me –
> But awed beyond my errand –
> I worshipped – did not "pray" –   (564)

Prayer collapses and she worships through simple wonder. What she worships is the impersonal, faceless firmament, since prayer is futile without an obvious "Object." His residence, much less the resident, is not to be found.[42]

The evidence seems overwhelming that, far from feeling herself to be one of God's children, Emily protested the Puritan heritage which promised a grace she desperately wanted but which she did not even halfway receive. She was left with an indelible suspicion, "As Children – swindled from the first / All Swindlers – be – infer."[43]

Perhaps Emily had her moments of reconsidering God's purpose, but they were not solid statements of a horizontal relationship toward a towering benevolence whom she had personally encountered. Rather, they were tentative and tenuous, sparsely revealed and delicately, highly originally perceived. For instance, one poem seems to describe a village as God's kingdom (immortality?), which may only be seen in March, Emily's favorite month,[44] because she savored the slow arrival of spring, denoting delighted expectancy. She asks:

> Have any like Myself
> Conjectured Who may be
> The Occupants of these Abodes –
> So easy to the Sky –
>
> Twould seem that God should be
> The nearest Neighbor to –
> And Heaven – a convenient Grace
> For Show, or Company –
>
> Have any like Myself
> Preserved the Charm secure
> By shunning carefully the Place
> All Seasons of the Year,
>
> Excepting March – 'Tis then
> My Villages be seen –
> And possibly a Steeple –
> Not afterward – by Men –   (736)

Though this poem is given the date 1863, it continues the familiar lack of witness to an earthly ecstasy with God. Instead, the scene described is dreamlike, a mirage perhaps, purposely avoided until March, the magic month (the moment of Emily's sense of oncoming grace?), when the mysterious "New Houses on the Hill" may be seen, including significantly, "a Steeple." This brief reference to a church hints of Emily's continuing but unfulfilled hope of communicating with her Puritan past. It echoes her statement, made near the end of her life, "On subjects of which we know nothing, . . . we both believe, and disbelieve a hundred times an Hour, which keeps Believing nimble."[45]

II.

If God's house were illusory, what then of Nature's? Emily's ambivalence toward "Great Nature" rested on a familiarity she did not have with God. Its tangibility, as well as its ultimate elusiveness, she could describe, while the faceless deity showed her little else but his vengeful will.

In the poem " 'Nature' is what we see," she sets scenes (a hill, an afternoon, an eclipse) or lists sounds (the sea, thunder, the cricket) or suggests that Nature is known by thought intuitively. But refuting her own enumerations, she finds the senses are not enough. The "Nature" we think we know by the eye, ear, and mind is only a fragment. "Nay," she says, Nature is deeper than appearances. It is Heaven, Harmony, and Simplicity, beyond the "art" of human wisdom.[46] Nonetheless, these are qualities which give some topography to the vista of Nature. God's visage remains for Emily an antique bas relief, present but eroded past recognition.

Nature might also be a "dissembling Friend," however, and parallel God's distance in its downright malevolence or imperviousness to man's destiny. Its potency for ill as well as good throbs simultaneously sometimes beneath her rejoicing. She cannot read it as only an apparent evil within God's larger plan, as the Puritans resolved the contradiction. In one poem, Emily observes that Nature's "fact" is "Beauty," and in another, that fact "scuttles" Emily's balloon, her illusions or aspirations. At such times, Emily sees past Nature as "gentle," "sweet," "sincere," "simple," "grand," and "wise." It becomes an ominous force contained in a "monstrous" house, a "Tempest" filled with thunder and lightning, which can "sear" and "scalp." More, Emily again confronts Nature's most treasonous envoy, that "guide to guile," the snake. Threatened by his swamp, she "sigh[s] for houses" for protection. The only positive role a malign Nature can play is to cure "Being's illness" by drawing the "curtain," death. And if it does not will actual harm, nonetheless, and perhaps worse, Nature like God "[does] not care."[47]

At this point, it helps to juxtapose Emerson's ideas with Emily's to dramatize her radically different findings about Nature and to illustrate again the reinforcement she received from him in using the figure of house.[48] His concept of the image, based on a personified Nature, she might mesh with her own while leaving the body of Transcendentalist thought to those who did not feel Nature's duplicity as acutely as she did. Emerson acknowledged that "Nature is no saint,"[49] but he saw imperfection as a way station to a final absorption of irregularities into a total unity, a neoplatonic, semipantheistic transcendent immanence of the Over-Soul merging with the world. The Puritans' cosmic optimism also underlay his confidence that a union between the viewer and the universe could be a reality through the soul's experience of sight, a transparent vision or "Revelation" of the fabric which weaves creatures into Creation.[50]

Emily could see the seamless side of existence, too, but at crucial times, "The Heavens were stitched."[51] In addition, she saw a rending of that fabric as well, most commonly, as with Emerson, in the context of immediate experience or by intuition, as she knew "Mightiest Things." ("If I feel physically as if the top of my head were taken off, I know that is poetry."[52]) Emerson's affirmation of harmony or correspondences between the orders of Nature was constantly questioned and sometimes fiercely denied by Emily's encounters either with the cosmos or with the concrete environment of the homestead. Not with a sense of fellowship but with an eye which transformed her father's hedge or her own door into a defending wall, Emily might look at the world.

At such moments of arch withdrawal, she could yet empathize with Nature's shortcomings, acknowledging her own. The reverse perspective echoes her understanding of divine anger. "Nature, like Us, is sometimes caught / Without her Diadem."[53] When Nature was "helpless," it touched Emily's core.[54] Its misfortunes and

her own were the basis for a certain affinity, though not a unity.
Emerson's harmony then was turned, not entirely upside down,
but at least was pulled askew.[55]

Two poems, both set within the language of houses, may be
studied to see Emily's awareness of Nature's contrasting potencies.
The first recalls Wyeth's Christina grasping toward a haven. It also
echoes Emily's remark that "Nature is what we know – / Yet have
no art to say."[56] Another poem, infused with the awe and comfort
she reserved for home, is expanded here for everyone:

> These are the Signs to Nature's Inns –
> Her invitation broad
> To Whosoever famishing
> To taste her mystic Bread –
>
> These are the rites of Nature's House –
> The Hospitality
> That opens with an equal width
> To Beggar and to Bee
>
> For Sureties of her staunch Estate
> Her undecaying Cheer
> The Purple in the East is set
> And in the North, the Star –   (1077)

The word "Inns" in the first line declares an openness and expectancy which contrast with a private house, reserved for its
owners' exclusive use. "Her invitation broad" is an open door for
all, especially to those who hunger for the special bread offered.
One recalls Emily's own talent for making bread, in frequent demand by her father. And one links it with the biblical word, "Man
does not live by bread alone," which infuses the "mystic" loaf with
a spiritual sustenance Emily no doubt intended both when she
made her literal bread and obviously in this poem.

The manners of this public house show the highest etiquette
because they are democratic. The inn opens equally to the beggar
and the bee. Emily as "a beggar / Before the door of God"[57] is here
always accepted, with her sometime companion, either as totally
other or as an alter ego, the bee. Finally, by the third stanza, she
envisions the permanence of this inn, though that assurance lasts
only within this poem. In the legal language of her father, she saw

certain "Sureties" of Nature's "staunch Estate," an undissolving blessing. The Sunset and Polaris are precise and timeworthy. They are intrinsic parts of the inn, assuring that it is regular and reliable. Here Emily reveals her need for structure and form, for security and guidance as an antidote to that part of her which was acutely antinomian.[58]

This poem would seem to echo Emerson's exuberance with Nature, and it does, but only to a certain degree. Its main theme is a paean to the availability and largesse of the world. However, within the image of inn (a mother symbol?[59]) and with the dominant note at the end of protection and constancy (a suggestion of her father's role in her life?), Emily's dependency is transparent, a qualification of Emerson's and her own self-reliance inside the walls of Nature's public house.

The X factor in Nature which separated Emily as perceiver tellingly emerges in a second poem using the house trope. One version substitutes the name of Sue for Nature. The change suggests how immediately Emily may have experienced the mystery, perhaps the duplicity of both. The following two verses end a six stanza poem:

> But nature is a stranger yet;
> The ones that cite her most
> Have never passed her haunted house,
> Nor simplified her ghost.
>
> To pity those that know her not
> Is helped by the regret
> That those who know her, know her less
> The nearer her they get.   (1400)

Just as Sue remained an intimate enigma to Emily, so Nature was ultimately anonymous, at best bountiful and inviting, at worst, unpredictable and potentially ruthless. This combination of Nature's warmth with her "imposing Negative" made her house "haunted," the ghosts there complex with the spirits of evil and good. Instead of repelling, however, the mystery infinitely attracted her. Emily patterned her vocation as poet on this fearful but fascinating vibrancy with which she, like Emerson, felt a profound relationship, even a kinship, at the same time that she knew herself to be totally distinct from it. The meshing of familiarity and distance underlie "Nature is a Haunted House – but Art – a House that tries to be haunted."

This aphorism, a scaffolding for the present chapter, was predicated on Emily's keen sense of the poet as creator and craftsman, fixed but free before Creator and Creation. "Myself was formed – a Carpenter," Emily announced.[60] The building became a mighty project as the poet rejected payment, publication, on anything but her own terms, that is, without editorial changes. Instead of constructing simple houses to be offered for sale, "We – Temples build – I said," again borrowing but not accepting the Puritan notion of prelapsarian man. This noble snobbery probably issued from a compensatory and stubborn self-esteem best illuminated by Emily's understanding of three interrelated but distinct concepts: consciousness, center, and circumference.

III.

In a letter to Maria Whitney, Emily observed, "Consciousness is the only home of which we *now* know."[61] Emily would have agreed with Emerson that this capacity of the mind was its primary order.[62] Without it, perception, awareness, sensitivity – human knowing, in sum – were all impossible. He precisely defined it as a range within each individual between awareness of a First Cause and a sense of one's own self in the flesh or Being. Emily's implied definition leaned toward the latter meaning. One's consciousness was impregnable, as she put it, a "Pyramidal Nerve,"[63] a given intuition or instinct, adequate unto itself. Typically, however, and unlike Emerson, Emily's consciousness was not whole and truly amoral in relation to herself, because she was continually and profoundly reminded that it could be split, "Of Consciousness, her awful Mate / The Soul cannot be rid."[64] It could be a "yawning Madness," "an awful stranger."[65]

These phrases not only describe a duality but again illustrate the way in which Emily saw consciousness operating. They register how primary the "felt life" was to her, as opposed to the categories of understanding and reason or virtue and vice. Her moral distinctions were primarily the Epicurean ones of pleasure and pain, which, in their highest expression, reach toward a good or attempt either to escape an evil or transform it to the virtue of emotional and poetic economy. If she borrowed Thoreau's attachment to the "*purely* sensuous life,"[66] by natural temperament and without specific reference to him, it was because her natural habit of mind characteristically united abstractions with sensations, never separating one from another.[67] The enmeshing of thought with perception, rather than an entirely intellectual explication of a body of ideas, freed her from either a didactic or a moralistic role. She had no message, simply a testimony to a pursuit of truth which was in constant flux because she grasped for a personal revelation.[68] This tactile and direct mode of encounter with life, including her inherited culture, resulted in an unstable, temporary body of expressions. And its nature and result forcefully arose in her contrasting sensitivity to space: "Captivity is Consciousness – / So's Liberty."[69] If it were the only home she now knew, that home was fraught with the insecurity generated in experiencing release in one moment and capture in another. Consciousness could be "Noon," the apex of perception, or it could be "suspended" in the vacuum of loneliness.[70]

Where did Emily locate the "Pyramidal Nerve?" It was either within the self or the goal of greater consciousness the self strove to attain. This double location appears to define Emily's sense of a "Centre." As the seat of consciousness, center was also a locus of both peace and anguish. Two poems reveal the combination of separate positions and opposite states of mind. One finds a universal and intimate crucifixion in the "Being's Centre."[71] Another, "Each Life converges to some Centre,"[72] speaks of the unattainable yet beckoning goal of self-fulfillment and foresees the pursuit continuing after death. She ultimately envisions this sense of center as infinite growth beyond time, "There is no first, or last, in Forever – It is Centre, there, all the time."[73]

Again Emerson provides a necessary touchstone for comparison and contrast to Emily's less fully stated views. In "Circles," he was at once more precise and more optimistic than Emily, clarifying the process out or in by which consciousness, "thought," pushes from its center, "a ring imperceptively small." Forging outside itself, the extent of one's "self-evolving circle" toward new and larger circles is a function only of the "force or truth of the individual soul." Such is the power of the quick, strong personality, that no boundaries can define an outside, a final wall, a circumference. Emerson stopped just short of promising infinity to the

noblest of human spirits. His theme was the ceaseless aggrandize-
ment of perspective, daily enlarged and abridged only by the
"word" which defines it. One's understanding then is a series of
generalizations continuously succeeding their predecessors. The
possibilities are endless.[74] So, too, the view inside onself – which
Emerson treated only briefly – shows infinite potential for comprehension. As the focus reverses to the interior life, the quintessential
center becomes fathomless: "The last chamber, the last closet, he
must feel never opened; there is always a residuum unknown,
unanalyzable. That is, every man believes that he has a greater
possibility."[75] In conceiving of the natural world as a series of
concentric circles, enlarging or contracting from the mind, Emerson at this moment in effect substituted consciousness for the position orthodox Christianity had reserved for God. He observed
that "St. Augustine described the nature of God as a circle whose
center was everywhere and its circumference nowhere."[76] Individual consciousness could not claim so much, but its potential
growth might progress infinitely.

Emily observed that "The Bible dealt with the Centre, not with
the Circumference,"[77] giving a simultaneous description and cri-
tique of the perspective and purpose of the Scriptural writers. The
implication is that their statements were a vertical exploration of
a universe visualized as triple-layered: heaven – earth – and hell.
And their focus was the divine will, the center of that world. Insofar as they subsumed the human mind and the objective world of
nature to this all-encompassing task, that is, slighted circumference, they committed a profound disservice to two essentially horizontal spheres of reality which Emily found nothing less than
fundamental. Not that the Bible failed to instruct her; we have
seen that the home image – not to mention numerous others –
depends upon it.[78] Nor did her curiosity bypass its purpose. Still,
she felt herself to be pushing beyond its concerns, as she makes
clear in a poem whose first version she entitled, "Diagnosis of a
Bible, by a Boy":

> The Bible is an antique Volume –
> Written by faded Men
> At the suggestion of Holy Spectres –
>
> .   .   .   .
>
> Had but the Tale a warbling Teller –

> All the Boys would come –
> Orpheus' Sermon captivated –
> It did not condemn – (1545)

Emily here again exposes her irritation with the Judaic-Christian message of God's wrath and with the faith dependent on the revealed word. She would be persuaded rather by a joyful song, such as, Orpheus, the Thracian bard, might sing, whose music celebrated the world and charmed all of nature, even the insentient, the trees and rocks as well as the animals. Emily remained respectful of the biblical authors for their insights into the world of spirit, particularly the books of promise, most notably *Revelation,* but as far as the Decalogue was concerned, she was less impressed. Accompanying a gift of her rare, red lilies to a newborn in Amherst, she wrote, "Let me commend to Baby's attention the only Commandment I ever obeyed – 'Consider the lilies.' "[79] Humanity was one of creation's flowers; human dogma denied its simplicity and thus its full blossom. Divinity was incorporated, at least in part, within. Consciousness alone then became her one sure religion.[80] A critic's comment that "the address on Main Street was the address of God," seems to illuminate still another facet of the poet's affirmation, "Home is the definition of God."

In July 1862, Emily wrote to T. W. Higginson, mildly embarrassed by her own seriousness, as if it would sound comical coming from so slight a person, "Perhaps you smile at me. I could not stop for that – My Business is Circumference."[81] In moments of confidence, Emily celebrated the conscious self as ultimate center. But her search for "Circumference" was more complex both in definition and direction. As the linear boundary enclosing a circular area, circumference could be a seemingly infinite perimeter progressing outward from the perceiver by "Processes of Size" toward "the Stupendous Vision / Of His diameters." But since the space defined by that curve might be limited, even quite small, circumference denoted circumscription as well: "I fear me this Circumference / Engross My Finity."[82]

Beyond describing space in this double sense, in the mode of Emerson, as expansion or as enclosure (with its corollary, protection), circumference sometimes abrogated or transcended time. This could be an event either in this world or in eternity; its arc overlapped both spheres. Moreover, it contained the paradoxical sensation of a "woe of Ecstasy." One critic has observed that cir-cumference was Emily's most frequent metaphor for the ecstatic moment.[83] But, as in this phrase, she chiefly knew that second of beauty and joy through the familiar guidance of pain.[84]

The several qualities of circumference appear in the poetry either separately or, more often and interestingly, in combination with one another. For example, the three elements of space, time, and joy emerging from suffering figure in "I saw no Way – / The Heavens were stitched." Kept from belief, she holds her vision on the tangible: "I touched the Universe" and alone "Went out upon Circumference – / Beyond the Dip of Bell –" (church bell?). Time and Christian faith are left behind by this solitary adventure to look at infinity.[85]

Two other poems concentrate on the spatial and temporal, leaving any aspects of bliss either unmentioned or only implied. She complains about the "minute Circumference / Of a single Brain" because it acutely feels the "Ages coil[ed] within" through agony's extension of time.[86] Ultimately that time becomes eternal and the space limitless within death: "A Coffin – is a small Domain, / Circumference without Relief – Or Estimate – or End."[87] There is an inescapable irony in the last lines. Only if immortality, not simply eternity, should ensue, then on Resurrection Day "Circumference [could] be full."[88] In this life, too, triumphal moments of circumference are possible because the "minute" Brain is "wider than the Sky," "deeper than the sea," and equal to ("just") the "weight of God."[89]

In endowing her enclosures of perception with divinity, Emily simultaneously protected herself from that final confrontation with God, defending her own center from his absolute judgment and wrath. The edge was a hair-fine limit, yet it "secures Eternity / From presenting – Here."[90] God's territory lay beyond Emily's circumference and threatened her independence, self-reliance, and identity. He was on the "frontier" where she could envi-sion another "House," and conclude that its owner must be a "Stranger," whose face "Is shunned, we must admit it, / Like an adversity."[91]

Emily's simultaneous use of the several meanings of circum-ference appear in succinct richness in "Circumference, thou bride / Of awe."[92] Parallel to her first line is Emerson's observation in "Experience," "The universe is the bride of the soul."[93] His statement is the culmination of an argument exposing the force of the perceiving "subject," its even ruthless exclusion of all others, "objects," and consequently its highly personalized, autocratic interpretation of the world. Here Emerson is saying that consciousness, as a tyrannical husband, bends his bride, the universe, to his will.

Emily's awe does not immediately seem identifiable with soul in Emerson's sense. But a certain similarity emerges in the poem's total context:

> Circumference, thou bride
> Of awe, – possessing, thou
> Shalt be possessed by
> Every hallowed knight
> That dares to covet thee.   (1620)

"Awe" functions as "soul" in the same sense that its source, consciousness, reaches out (or in) to comprehend and define the world. Yet wonder, not domination, is its motivation, the difference perhaps reflecting the sexuality of each writer.

In any case, the distinction becomes clearer if the letter with which Emily prefaced the poem is considered. She was writing to congratulate the sculptor Daniel Chester French upon the unveiling of his statute of John Harvard in front of University Hall in Cambridge. And her brief accompanying note included the statement, "Success is dust, but an aim forever touched with dew." Circumference becomes more tangible in this instance because it is attached to a palpable piece of sculpture. And it bears the double definition of total creation and the object produced by creativity, because at the same time as it encompasses, possessing all, it is possessed, in the role of bride, chosen by the artist's will. Further, embodying awe, circumference becomes the sculptor's success, finite but original. Emily transforms Emerson's soul from the exclusive possessor of the universe, a superior generator, to the mind infused with wonder. That awe – first felt by the artist – is transferable to all sensitive observers, "every hallowed knight." For both creator and observer, circumference in its contrasting dimensions and complex associations becomes expansion, enclosure, and ecstasy in one.

This invitation to the sensitive public to share in the artist's imaginative effort was a specific concern of Emily's. It expressed a hope in the infinite growth of circumference. "When Cogs – stop – that's Circumference – / The Ultimate – of Wheels."[94] At the moment of "stop" (death), she will have expressed from her "Vital Axle" the fullest, "Ultimate" perception of which she is capable. Beyond life, she hopes that "Circumference be full," personally in immortality. But her poetry will remain, the vision of circumference then becoming the burden or pleasure of posterity. The gentle openness and expectancy toward future readers of "The Poets light but Lamps / Themselves – go out –" (883) contrasts sharply with Emerson's imperious soul.

Emily tested her place in the inherited categories of time and space. In discovering her own sense of them largely by disjunction (time could increase or diminish according to the experience of pain; limit was defined by one's own consciousness, now captivity, now liberty), she found a freedom within a dependency upon God's House of Time and Nature's House of Objects. She could then establish a self-defined status. Within consciousness and in the process of exploring circumference, she could literally and figuratively be at home. With a position and purpose located, she made explicit the task: "Nature is a Haunted House – but Art – a House that tries to be haunted."

The Emersonian basis of this statement is obvious from what has gone before, but the word "haunted" makes it peculiarly Dickinson. In her sense of the ghostly, she reached back to Hawthorne and forward to Eliot, but knew the haunted world with a singular intimacy. It was so much a part of her mind that she nearly touched it. The accustomed spectral company of her psyche's selves and of her friends enlarged here to encompass the spirit of the universe past and present. This world haunted her, inspiring wonder and fear, by both its majesty and its monstrosity. It was the Holy Ghost newly viewed.

Emily's purpose was to create a similar, but not identical house, enclosing the entire range of her experience, the radiant and the oppressive under one roof. Her open, sophisticated eye saw the ambiguous life force beyond her reach and attempted to create a comprehensible model of it. Circumference as vision (expansion) and circumference as creation (enclosure) merged in this House of Art. Its subject matter was beyond boundary but its design had specific, personal form. Emerson stated the structure simply, "The visible creation is the terminus or circumference of the invisible world."[95]

Emily's haunted house, her temple of poetry, was to be furnished with her form of the "felt" spirit of the unseen universe. She implied that only in a manageable replica of reality can consciousness know life, that, in fact, consciousness gives birth to the construction of Self, God, and Nature. The interdependency of the artist as creator and creation was quite clear to her, however, and her own attempt to be "true" was expressed in the remark, "Art's inner Summer, never Treason to Nature's."[96]

If circumference as enclosure was basic to Emily's aesthetic method, it was encouraged, if not directly shaped, by her increasing attachment to a life circumscribed by her father's hedge. In 1870, when Higginson visited her for the first time, he asked "if she never felt want of employment" and if she missed going out or receiving visitors. Emily replied, "I never thought of conceiving that I could ever have the slightest approach to such a want in all future time." To seal the force underlying this statement, and perhaps also belying it somewhat, she added, "I feel that I have not expressed myself strongly enough."[97] Her statement may have been so strident because old anxieties constantly threatened, which she had force to meet only in seclusion or which she sometimes could not surmount, needing then a shield to mask her failure: "In all circumference of Expression, those guileless words of Adam and Eve never were surpassed, 'I was afraid and hid Myself.'"[98]

Emily's arduously won royalty placed her in a kingdom at home, "My Blue Peninsula," access to which was possible only on her allowance. Blossoms and poetry were her communications, fragile but tangible substitutes for self, reminders first to society and then to eternity of her existence:

> Between My Country – and the Others –
> There is a Sea –
> But Flowers – negotiate between us –
> As Ministry.   (905)

This brief quatrain summarizes the emphases of this chapter, if "Others" may be read not only as other people but as God or Nature. Such economy we have learned to expect from a poet for whom limitation was a surpassing virtue. "My Country" may be read figuratively for the moment as the conservatory which defined

Emily's shore of the "Sea," keeping her apart from anyone or any spirit. Deity and universe signified their separation by insincerity, and people who followed suit were no part of the poet's "Estate." Thus Emily here stood alone. But she found assuagement in a "Ministry," as she says in the last line, which allowed her to serve others by creating in imitation of the cosmic life spirit. This service defined her position as poet, unlike Emerson, quite distinct in herself but finally at one with her view of the universe. Now set, her course developed in successive stages, a progress traced in the next chapter once again through the prism of home.

Chapter 6
Changing views of the Mansion and the image of home

Vesuvius at Home

Emily's verse has a quality of suspended time about it, if Thomas Johnson's dating can be taken as largely accurate.[1] It relates to her habitual pose as a child as well as to the surface sameness of her schedule. Not that life was placid. Once she described herself in a familiar image as "Vesuvius at Home," capturing in the epithet the pressures she felt within her father's house and the additional weight of her own anxieties. The volcanic cycle of submerged anguish, abrupt eruption, and return to relative peace was a constant pattern.

But even if poems of quite similar theme and tone appear at any time in her writing, definite changes of emphasis occur. The seismographic record varied measurably in response to shifting forces within and without. Approximately five overlapping periods are registered in her poetry and prose, each illustrated by selections which use the house-home figure: her return to the Mansion, 1855–60; the crisis, 1861–63, which calls for exploration focusing upon her use of the cup image, a corollary to the house figure; an unsettled resignation, 1864–70; a poised remorse, 1870–74; and an expectation of eternity, 1874–86.

I.

In chapter 3, I noted Emily's reaction to the family's return to the Mansion. Three years later, in the summer of 1858, Emily described the circumstances of life at the homestead which help explain the depth of her rebellion. She wrote to decline a neighbor's invitation to visit:

> I do not go out at all, lest father will come and miss me, or miss some little act, which I might forget, should I run away

> – Mother is much as usual. I know not what to hope of her.
> Please remember Vinnie and I, for we are perplexed often –[2]

Not only were her father's needs overshadowing her social life, at
least as she saw it, but her mother's recurring illness caused her
alternating alarm and depression. This pattern had prevailed since
1850, when Emily was nineteen,[3] and despite the surface tone of
calm and acceptance in this passage, the deep-rooted confusion
Mrs. Dickinson's invalidism wrought in her daughter is obvious.

Several poems written in the late 1850s explicitly etch Emily's
agitation. One written about 1859 shows how expertly she could
contrast a playful tone with a hauntingly serious theme. With
deceptive flippancy she appeals to God:

> Papa above!
> Regard a Mouse
> O'erpowered by the Cat!
> Reserve within thy kindom
> A "Mansion" for the Rat!
>
> Snug in seraphic Cupboards
> To nibble all the day,
> While unsuspecting Cycles
> Wheel solemnly away!   (61)

The request may be a description of the situation in her present
Mansion at the same time it asks for refuge in another. Yet the
only difference between them is that presumably the "unsuspecting
Cycles" can wheel away there eternally. She considers escape from
the Cat, quite possibly her father, whom she once called an excellent "Mouser,"[4] impossible for the rat, here or "above". Fatalism,
dependency, and sense of capture seem subtly skewered by Emily's
defiant tone and ironic prose as one of the meanest of God's creatures, hinting, especially at this date, of a probable revolt against
a required role.

In the same year, she wrote at greater length and with more
direct defiance:

> Bring me the sunset in a cup,
> Reckon the morning's flagon's up
> And say how many Dew,
> Tell me how far the morning leaps –

Tell me what time the weaver sleeps
Who spun the breadths of blue!

Write me how many notes there be
In the new Robin's extasy
Among astonished boughs –
How many trips the Tortoise makes –
How many cups the Bee partakes,
The Debauchee of Dews!

Also, who laid the Rainbow's piers,
Also, who leads the docile spheres
By withes of supple blue?
Whose fingers string the stalactite –
Who counts the wampum of the night
To see that none is due?

Who built this little Alban House
And shut the windows down so close
My spirit cannot see?
Who'll let me out some gala day
With implements to fly away,
Passing Pomposity?   (128)

If one reads only the first line, imagining that fury motivated it, the letters almost jump with the force of Emily's anger. She defies anyone to measure nature's work from its largest to its smallest phenomenon, sunset or dew, robin's note to bee's drink. By implication she protests – probably to the author of this infinite creation – why should she, a child of nature, be caught as in a cup, confined? Her list is endless and dimensionless as she moves beyond the visible world to probe its origins. Who made the rainbow's "piers," its scientific, even microscopic, supports? Who directs the movements of the spheres? Who gives form to the precise and delicate in nature like the stalactite? And above all, who is the accountant to implement justice in this wide-ranging panoply of objects?

In the final stanza, Emily abruptly moves from cosmic spatial extremes to herself at home, but this does not surprise us. Her assumption of being one with itemized nature in the preceding three stanzas has built toward this narrowing focus. Whether she means her body or her father's Mansion when she asks who built "this little Alban House" is unclear,[5] but within that house, she is as stifled as nature is free in all the examples she has just given. Who may rescue her? Perhaps she unconsciously knew that it would have to be herself, if her question is not already rhetorical. In any case, "Passing Pomposity" may suggest Emily's evaluation of the Mansion's grandeur and what its impressive dignity meant to her father.

II.

In September 1861, Emily experienced a "terror . . . I could tell to none."[6] Unspecified by her, this trauma remains untold, though there is increasing reason to think it may be related to the health of Samuel Bowles, a matter to be discussed in the next section. Nonetheless, during the following year, she produced fair copies of approximately 366 poems, some of which may have been composed a few years earlier.[7] Her tremendous productivity measures the full flowering of a creative drive which had been mounting since 1858.[8] All this is well known. A point not previously made, however, is that in the period from 1861 to 1863, allowing for errors in dating, she put into final form about 35 percent of her total poems which use the house-home metaphor.[9] This evidence may suggest her awareness of a new role within the family. Did she then, because of the crucial experience in September 1861, anticipate that she would never have another life outside "this little Alban house"?

The poems which date from this period show a shift from the protest of the late fifties to a victorious lament. The former were defiant possibly because of some hope that her circumstance might be changed. She wrote her cousin in December 1860, ". . . I feel rather confused to-day, and the future looks 'higglety-pigglety.' "[10] At least the situation was open.

In contrast, the tone of the poems of the 1861–63 period is often heightened with tragic anguish which may turn to apparent triumph. Interestingly, the word "Calvary" appears nine times in the poems of about 1862, which are of the most intensely emotional sort.[11] She now becomes the Empress or Queen of Calvary, the former, adolescent image of royalty, self-elected and self-denying, raised to its highest point of identification with the suffering rather than the divinity of Christ. She does not become his bride, she becomes her own. Implied in this singular wifehood is a certain sexual duality, perhaps because she takes on Jesus' role both as solitary sufferer and as bridegroom. Simultaneously, she is "Wife" and "Czar" by finishing the "other state" of simple girl-hood, even though she cannot fully leave it behind in actuality. "It's safer so," she concludes, because she is beyond being hurt. Yet the autonomy gained and stridently affirmed sometimes com-pensates, sometimes just disguises the pain of her anguish.

The masculine element, an imperious aloofness not unlike her father's, in Emily's essentially feminine coronation and marriage reappears in the meaning of the white dress which she chose to wear exclusively about this time. It symbolized at once her unpub-licized, secret trial, her betrothal (self to self, the second self assuming Christ's roles), her virginity, her royalty, and, possibly, her immortality. In a poem of about 1861, she affirms a "size," status, that she alone knows now because she anticipates its con-firmation in eternity:

> A solemn thing – it was – I said –
> A Woman – white – to be –
> And wear – if God should count me fit –
> Her blameless mystery –
>
> .   .   .   .
>
> I pondered how the bliss [Eternity] would look –
> And would it feel as big –
> When I could take it in my hand –
> As hovering – seen – through fog –
>
> And then – the size of this "small" life –
> The Sages – call it small –
> Swelled – like Horizons – in my breast –
> And I sneered – softly – "small"!   (271)

From a perspective of timelessness, Emily's small life, clothed in white by her own choice, not God's, enlarges to the dignity and significance she so keenly felt at times was already hers, mocking the "Sages'" estimate of a human lifetime.

This idea continues in a second poem of about 1862 in which she asks, "Dare you see a Soul *at the White Heat?*"[12] At this in-

FIGURE 15. *White cotton dress of Emily Dickinson's, probably dating from the last decade of her life. Photograph by James Gerhard. Courtesy of the Amherst Historical Society.*

FIGURE 16. *Back view of the same dress.*

candescent moment, Emily's inner, invisible forge produces such a light. And she dresses to witness to this luminous height, its urgency purified in time by patience, in an essentially androgynous costume suggested by its probable symbolism (in part, self-marriage) and by its material. Her only known remaining white dress is made of men's formal shirting fabric of embossed cotton, fashioned in a severe but womanly tailored style. Above earthly reward, she set herself apart in a "Scarlet prison,"[13] signifying suffering perhaps, to become the Amherst nun, a self-defined sisterhood of one, as impregnable to others as the world was to her.

The nature of Emily's crisis, at least in part, can be guessed, knowing her exposed sensitivity, her inconsistent views about home, the information of her family, and the work of recent scholars. All such sources point to a romantic crisis. Certain poems are more explicit than others about a possible love affair. One written about 1862, mentioned in this study at least twice before, beautifully evokes such an encounter, more than appropriately with the vision of a house and with the fervor of actuality:

> To my small Hearth His fire came –
> And all my House aglow
> Did fan and rock, with sudden light –
> 'Twas Sunrise – 'twas the Sky –
>
> Impanelled from no Summer brief –
> With limit of Decay –
> 'Twas Noon – without the News of Night –
> Nay, Nature, it was Day –   (638)

Emily's house feels the sure progress of the lover's fire. It begins properly enough in her heart but then leaves this safe, accustomed place to enlarge, illuminate, and engulf the whole structure. The experience is the beginning, "Sunrise," of a sense of great expansiveness, "Sky." Then past any panel of time, the summer it has begun, untouched by decay or darkness, the fire, burning on the entire building, becomes total light. It is more than Noon, elsewhere Emily's moment of ecstasy. It is Day, capitalized to signify timeless, perpetual sun. Not only is the consummation complete, however chaste, but what it has wrought is immutable and permanent.

In a poem apparently written the same year, she soberly forswears the ecstasy of the fire. In its focus on the image of a cup, it

recalls the Twenty-third Psalm, "My cup runneth over. . . ."
Emily's theme is just the opposite. Her cup is cracked. Significantly, this is the longest poem she ever wrote:

I cannot live with You –
It would be Life –
And Life is over there –
Behind the Shelf

The Sexton keeps the Key to –
Putting up
Our Life – His Porcelain –
Like a Cup –

Discarded of the Housewife –
Quaint – or Broke –
A newer Sevres pleases –
Old Ones crack –

I could not die – with You –
For One must wait
To shut the Other's Gaze down –
You – could not –

And I – Could I stand by
And see You – freeze –
Without my Right of Frost –
Death's privilege?

Nor could I rise – with You –
Because Your Face
Would put out Jesus' –
That New Grace

Glow plain – and foreign
On my homesick Eye –
Except that You than He
Shone closer by –

They'd judge Us – How –
For You – served Heaven – You know,
Or sought to –
I could not –

Because You saturated Sight –
And I had no more Eyes
For sordid excellence
As Paradise

And were You lost, I would be –
Though My Name
Rang loudest
On the Heavenly fame –

And were You – saved –
And I – condemned to be
Where You were not –
That self – were Hell to Me –

So We must meet apart –
You there – I – here –
With just the Door ajar
That Oceans are – and Prayer –
And that White Sustenance –
Despair –   (640)

As a broken cup, discarded, lifeless, shelved, Emily's possible
conjugal life is set aside. And she views her beloved from a distance, still athirst for the contents of that cup, but forced to feed
on the very tangible, yet intangible and mysterious, white sustenance, despair. Such tragedy is double, for the cup is not only
empty but unusable. She, as woman, will never know it to be
used, and the psychic sense of void and unfulfillment makes that
fact even more tragic. The "Door," which she sometimes uses to
symbolize freedom, here pictures a fragmented communication,
and a vast, probably permanent separation.[14] Finally, all that is
left is prayer and despair, which vie for comfort, the former
assuaging the cupboarded cup with the suggestion that it was
quaint.[15]

In a digression from the chronological movement of the chapter,
can we identify beyond question the figure to whom these poems
are addressed? Should we for any other reason than to discover the
personality who consumed her house and left her marriageable self
a useless cup? "No" answers both questions. And that is because
the search penetrates the biographic fact to reach a poetic truth,
her synthesis of imagery and theme. Once again, one sees Emily's

essential dependency upon a specific object as the precise medium for expressing the spirit of her intent. The vibrancies of actual encounter breathe through the images of home and house, or in this case, their surrogate, broken chinaware, to specify the intensity generated by the subject of her love poems.

One cannot safely read these expressions as one-to-one accounts of an affair, although they appear accurately to report Emily's reactions to the swell and ebb of it. But conversely, one cannot dismiss them, as critics have done, as emerging solely from fantasy, however richly imaginative and wishful Emily uncontestably was. Also – almost as an aside – the issue is not whether her love was unilateral or not; her sorrow testifies to that sad fact. The point is that she did not spin yearning into poetic form without a real, and as it turned out "Near, but remote" man in mind.[16] Exposing him then does not serve to satisfy simple curiosity. It shows the poet's characteristic use of an actual object, real person, or fictional but "extant" character or situation as highly selected emblems of her sensitivity. The metaphors of the two poems just considered recur in others and also, most importantly, in Emily's letters, which provide a resounding board of clues confirming the verse.

Samuel Bowles, editor of the *Springfield Republican* and close family friend, has been persuasively documented by David Higgins and Ruth Miller as the person who inspired Emily's lyrics.[17] He now replaces Charles Wadsworth, the prominent Philadelphia minister and longtime leading candidate, as the unknown man whom she supposedly obliquely and distantly adored, though Bowles was directly and closely cherished. It is sufficient for present purposes to accept Bowles as the unnamed man on the basis of accumulated evidence; interested readers will find the detailed case for Bowles in the Higgins and Miller books.[18]

What concerns us now are figures which seem especially appropriate to Bowles as Emily's beloved, those relating to house and home and to the humble but holy cup. In late summer, perhaps August 1858, Emily wrote a letter to Bowles, the second one she had ever sent and the first written to him only, excluding Mrs. Bowles this time. She knew him so briefly that she was unsure if a pamphlet she had just received came from him, so unfamiliar was his handwriting. At their first meeting she had made both Bowleses immediate intimates definitively and possessively.

In this letter, she now includes Bowles in her "estate," which is solely composed of friends, her single cherished possessions. And she extravagantly admits that "Summer stopped since you were here."[19] More, she alludes to her theological doubts and asks questions about them in a whimsical tone. Her references to gold, morning, and daybreak are all a mixture of her religious concerns as well as her growing desire to establish continuing ties with this man. But even more interesting, she makes two references to cups, one in the second paragraph and another toward the end of the letter. The first expresses a wish, almost as a benediction:

> I hope your cups are full. I hope your vintage is untouched. In such a porcelain life, one likes to be *sure* that all is well, lest one stumble upon one's hopes in a pile of broken crockery.[20]

The use of this imagery parallels as it foreshadows the poem, "I cannot live with You," dated about four years later. But obviously the cautious optimism and exuberance of these sentences contrasts with the jarring pain of the poetry. There the cup has become not Bowles's life but the one they might have shared, her fulfillment. In the letter, she has precisely, though unknowingly, predicted her own "stumbling."

The second mention of the cup states a grand purpose in a prose poem:

> I would distill a cup, and bear to all my friends, drinking to her [Summer?] no more astir, by beck, or burn, or moor![21]

Summer's warmth, flavor, and blossoms are to be captured and condensed into Emily's own "wine," her supreme gift for her friends. She now makes the cup image carry at least two major meanings. It is her creative center. It also determines the form of that creation, the poetry. The elixir, a blend of summer's fruit, offered in her cup, a composite of "inner space" and poetic structure, symbolizes the potency of her first June meeting with Bowles. Metaphor and message have become almost one, and Bowles received oblique warning that he might be among those to whom Emily would frequently "bring an unaccustomed wine" and to whom she would "always bear the cup" as she, dreaming, imagined in a poem of about 1859.[22]

Between this letter of late summer 1858, and another of about February 1861, in which the cup figure reappears, only four letters to Bowles are now extant. But Emily testifies that there were many more, "I write you frequently, and am much ashamed."[23] More important, these four show an increasing intimacy, at least on Emily's part, and the beginning of a sense of inadequacy and apology toward "Mr. Bowles" (she never addressed him by his first name, at most, simply, "Dear friend") which suggest a mounting of emotion toward a climatic encounter and her continuing adoration of him in the wake of it.[24]

In the letter of February 1861, this event is marked when Emily recalls a "little 'Meeting' " of the previous spring which apparently concluded with a deathless promise of friendship, reaffirmed the Saturday before. "We voted to remember you – so long as both should live – including Immortality." Thus, she says, "I bring the Bond – we sign so many times – for you to read, when Chaos comes – or Treason – or Decay – still witnessing for Morning." The "we" may be both sides of her psyche, united now in this love, or it could refer to Sue and Lavinia. A second "we," however, is clearly editorial, when Emily submits another tonic, especially warranted since Bowles is ill, saying, "We offer you our cups – stintless – as to the Bee – the Lily, her new Liquors." Then follows her distilled spirits in the poem, "Would you like Summer? Taste of our's." It is a "Fairy Medicine" even in the face of death, and Emily hopes it will work its magic if Bowles will only drink.[25]

A final reference to cup occurs in a letter dated January 11, 1862. She begins it, "Are you willing? I am so far from Land – To offer *you* the cup – it might some Sabbath come *my* turn – Of wine how solemn – full!"[26] Emily's own habit of providing a revivifying liquor, now by letter, now by poem, now by actual bottle of home-made sherry, is here transfigured to the sense of holy communion. She is unsure ("I am so far from Land," true faith), but she hopes that her offering, so alive and forceful is it within her, can effect a grace similar to what the believer would find in drinking the "solemn" (consecrating) communion wine. Sabbath as holy day represents either an impossibly hoped-for second "Meeting," or their encounter in eternity.[27]

Like the cup image, the house figure carries a wealth of allusion to the nature of the Emily-Bowles relationship. And "house" or "home" are intimately linked to the words "heart" and "room." In her first letter to the Bowleses in 1858, Emily had asked, "How are your Hearts today?"[28] And in another to Bowles alone in late April 1859, she wrote, "I hope the hearts in Springfield are not so heavy as they were – God bless the hearts in Springfield!"[29] Three years later, in early April 1862, though there may have been many other similar references, Emily clarifies the state of her own heart, "The Hearts in Amherst – ache – tonight – You could not know how hard – They thought they could not wait – last night – until the Engine – sang – a pleasant tune – that time – because that you were coming."[30]

Then about August, the same year, she wrote to Bowles on the eve of his return from Europe, "How sweet it must be to one to come Home – whose Home is in so many Houses – and every Heart a "Best Room." I mean you, Mr. Bowles.[31] "Heart," "Home," and "Room" all come together in a single sentence. And in the same way that "cup" images Emily's distilled elixir of poetry and her own morphology so aptly, so these words perfectly combine metaphor and theme, as in the poem "To my small Hearth His fire came," also written about 1862. The reference to "Best Room" recalls the argument of chapter 3, by which "room" denotes Emily's vital center. Obviously, Emily's heart is one of the "Best Room[s]." And fifteen years later, in 1877, just a year before Bowles's death, Emily again refers to a room, meaning it literally this time, but following the mention of it with one of her most explicit poems:

I went to the Room as soon as you left, to confirm your presence – recalling the Psalmist's sonnet to God, beginning

> I have no Life but this –
> To lead it here –
> Nor any Death – but lest
> Dispelled from there –
> Nor tie to Earths to come –
> Nor Action new
> Except through this extent
> The love of you.   (1398)[32]

The linking of heart, home, and house allows us to look at other poems, not known to have been written for Bowles, which use these images, assuming now that she probably wrote for him. One in particular, dated 1863, tolerates extreme differences in the definition of home only if that place also includes the beloved. With all the hyperbole of the ravished heart, she records the heights and depths of her reactions, against which Bowles fits as an authentic foil:

Where Thou art – that – is Home –
Cashmere – or Calvary – the same –
Degree – or Shame –
I scarce esteem Location's Name –
So I may Come –

What Thou dost – is Delight –
Bondage as Play – be sweet –
Imprisonment – Content –
And Sentence – Sacrament –
Just We two – meet –

Where Thou art not – is Wo –
Tho' Bands of Spices – row –
What Thou dost not – Despair –
Tho' Gabriel – praise me – Sir –   (725)

The first line seems to condense Emily's already succinct statement, "How sweet it must be to one to come Home – whose Home is in so many Houses – and every Heart a 'Best Room.'" Conventional considerations about that home are discarded. Emily doesn't care if pain or shame accompany the place, because they will be ignored. Or, difficulties will dissolve in their opposites. And if the beloved is not there, despite any exotic alternative (her "Bands of Spices") or heavenly blessing for her discipline, that place is, simply, "Wo."

Other poems of this period using the same images show clues which may be linked to Bowles: "Her breast is fit for pearls" (84); "The Malay – took the Pearl –" (452); "He found my Being –" (603); "Again – His voice is at the door –" (663); "If Blame be my side – forfeit Me –" (775). But the point has been made. First, the cup, home, and house metaphors supplement the more explicit evidence of the letters to corroborate other evidence that Bowles was the subject of the love poetry. Second, the use of these figures is freighted with the exuberance and anguish of the whole relationship in such a way that they become fully meaningful only if Bowles were the person whom Emily had in mind. She had been looking for home ever since she left the house on Pleasant Street, that haven of childhood she sought to extend at the Mansion. Now this man alone could have evoked a true home and house, a new place, obviously not the present one, as appropriate figures. Only he could have made her cups of poetry and of yearning crack, since he was the single person who rejected both her writings and her adoration. With the specific subject identified, the imagery can all the more fully feed the poet's overflowing intent to the reader's perception. The marriage of poetic form and content is small but brilliant compensation for the failure of actual marriage, which Emily may ultimately have avoided, but which she surely contemplated as a cherished though hopeless possibility with Bowles. That was her apparent dedication, or "business," after the storm of this affair began to subside in the mid-1860s.[33]

III.

I now move to a third traceable period in Emily's reaction to the Mansion, one of restless acceptance, datable roughly from 1864 to 1870, and partially revealed earlier. By choice and necessity, especially because of her mother's chronic ill health,[34] Emily had remained at home. Now in the early 1860s, she was painfully pressed into the first stages of her self-isolation within the house and grounds. Was this "an extension of a particularized exile," as one critic has called it?[35] Did she turn her refusal to see Bowles, based on a fear of exposing her sensitivity toward him, into a life strategy, easily accomplished because of her earlier pattern of semi-seclusion? She seems to say so retrospectively in a prose fragment written in the last decade of her life, ". . . a climate of Escape is natural to Fondness. . . ."[36] The preference or need to be at home appears to have become a defense against further abrasion. Also, by 1862, her vocation as poet was set, and she needed time to work. For these reasons, her earlier revolt and renunciation led to a period of fitful acceptance of, if not ever profound affection for, the Mansion.

The first line of a poem of about 1864 clearly states the wistful theme of these years, again probably inspired by Bowles: "I learned – at least – what Home could be"; however, as she concluded, ". . . Home is not – / But what that Place could be – / Afflicts me . . ." (944). The resignation was possible because by then, redirected from romance, imaginative expansiveness pushed her past the homestead or any home with Bowles to build her own temple, poetry: "Myself was formed – a Carpenter," an image, which, as we have seen, reflects her major imitation of Christ. She began to define her own circumference and encompass the cosmos and time from her poetic center. An excellent picture of this diastole-systole beat, projecting and gathering, injecting lifeblood with its workings, is apparent in a poem written two years earlier:

> I dwell in Possibility –
> A fairer House than Prose –
> More numerous of Windows –
> Superior – for Doors –
>
> Of Chambers as the Cedars –
> Impregnable of Eye –
> And for an Everlasting Roof
> The Gambrels of the Sky –
>
> Of Visiters – the fairest –
> For Occupation – This –
> The spreading wide my narrow Hands
> To gather Paradise –   (657)

The theme of limitlessness is ironically built on the details of the house which held her. All the rooms are as "impregnable" to any sight as those of the cedar, and the roof is as high and as permanent as the sky. More, all the visitors are fair because, she concludes, in contrast to the broad emphasis which began the poem, her outstretched hands are all that is needed to make a passageway for paradise.

The day-to-day static aspect of Emily's life meant that living within the Mansion was more than an environment; it was a continuation of time past. The seasons changed but the years did not. For, at moments, she remained a little girl with all the preferences and problems of her younger self. In 1859, she acknowledged that, ". . . we're children still, and children fear the dark."[37] This dark was filled with the threatening unknowns discussed previously in chapter 3. It was much more than the hopelessly invalided mother, her own problems with her eyes, her father's need to have her near, and her continuing disdain for housekeeping.[38] It was the mountain of fear challenges to which were her final guards for sanity and for security.

She maintained the pose of a child through the late 1860s, clearly stating in 1869 to Higginson that her withdrawal was nearly complete: "You noticed my dwelling alone – To an Emigrant, Country is idle except it be his own. . . . I do not cross my Father's ground to any House or town."[39] In a sense she was paralyzed where she was. Remaining a little girl was both a defense against and a result of the anxieties which kept her restless. On the one hand, it allowed her the measure of liberty and simple joy she could have in watching a circus caravan pass by the house or, similarly, in walking through the grove of oaks to the north of the house where, she said, ". . . I play every day." On the other hand, as she frankly admitted, ". . . I am so hurried with Parents that I run all Day with my tongue abroad, like a Summer Dog."[40] Probably it was only with the deaths of Edward and Emily Norcross Dickinson that Emily awakened more fully to the adult world. Her clinging to girlhood partially explains her utter sense of loss when those deaths eventually took place.

Paradoxically, while Emily was still protected in the family, her more independent life was maturing. The following poem, first written about 1863, was revised to the following form about six years later. One pictures Emily, in much the same way that she may have toiled over the lines, working beyond the poem's creation to its goal, a self standing as invulnerable and straight as the Mansion itself.

> The Props assist the House
> Until the House is built
> And then the Props withdraw
> And adequate, erect,
> The House support itself
> And cease to recollect
> The Augur and the Carpenter –
> Just such a retrospect
> Hath the perfected Life –
> A path of Plank and Nail
> And slowness – then the Scaffolds drop
> Affirming it a Soul.   (1142)

Emily's sense of being "adequate, erect" (like her father) was a long-sought wish. Were the "Props" traditional faith or her parents? In "I'm ceded – I've stopped being Their's –" (508) she uses the same words to describe herself as the fully conscious, crowned queen, even though the crown may be of thorns. Self-elected to sovereignty, however tragic, she is beyond "Them," her parents. Further, the rich, root meaning of "adequate," "in exact proportion," is especially appropriate to her identification with the house,[41] expressing wholeness and status simultaneously.

IV.

The completed house represents Emily well at this age because, after forty, she used the house-home image to express not so much an acceptance of life in the Mansion as a churning born by resuscitating old hurts. In this period, from about 1870 to 1874, she was composed but remorseful. She was built as a personality, but still felt the augur and the nail of remembered agonies. And she did so with a strong sense of martyrdom, perhaps masochism, just missing sentimentality and self-pity. In lines written about 1871, noted in chapter 1, she describes her mind in familiar architectural terms:

> Remembrance has a Rear and Front –
> 'Tis something like a House –
> It has a Garret also
> For Refuse and the Mouse.
>
> Besides the deepest Cellar
> That ever Mason laid –
> Look to it by it's Fathoms
> Ourselves be not pursued –   (1182)

In the same way that such poems as "I dwell in Possibility" foreshadow a later period, so "Remorse – is Memory – awake," written about 1863, seems to adumbrate this one:

> Remorse – is Memory – awake –
> Her Parties all astir –
> A Presence of Departed Acts –
> At window – and at Door –
>
> It's Past – set down before the Soul
> And lighted with a Match –
> Perusal – to facilitate –
> And help Belief to stretch –

Remorse is cureless – the Disease
Not even God – can heal –
For 'tis His institution – and
The Adequate of Hell –   (744)

In the last line, the experience of pain still seems very much
alive, as if memory at this moment did not need to return far into
its past. The beginning lines second this sense of recent sorrow
with the parties of remorse everywhere, all the "Departed Acts"
perhaps recalled in some detail since they are present at each window and door. The poet seems feverish, hot with the discomfort of
her disease as she writes.

In contrast, "Remembrance has a Rear and Front," written
about eight years later, is a statement about memory with a greater
distance, a larger perspective on the subject with the poet's tem-
perature returned to "normal." The whole house, Remembrance,
is now the subject, not simply Remorse, the darker side of memory. Further, memory's parts are assigned appropriate areas in the
house. Earlier ones presumably are at the rear, later ones toward
the front, and while cherished thoughts are preserved upstairs in
the garret, others which trouble but cannot be dismissed are in the
cellar. That these last are perhaps unsurpassed by any others in
quantity or effect is suggested by the fact that they are kept in "the
deepest Cellar / That ever Mason laid." But they are separate and
controlled. They do not dominate the poet here as the pervasive
presence of remorse did in the earlier poem. The ending of the
1871 poem could also be read not only as an admission of the cellar's ominous potentiality but as a firm resolve, "Ourselves be not
pursued."

Another poem of about 1873, beginning "That sacred Closet
when you sweep – / Entitled 'Memory' –" (1273), asks that the job
of cleaning memory's closet be done reverentially, because disturbing the dust of the past does no good. Besides, there is a certain
sanctity about that past. Old patterns cannot be readjusted like a
kaleidescope, rather, scrutinizing them again can silence one. The
implication is that the silencer is either fear or the utter futility of
change.

In this period of controlled but vivid recall, Emily's pattern of
semiestrangement in the Mansion was still clear, but reliance on a

country of truth, beyond the house, was not always sufficient substitute. When Higginson first met Emily in August 1870, he reported this startling question from her: "Could you tell me what home is?"[42] For the fifteen years she had been back at the homestead, apparently no people or events had answered that question for her.[43] Bowles certainly had not. She now confessed to Higginson, at least to reveal her own feelings, if not reality, "I never had a mother. I suppose a mother is one to whom you hurry when you are troubled."[44] And whatever Edward Dickinson was to Emily privately or even publicly in the past, Higginson's impression was clear on this visit: "I saw Mr. Dickinson this morning a little – thin dry & speechless – I saw what her life has been. Dr. S [Stearns] says her sister is proud of her."[45]

After Higginson's second and final visit in January 1874, Emily wrote him: "I always ran Home to Awe when a child, if anything befell me. He was an awful Mother, but I liked him better than none. There remained this shelter after you left me the other Day."[46] In statements such as these, one has the feeling that Emily's search for a "Preceptor" in Higginson, which began ten days after Bowles left for Europe,[47] was as much for personal warmth and compensation for renouncing Bowles, perhaps even for affection from the senior generation which *she* felt inadequate at home, as it was, initially, at least, for literary recognition and criticism.

V.

One of the few aspects of Emily's mind which dates her for most modern readers is her constant curiosity and apprehension about the end of life. Often death is as attractive as an imperious lover, now gentlemanly, now ruthless, magnetizing her response. Nineteenth-century New England was still plagued with the empirical reasons which had caused the Puritans two centuries before to be perpetually contemplating life under the omnipresence of death. Arduous winters and uncontrollable epidemics, no matter the season, might carry off many of Emily's closest friends and relatives in a single year.[48] The imminent possibility of her own dying understandably arose as a vivid and, at times, pleasurable preoccupation, particularly when linked with the hope of joining her beloved or when self-pity overwhelmed her.

From her earliest years, both parents, especially her father, had been unremittingly solicitous whenever Emily was ill. Poor health had been reason in part for her return home from Mount Holyoke. Mrs. Dickinson's neuralgia and successive complaints were daily reminders of the weakness of the flesh. Whether or not Emily worried much about her father's physical state can only be surmised, but she probably was both concerned as a devoted daughter and yet freed by her role as child, taking as almost permanent his paternal strength and sheltering.

Assuming this to be her attitude, one can understand why Edward Dickinson's death in June 1874 was a shock from which Emily may never have really recovered. In the twelve remaining years of her own life, its impact forced her to consider eternity with a new urgency. The Biblical definition of home as the place beyond, the "long home" of Ecclesiastes, entered her life at the most sensitive points, touching her dependency as a perpetual little girl and her role as housekeeper. For years afterward, she wondered where her father was. In a letter to her cousins, Louise and Fanny Norcross, in the summer of 1874, she wrote that her father was "in a new house." In her comment that, even though it took just an hour to build, "it is better than this,"[49] she implied a Christian one.

A few months later, however, she was less certain. The first stanza of the following poem she enclosed in a letter written in late January 1875 to her close friend, Mrs. Josiah Holland; perhaps the second verse, even more revealing, was composed shortly afterward. The letter introduces the first four lines, "Mother is asleep in the Library – Vinnie – in the Dining Room – Father – in the Masked Bed – in the Marl House."[50]

> How soft his Prison is –
> How sweet those sullen bars –
> No Despot but the King of Down
> Invented that Repose!

The second stanza reads:

> Of Fate if this is All
> Has he no added Realm
> A Dungeon but a Kinsman is
> Incarceration – Home.   (1334)

The contrast between the skepticism, even cynicism, of the poem and the veiled faith of the letter to the cousins is sharp. Here the King of Down is triumphant, assigning her father the circumscribed tomb. There is no hint of the spaciousness of a "new house" "better than this." Incarceration is his only home, not a millimeter extra for an ounce of paradise.

Emily apologized to Mrs. Holland for focusing on what she called the "first Mystery of the House," but Edward Dickinson was the first member of the immediate family to have had an experience "distinctly of the Spirit." Further, she thanked Mrs. Holland for affectionate support: "It helps me up the Stairs at Night, where as I passed my Father's Door – I used to think was safety.[51]

Afterward, Emily's seclusion became total. Her mother suffered a paralyzing stroke exactly a year after her husband's death, becoming a bed patient and requiring even more attention than before. Mrs. Dickinson died in November 1882. In a manner quite distinct from her reaction to her father's death, Emily now admitted, "We don't know where she is, though so many tell us."[52] Yet in a poem about her mother's death she assumes it is eternity and asks the "Brothers of Paradise" to "remit her home." She herself wanders here, "homeless at home."[53]

If the sense of being at home always eluded Emily, especially after her parents' deaths, then the continued correspondence with Higginson was partial assuagement. In July 1875, she wrote him, "Home is so far from Home, since my Father died."[54] Then in February, the following year, she implied that communicating with her preceptor was more than a literary lifeline of letters, but rather a real "place" of solace. She told him, "I often go Home in thought to you."[55]

Emily's attempt to find out from Higginson what home might mean seems slightly pathetic in view of his consistently patronizing attitude. But she searched elsewhere. Judge Otis Phillips Lord, a younger friend of her father's, knew her well before his wife's death in 1877. Sometime afterward, the two began exchanging what appear to have been weekly letters, and Lord called on Emily in Amherst. The delight and restraint of this one documented love affair in Emily's later life has been clearly described elsewhere.[56] It is hardly strange that in rejecting a possible marriage, but professing great devotion to this man, Emily questioned Lord about home. She wrote him in 1879, . . . You spoke of "Hope" surpassing

"Home" – I thought that Hope *was* Home – a misapprehension of Architecture – but then if I knew . . ."[57]

Obviously, she did not know, nor would she ever cease to ask. She leaned toward accepting an intangible definition, in the style of her earlier fantasizing. In 1878, she wrote Sue Dickinson, "In a Life that stopped guessing, you and I should not feel at home."[58] About the same time, she defined the central word, consciousness, as "the only home of which we *now* know."[59] Then in 1880, again to Lord, she was more specific about her intent: "I wonder we ever leave the Improbable – it is so fair a Home, and perhaps we don't."[60]

The fleeting, unsystematic, but recurring quest for a definition of home is typical, too, of Emily's use of the image during the last decade of her life. In the 1880s, she retained the measured optimism expressed ten years earlier when, in a letter to Higginson, she weighed the concept of immortality: "The larger Haunted House it seems, of maturer Childhood – distant, an alarm – entered intimate at last as a neighbor's Cottage."[61] Yet the stinger of uncertainty punctured the unqualified ideal for her. The new home is a "strange" one. Also, there was no guarantee of a life beyond: "Parting is all we know of heaven & all we need of hell."[62] Nonetheless, she spoke of Charles Wadsworth's death as "Going Home."[63] And although she became a "homeless bird" after Lord died, she hoped he had been taken home.[64] One of the last things she wrote, borrowing the title of a book she had recently read, were two words, the extent of a note to the Norcross cousins, "Called back."[65]

At this point, the difference between house and home – never made distinct by Emily herself – becomes clearer. As figures, they appear to represent certain polar temporal or eternal attitudes: the house – Emily's vision of the past or the historical known; home – her expectation of the future through the familiar present, the anticipated. But, at the same time, both terms encompass ambiguous assets. If the house of her fathers symbolized the protection she needed psychologically as an "old-fashioned" little girl, then it also could be her "Pearl Jail,"[66] separating her from "Nature's Inns," and "staunch Estate," where as a child of creation she might be free. If it was the sanctuary where she could be safely alone and have the time to write poetry, then it was also "that old castle" where "Paradise" was supposed to be, that is, traditional faith.[67]

Her free spirit and the appeal of Christianity met head-on in the image; compare "The Props assist the House" with " 'Houses' – so the Wise Men tell me."[68]

In the same way, although less sharply, home was a mixed gift. Early, as a concrete place, it combined the awe and the warmth of family affection. In 1850, referring to the house on Pleasant Street, she found it was her one sure object of worship: "Home is a holy thing. . . ."[69] But later, as an ideal, it teased not only by its ambiguity but by its elusiveness. In part, this was her preference, a corollary of her royal renunciation. She characteristically savored the freedom and the elixir of expectation that impalpability allowed, holding back from completion of her most profound wishes. "Of our deepest delights there is a solemn shyness."[70] Home not only became such a delight but, being beyond definition, was beyond possession. Actually, it best remained an image, because "Emblem is immeasurable – that is why it is better than Fulfillment, which can be drained."[71]

Chapter 7
Amherst and Emily Dickinson

The Amherst Heart is plain and whole
and permanent and warm.
  E M I L Y   D I C K I N S O N

Emily Dickinson, as person and as poet, has no close parallel among American writers of any generation in her intimate relation to a particular town or family homestead. Sex, situation, and period formed the portcullis of sociological factors keeping her in the "old castle." The moat was Emily's own preference to stay near the family circle deepened by the crisis of her early thirties. She was not a frustrated feminist.[1] But the constant, inelastic attitude about leaving home hardly hid the essential turmoil and rebellion in retreat which finally left her homeless. In some ways, Emily's predicament parallels Isabel's in James's *Portrait of a Lady,* where Isabel's house is the subtle, suffocating mind of her husband, in which she fatalistically, even pridefully, wills to remain imprisoned.

If Emily cherished security and liberty from convention inside her father's house, still she almost perpetually waged a personal battle for psychological freedom and religious affirmation. And if she chose to erect a private temple of poetry, still she obviously felt the force of her own potential and for a time smarted under her lack of a public literary status, assuaging her pride with such thrusts as:

> Fame is the tint that Scholars leave
> Upon their Setting Names –
> The Iris not of Occident
> That disappears as comes –   (866)

Building temples, she repeatedly relied on the imagery of houses or parts of them as self-revelations. Throughout her adult life, prose comments second the strength of her poetic leaning on this symbol. Together they emphasize Emily's concentration on the self in self-communion. With no public life, even marriage, she

found her limited setting forcing the psychic life into major focus
as if she had been a model for one of Hawthorne's heroines. In an
1860 letter to the Norcross cousins, she described her heart as the
"smallest parlor in the world," but always ready with a chair for
them, echoing similar comments to Samuel Bowles.[2] She wrote
Mary Bowles in 1878 after her husband's death, "I felt it sweet that
you needed me – though but a simple shelter I will always last,"
showing how her center could expand and encompass.[3] And again,
in 1881, she asked the Norcross girls to share their sorrows with
her, "for Emily's heart is the edifice where the 'wicked cease from
troubling.' "[4]

To interchange heart and house was a natural substitution for a
woman most of whose life, now nearly at an end, had been like the
evasive butterfly she often observed, first cocooned, then screened
inside the Mansion and its grounds. But any barrier was negligible
considering one was "Immured the whole of Life / Within a magic
Prison."[5] The prison was the inescapable disparity between human
knowledge and the omniscience of God, Nature, and Immortality.
The saving feature of this cage, whether world or self, was that it
was "magic," vibrant with possibilities. What personal qualities
made it so alive Emily described in a summary self-portrait written
just a few months before she died, "The Amherst Heart is plain and
whole and permanent and warm."[6] If the adjectives picture her,
they apply equally to her house and her poetry.

Emily occasionally dropped "heart" and simply denoted herself,
"Amherst."[7] The identification seems triply significant. In the first
place, she sometimes addressed intimates, such as the Bowleses, as
the "Springfield hearts" or just "Springfield." Charles Wadsworth
was Emily's "Philadelphia." And Judge Otis P. Lord became "My
lovely Salem."[8] They alone gave their cities final importance. Perhaps she adopted the compliment in assuming "Amherst" for herself. The sense of self-importance behind the wall of withdrawal
was early, almost apparently, inherent. If she felt that she and her
family were "different," that suggested specialness, even superiority. Yet secondly, she was intimately part of the community, loving
first her home, almost pathologically at times, and then the aca-
demic, social, and also religious (where they became personal) associations of the town.[9] In this way, she reached beyond Amherst
(beyond its antiintellectual evangelizing, its Main Street manners,
its plump politesse, and its sewing circle simpery[10]) yet remained a

FIGURE 17. *Detail of 1886 lithograph of Amherst. Courtesy of the Jones Library, Amherst.*

FIGURE 18. *Lithograph of Amherst, 1886. Photograph by Lewis Mudge. Courtesy of Amherst College.*

devoted daughter of it. In a word, she could criticize or surpass the citizenry and its conventions, using the speech and accents of the town. Thirdly, then, it is easy to see that the timeless quality of Emily's poetry emerges from the provincial moments of a separate but intrinsic life. The stamp of Amherst is always there; it shaped both the content and form of her work. The capital "A," like Hester Prynne's scarlet letter, universalizes as it particularizes the poet and her "Act," the poetry.

In what way do Emily's thought and style transcend the culture which made her "Amherst," yet remain distinctly dependent on their regional sources? Her own brand of Protestantism, carrying the Reformation principle past community to one aspect of the center of its logic, chilling self-reliance, excelled in quality and intensity what she found at the church across the street. But it had its history there. She recaptured an earlier Puritan individualism and practicality which temporarily had been expunged from the tradition by the enthusiastic absolutism of contemporary church-focused revivals. As artist, she was free from her father's faith. As woman, she was never wholly unburdened by the weight of the past. And the two perspectives were often one. Her persistent, probing note was a plaintive plea for belief. Early in the month she died, she asked Higginson, "Deity – does He live now? My friend – does he breathe?"[11]

Amherst also dictated Emily's technique, though again not without importations suggested by either her reading or her inventions. In the particulars of her prosody, Emily saw "New Englandly," that is, provincially, but her poetic method parallelled the thought in its combination of the original with the commonly known. Emily's "voice" has recently been extensively analyzed in absorbing detail by Brita Lindberg-Seyersted.[12] Here only the major distinguishing aspects of her verse illustrate Emily's steps, more often in time with tradition than one might think. In fact, her style deviated less from the orthodox than did her ideas. It is her use of convention which makes the poetry shimmeringly fresh. She stayed close to the hymn meters of Isaac Watts, even though she sometimes used them ironically to enclose impious themes.[13] And though she selected inexact rhymes for her private euphony, she was not unlike Watts, whose lyrics have an equal number of approximate and exact rhymes.[14]

Actually, her one real innovation was simply an unpredictable

FIGURE 19. *The original First Congregational Church (now College Hall) in Amherst, where Emily attended services with her family as a child and young adult. Photograph by Jean Mudge.*

line arrangement.[15] Line irregularities, however, are hardly the only feature which marks her work. She used other techniques, not unique to her, in a fashion which gave her total product a high intensity and most private effect. For instance, she broke up a basic meter by superimposing speech rhythms upon it, introducing a contrapuntal beat. What was new was her selection of the rhythms and their novel result. Or perhaps the most striking aspect of her style is the juxtaposition of everyday words with the abstract, literary, dignified, solemn, or foreign.[16] This habit, accentuated by her lexical economies, became Emily's own because of her special choice of words, as in "homely Anguish," "feeble Mountains," and the "Heft of Cathedral Tunes." The hybridization of terms is more typical than her coinages or regionalisms, both of which are few and do not often bear the weight of a poem.[17] (An exception may be a poem about herself as an "Angle worm," a regional synonym for the urban "earthworm."[18]) Emily's unique style, then, was rooted in familiar forms and devices. She merely manipulated the modes which, with her searching themes, finally made the poems like no one else's.

One is reminded of the untutored and rough secular folk roots of many of the hymn tunes on which Watts based his lyrics. Emily's work seems to return to the worldly folk song tradition before its borrowing by the church, while retaining the spiritual longing pervading the hymns.[19] The point is that Protestant Amherst was pulsing to the foursquare iambic tetrameters upon which Emily based her poetry. The difference was that while churchgoers metronomically sang about "our eternal home," Emily was observing that "Consciousness is the only home of which we *now* know."[20] And she was also matching her technique of poetic contrasts to her mode of thought and to the thought itself, as if to parallel her feeling that life was basically immeasurable, beyond a fixed focus, as she was, homeless at home.

Living beyond the Mansion, Emily's loyalty and measured devotion to it are nonetheless almost poignantly apparent in the plans she made for her funeral. Its focus was the house, the scene of her birth and death, and it ended within view of the Pleasant Street home. On this occasion, the worldly and otherworldly intersected in the house image with profound appropriateness to her life and expectations. As Higginson described it, May 19, 1886, was a matchless spring day with an atmosphere of its own, fine & strange about the whole house & grounds – a more saintly & elevated "House of Usher." The grass of the lawn full of buttercups violet & wild geranium; in [the] house a handful of pansies & another of lilies of the valley on [the] piano.[21]

The service was held in the Mansion. The Reverend Mr. George S. Dickerman, pastor of the First Congregational Church, read her favorite scriptural passage, identified by a friend, Mrs. John Jameson, "on putting off the earthly and putting on immortality."[22] Doubtless, it was the familiar verses of 1 Cor. 15, ending, "O death, where is thy sting? O grave, where is thy victory?" Higginson continued with Emily Brontë's poem "Immortality," passages of which Emily had often read to Vinnie, commenting that it was to honor one who had taken on immortality but never seemed to have been without it. The Reverend Mr. Jonathan L. Jenkins, former First Church pastor and old family friend, concluded, saying "a good [unrecorded] prayer."[23]

Emily, dressed in a new white gown, was fitted to her "dainty, white casket."[24] Violets were placed at her neck with one pink cypripedium, and Vinnie put two heliotropes by her hand " 'to take to Judge Lord,' " according to Higginson. The buttercups she had hoped would be a final corsage were inexplicably excluded, remaining unpicked in the grass. Robed like an angel, and with certain chosen emblems of eternity showering her, little wonder that Higginson thought she looked transformed from her actual years, fifty-five, to thirty. He noted that she had "not a gray hair or wrinkle, & perfect peace on the beautiful brow."[25] Mrs. Jameson also observed a special aura about her, "She looked more like her brother than her sister, with a wealth of auburn hair and a very spirituelle face."[26] The French adjective imparts Mrs. Jameson's impression of ethereality, though it may have been unconsciously, even ignorantly, used.

Following Emily's request, her casket, laden with ground pine and violets, was "lifted by the stout arms of six or eight Irish workmen"[27] out the rear door of the Mansion, through the garden, then into the opened barn from front to back, and finally through the fields via footpaths to the family plot, in sight of the house for most of the procession.[28] It was as if she were in final review of the whole property.

In visiting her grave in the town cemetery, one can envision Emily's life telescoped backward in time. The graveyard was adjacent to the grounds of her old home on Pleasant Street. She was returning there from the homestead of her birth, the scene of a brilliant conflict against a crippled life, to a formerly hallowed hearth. Buried, she was finally with her parents, who had preceded her to each house and to the "House not made with Hands."[29]

In one of her best poems, with Death as a lover-guide, she had paused to inspect, then to pass, "a House that seemed / A Swelling of the Ground – / The Roof was scarcely visible – / The Cornice in the Ground –" (712). No actual or metaphoric mausoleum would be a final dwelling place. But the elusive, timeless "location" gains some tangibility if one imagines transparent views of the house on Pleasant Street and the Mansion superimposed on her simple headstone. Such an image makes immediate and immutable the report of the Amherst town clerk in recording her death, "Occupation: At Home."[30]

Chapter 8
The image of home: a key to the poet's inscape of enclosure

I am alive — because
I do not own a House —
Entitled to myself — precise —
And fitting no one else —
EMILY DICKINSON

Emily's separation from a physical house, illustrated in the opening quatrain, suggests the way in which tangible scenes hardly delimited her musings about ideas, feelings, or beliefs. She escaped her house and its surroundings in her search for home in the same way she avoided the world, by dwelling in her highly imaginative, eclectically informed, cosmos-encompassing, quick, clever mind. Home was consciousness alone. She once noted, "As it takes but a moment of imagination to place us anywhere, it would not seem worth while to stay where it was stale."[1] But she made those journeys into new apartments of the mind with the help of familiar and palpable props, whether they were real or fictional persons, places, or objects. That sensitivity to the inner life in terms of determined outer space just at hand, including her own body, is a primary characteristic of her spatial inscape and provides the underlying theme throughout the chapters which have brought us to this point.

Now, a summary view of the poet's inscape attempts to bring together the several nuances of Emily's poetic sensitivity to enclosure: her views of physical self or actual buildings, of cherished persons, and of life's primary questions as they related to her situation: the scholar-poet at home. The poems selected here, some of which will be familiar, others new, may or may not be of the house-home category, but all describe "location" and reflect the pattern of mind which would say "Dickinson" even if we did not know the author. Just such a poem is the following:

> The Body grows without —
> The more convenient way —

FIGURE 20. *The manse of the second First Congregational Church with the church steeple visible behind. Residence of the Reverend and Mrs. Jonathan Jenkins. Photograph by Jean Mudge.*

FIGURE 21. *Edward Dickinson family plot, West Cemetery, Amherst.* Left to right: *the graves of Lavinia, Emily, Emily Norcross, and Edward. Photograph by James Gerhard. Courtesy of Amherst College.*

That if the Spirit – like to hide
It's Temple stands, alway,

Ajar – secure – inviting –
It never did betray
The Soul that asked it's shelter
In solemn honesty.   (578)²

   Though Emily wrote this poem about seven years after her return to the Mansion, the first line might hint of an earlier period
when she was still developing at the house on Pleasant Street.
Otherwise, she could simply have stated that "The Body *lives* without." But the primary interest here is the tremendous value given
the flesh as house, even a temple (like home, a holy thing), almost
above consciousness, that is, "Spirit" or "Soul." The body is the
spirit's only source of protection, a nest of security and shelter, the
home of homes, the supreme enclosure in life, at least at this moment. These lines expand the idea found in the quatrain which
begins this chapter, "Entitled to myself – precise – / And fitting no
one else." The body, offering harbor to the soul, cannot do so for
any but its own, and that housing affirms being's independence of
anything or anyone else. Notably in the above poem, the stress is
upon this world and this body, so that even in separation from
others, Emily does not become ethereal and remove herself to an
imagined angelic realm. On the strength of this poem, one could
amend the poet's now familiar remark to read, "The body and
consciousness are the only homes we *now* know." And the body has
a function that the soul cannot provide: it shelters and, if necessary, hides the spirit. Harboring, it serves a specifically feminine,
nurturing role.

   Enclosure as body and as earthly existence, both giving assurance or pleasure, is the central assumption of the following poem:

Their Hight in Heaven comforts not –
Their Glory – nought to me –
'Twas best imperfect – as it was –
I'm finite – I cant see –

The House of Supposition –
The Glimmering Frontier that
skirts the Acres of Perhaps –
To Me – shows insecure –

The Wealth I had – contented me –
If 'twas a meaner size –
Then I had counted it until
It pleased my narrow Eyes –

Better than larger values –
That show however true –
This timid life of Evidence
Keeps pleading – "I don't know."   (696)[3]

Emily clings to ignorance in the face of heaven's unsure promises. "The Glimmering Frontier," miragelike, suffers from a suspect reality. Thus, despite the imperfections of this life, the first of
which again echoes Emily's self-image, "a meaner size," it is preferred by her "narrow Eyes." "Narrow" is a term of limitation with
which Emily often demarcates an avenue of invaluable insight, as
in "I dwell in Possibility," which ends with the poet's "narrow
hands" making a pathway for paradise, and in "A Prison Gets to
be a Friend," with narrow eyes and narrow round cherished (to be
discussed later in this chapter). Here the poet's narrow eyes denote
evaluation or judgment of the "larger values" which, though they
be true for others, are finally eschewed by Emily's evidence and
dismissed with, "I dont know." Life-after-death enclosure could
not compete with the body or consciousness.

This sentiment is nowhere better expressed than in a poem
which would make an excellent sequel to "The Body grows without":

Exhiliration – is within –
There can no Outer Wine
So royally intoxicate
As that diviner Brand

The Soul achieves – Herself –
To drink – or set away
For Visiter – Or Sacrament –
'Tis not of Holiday

To stimulate a Man
Who hath the Ample Rhine
Within his Closet – Best you can
Exhale in offering.   (383)

The body is enlivened by its spirit past any competition of material elixir. Through this highly idiosyncratic alchemy, the "Soul achieves – Herself," reaches the heights of identity or ability. And this interior apex can be presented to another in a similar state –"a Man / Who hath Ample Rhine / Within his Closet" – by "exhaling," presumably finding words for this exhiliration, as in the poem. Again, Emily denotes the life of limit, within one's "Closet," to be the superior, even the divine one.

In her later years, it is true, Dickinson approached death with an expectation of eternity and a longing for the heavenly mansions promised by Christ. She wanted to be "called back." And yet the distance felt between herself and Deity would not close. At the same time, Emily never failed to explore her lack of belief:

> A House upon the Hight –
> That Wagon never reached –
> No Dead, were ever carried down –
> No Peddlar's Cart – approached –
>
> Whose Chimney never smoked –
> Whose Windows – Night and Morn –
> Caught Sunrise first – and Sunset – last –
> Then – held an Empty Pane
>
> Whose fate – Conjecture knew –
> No other neighbor – did –
> And what it was – we never lisped –
> Because He – never told – (399)

The final "He" suggests that the house in question is God's, all the more because this first line corresponds with the poem above, "Their Hight in Heaven comforts not." From the dearth of activity – no wagons, peddlers, or even dead come and go – this house resembles a mausoleum. In fact, apparently there is no inhabitant; the fireplace is unused and the windows only reflect light and at night reveal none. Is God Nothingness? And the future? Will he appear? Divine silence. Significantly, though the exterior of God's house appears here, it is the inside which most interests the poet. Where is the master of the house? Her scrutiny of the façade unveils her wish that he were at home.

The meaning of "House" in the following poem takes direction if it is understood to be akin to that "House upon the Hight," but this time Death's rather than God's:

> Too little way the House must lie
> From every Human Heart
> That holds in undisputed Lease
> A white inhabitant –
>
> Too narrow is the Right between –
> Too imminent the chance –
> Each Consciousness must emigrate
> And lose it's neighbor once –   (911)[4]

Besides "house," a number of Dickinsonian terms relating to limitation or space recur in these lines, especially "narrow," "Consciousness," "emigrate," and "neighbor." The first two have been discussed. "Neighbor" in this poem and the last illustrates Emily's awareness of the literal proximity of others to whom she sent messages, flowers, kitchen specialties, and poems, though she might not see them, such as the Luke Sweetsers, who lived on a rise to the north of the Mansion, the Hills families living east of the Dickinsons on Main Street, and of course, her brother and his family next door to the west.

"Each Consciousness must emigrate" bears more weight than a surface reading might suggest. About five years after this poem was written, Emily notified Higginson in a passage previously noted, "To an Emigrant, Country is idle except it be his own. . . . I do not cross my Father's ground to any House or town."[5] Death's mandatory uprooting not only from neighbor but from native place thus becomes all the more poignant for Emily. And in this extreme moment, the poet calls upon potent words, "little," "narrow," and "white," to express the total confinement fated for the soul in a house whose lease it cannot escape. Years later she expressed a qualified acceptance of this imminent, blank house of extinction in a letter to Higginson upon the death of his infant daughter in 1880: "A Dimple in the Tomb / Makes that Ferocious Room / A Home –" (1489). But these lines were written in the twilight years of her life when immortality seemed increasingly possible, thus their more muted protest against the "little" way to death.

A lean, apparently slight quatrain returns us, as she habitually, fleetingly returned, to ecstasy in existence, using the architectural language to which she was accustomed and applying it to the daily round:

> Noon – is the Hinge of Day
> Evening – the Tissue Door –
> Morning – the East compelling the sill
> Till all the World is ajar –   (931)

Dickinson begins with the favored term, noon, to emphasize the height of feeling accompanying the apex of day. By ascribing "hinge" functions to it, she prepares for her next line, when that hinge has swung almost shut at evening, though its door may be "seen through" in twilight, thus "Tissue." Night has no place here at all. But morning works upon "the sill" of the horizon to open or stir ("ajar" may be read as "jarred") the world, whose enumerated parts imply a house.

At first, such a poem seems to speak of exposure rather than enclosure, yet the speaker here is placed under the arc of time (the sun's course across the sky) and within the house which opens or awakes. Not so in a poem whose voice simultaneously complains of a living closure as it mourns the deceased:

> Safe in their Alabaster Chambers –
> Untouched by Morning
> And untouched by Noon –
> Sleep the meek members of the Resurrection –
> Rafter of satin,
> And Roof of stone.
>
> Light laughs the breeze
> In her Castle above them –
> Babbles the Bee in a stolid Ear,
> Pipe the Sweet Birds in ignorant cadence –
> Ah, what sagacity perished here!   (216, 1859 version)

The poem's second version of 1861 retains the first stanza except for a change in the last line, "Rafter of Satin – and Roof of Stone!" But the second one has been radically altered to express a similar intent in the words of remote rather than near space:

> Grand go the Years – in the Crescent – above them
> Worlds scoop their Arcs –

> And Firmaments – row –
> Diadems – drop – and Doges – surrender –
> Soundless as dots – on a Disc of Snow –[6]

It is not so much that this poem expresses Dickinson's cynicism about the resurrection hope but that in the length of time and the order of nature the dead are forgotten on *this* earth, in *this* world. In the first version, Emily mourns the passing of one generation's "sagacity," but by the second version, she only indirectly opposes the indifference delineated earlier by the light, laughing breeze. No exclamation protests the movement of the great spheres of the cosmos in time and place in the second stanza of 1861. That exclamation is reserved only for the rafters and roofs of the deceased's "Alabaster Chambers," mocking their security. But the final emptiness is in the voice of the poet herself, whose silent snow speaks of a great sense of void in the wake of great dismay, a void which encloses.

A poem which dramatically contrasts with this one was composed for Emily's nephew Edward, about three years old in 1864, the poem's approximate date. Instead of death, the theme is a protected, developing life, quite appropriate for the recipient and somehow reflecting the sender as well. The poem was sent with a cocoon the poet must have found on the grounds of the Mansion:

> Drab Habitation of Whom?
> Tabernacle or Tomb –
> Or Dome of Worm –
> Or Porch of Gnome –
> Or some Elf's Catacomb?   (893)

Considering Emily's fascination with the small and particular in creation, this gift and poem are no surprise, nor is her emphasis upon inner space in each line. One guesses that she feels an unconscious identification for the resident of this "Drab Habitation," likening herself, as she does sometimes, to the butterfly. In a poem written about two years later, she begins, "My Cocoon tightens – Colors teaze [sic] – / I'm feeling for the Air – / A dim capacity for Wings / Demeans the Dress I wear," in which the cocoon represents a spiritual confinement beyond which, if the poet had "The Aptitude to fly," she might "take the clue divine," that is, reach true faith.[7] Ready to burst her cocoon of doubt, God never offered her convincing reason to do so.

Another impasse besides disbelief was despair, that enclosure whose nursing required withdrawal:

> The Heart has narrow Banks
> It measures like the Sea
> In mighty – unremitting Bass
> And Blue Monotony
>
> Til Hurricane bisect
> And as itself discerns
> It's insufficient Area
> The Heart convulsive learns
>
> That Calm is but a Wall
> Of unattempted Gauze
> An instant's Push demolishes
> A Questioning – dissolves.   (928)

It has often been said that Dickinson never saw the sea, perhaps because she says so in a poem, but that might have been typical overstatement.[8] Her infrequent trips to Boston would have brought her too close for curiosity not to lead her there, if only briefly. Some familiarity of a firsthand sort seems to echo in the first stanza when she speaks of the Sea's "unremitting Bass." This observation would be hard to absorb from another's written or verbal description. But these conjectures are digressions. The subject is the poet's control or lack of control in bereavement. And it is the heart's "Area" which is deficient, so that even though she equates heart with sea, it is not sea *per se* but ocean floor she intends as a metaphor. This is not large enough to contain emotion (sea), for the wall of calm collapses under even a momentary wave of push or question. Again, "narrow" defines the heart's inadequacies, and Dickinson wishes at this moment for a larger size.

A more metaphorically simple, less stylistically confused poem speaks more directly and at length of the poet's problem, to know and to have a home:

> I learned – at least – what Home could be –
> How ignorant I had been
> Of pretty ways of Covenant –
> How awkward at the Hymn

Round our new Fireside – but for this –
This pattern – of the Way –
Whose Memory drowns me, like the Dip
Of a Celestial Sea –

What Mornings in our Garden – guessed
What Bees – for us – to hum –
With only Birds to interrupt
The Ripple of our Theme –

The Task for Both – ˎ
When Play be done –
Your Problem – of the Brain –
And mine – some foolisher effect –
A Ruffle – or a Tune –

The Afternoons – Together spent –
And Twilight – in the Lanes –
Some ministry to poorer lives –
Seen poorest – thro' our gains –

And then Return – and Night – and Home –

And then away to You to pass –
A new – diviner – care –
Till Sunrise take us back to Scene –
Transmuted – Vivider –

This seems a Home –
And Home is not –
But what that Place could be –
Afflicts me – as a Setting Sun –
Where Dawn – knows how to be –   (944)

From the theological references in the first stanza, one might
believe Emily was envisioning a spiritual or heavenly home, but
the first line of the second stanza which refers to the "Hymn /
Round our new Fireside" suggests family devotions such as the
Dickinsons daily practiced. This idyllic scene had been prompted
by an allusive "pattern of the Way," the way to what? Potential
marriage? Perhaps. The memory of its possibility, she seems to
say, swamps her in its cosmic proportions. Then by the beginning
of the third stanza, she returns to her vision of "the Way," for she

admits that mornings in "our" garden, bees and birds their special orchestra, was "guessed." Her fancied scenes proceed chronologically through a day's pattern of work and play until "Return – and Night – and Home." The consecration of that time, during which a "new – diviner – care" of the husband or lover ensues, enlarges the next day's round, in fact, it becomes "Transmuted – Vivider." This thoroughly worldly scene of what home might be at its romantic best, but is not, wounds the natural woman in a manner parallel to the reversal of nature should the sun suddenly set at dawn. In these lines, Dickinson again reveals her proclivity toward delimitation, the "new Fireside" and by implication, the conjugal bed, her primary synecdoches for home.

Seeing home idyllically but not possessing it, Dickinson turned to one much diminished in comparison which she could have as compensation:

> Mine – by the Right of the White Election!
> Mine – by the Royal Seal!
> Mine – by the Sign in the Scarlet prison –
> Bars – cannot conceal!
>
> Mine – here – in Vision – and in Veto!
> Mine – by the Grave's Repeal –
> Titled – Confirmed –
> Delirious Charter!
> Mine – long as Ages steal!   (528)

What is "mine" in this poem of about 1862 is not exactly a home *per se* but a substitute, a crown comparable to that of wifehood, as she made more explicit in "Title Divine – is Mine." Though within a prison of pain, her fresh wound coloring it, still she may be "seen" through her bars to have the domestic status she sought even if that would have to wait until death for fulfillment.

That this desire still had a burning *and* overflowing place within her, Emily testifies to in a poem of the same year:

> You cannot put a Fire out –
> A Thing that can ignite
> Can go, itself, without a Fan –
> Upon the slowest Night –

> You cannot fold a Flood –
> And put it in a Drawer –
> Because the Winds would find it out –
> And tell your Cedar Floor –   (530)

The poet's allusion to fireplace by indicating "Fan," or bellows, expands her setting to the hearth or heart. Changing the metaphor, that place becomes a drawer by the second stanza, where both water and wind seem ridiculous captives. Just such a container is the poet's inner life, and the poem helps, if help is needed, to see Emily once more as "Vesuvius at Home."

If Dickinson's withdrawal was in part self-willed, other powers worked toward that same effect as she reveals in the first stanza of a poem of about 1862:

> 'Tis true – They shut me in the Cold –
> But then – Themselves were warm
> And could not know the feeling 'twas
> Forget it – Lord – of Them –   (538)

Was she referring to her parents? Austin and Sue? At least the harm inflicted "was short," as she says in the third stanza, but if short, hardly sweet.

Another poem of similar date identifies "they" as Edward and Emily N. Dickinson. It also suggests that occasionally Emily did suffer the punishment proscribed by the Reverend Mr. Abbott in *The Mother at Home:*

> They shut me up in Prose –
> As when a little Girl
> They put me in the Closet –
> Because they liked me "still" –
>
> Still! Could themselves have peeped
> And seen my Brain – go round –
> They might as wise have lodged a Bird
> For Treason – in the Pound –
>
> Himself has but to will
> And easy as a Star
> Look down upon Captivity –
> And laugh – No more have I –   (613)

FIGURE 22. *Child's chair used by Emily Dickinson in the closet of her bedroom at the Mansion. Photograph by Jean Mudge.*

Possibly, one element in Emily's self-sequestration was the extension of a punishment inflicted in her youth, an unconscious operation of the "parent" or superego inflicting retribution for a supposed misdemeanor. That error may have been as harmless as the offering of love but interpreted by the authoritation "my spirit" in Emily's psyche to be shameful, thus deserving chastisement. Yet the poet's final independence seems affirmed in the last two lines of this poem, even if their tone rings with some insecurity.

That suggestion of instability becomes much more predominant in the poems which reveal Emily's inner splintering so that captivity might become escapeless:

> Me from Myself – to banish –
> Had I Art –
> Invincible my Fortress
> Unto All Heart –
>
> But since Myself – assault Me –
> How have I peace
> Except by subjugating
> Consciousness?
>
> And since We're mutual Monarch
> How this be
> Except by Abdication
> Me – of Me?   (642)

The same sort of civil war within appears in several other poems, "The Soul unto itself / Is an imperial friend – / Or the most agonizing Spy – / An Enemy – could send –" (683), or "My Soul – accused me – And I quailed –" (753). But the most chilling revelation of the severed self is:

> One need not be a Chamber – to be Haunted –
> One need not be a House –
> The Brain has Corridors – surpassing
> Material Place –
>
> Far safer, of a Midnight Meeting
> External Ghost
> Than it's interior Confronting –
> That Cooler Host.

Far safer, through an Abbey gallop,
The Stones a'chase –
Than Unarmed, one's a'self encounter –
In lonesome Place –

Ourself behind ourself, concealed –
Should startle most –
Assassin hid in our Apartment
Be Horror's least.

The Body – borrows a Revolver –
He bolts the Door –
O'erlooking a superior spectre –
Or more –   (670)

In this poem, the antagonism of intimates seems to reach a height, since it is not direct encounter so much as the fear of that encounter, experienced before in all its horror, which plagues the speaker. The first four stanzas are straightforward enough, borrowing images from architecture. But the frenzy built up reaches an enigmatic pitch at Emily's center, represented by her own chamber, in the last two lines. Does Emily intend to suggest that the body is faced with or itself faces, revolver in hand, "a superior spectre," and what or who is referred to when she says "Or More" – remembrances of selves past or God? Another poem (1225), speaks of the noise generated by this division in the "Cellars of the Soul" and thanks God that "the loudest Place he made / Is licensed to be still."

This central rift closed at moments, however, and unity, if not calm, could prevail. Emily describes her "Country" at such a moment:

The Heart is the Capital of the Mind –
The Mind is a single State –
The Heart and the Mind together make
A single Continent –

One – is the Population –
Numerous enough –
This ecstatic Nation
Seek – it is Yourself.   (1354)

The two principles of the psyche are not in conflict here, though they might be at other times. Rather, the poem's theme is a satisfaction with reposeful solitude in which the heart dominates the rest of one's inner space in a joyous, "ecstatic" state. This interior calm becomes all the more pronounced in a poem which begins with outer space and works inward:

> There is a solitude of space
> A solitude of sea
> A solitude of death, but these
> Society shall be
> Compared with that profounder site
> That polar privacy
> A soul admitted to itself –
> Finite Infinity.   (1695)

It is true that a transcending sense of loneliness haunts these lines, but that tone competes with the content, namely the poet's enjoyment of a polar privacy because it is the supreme solitude, a temporary "shelter" into which the soul is "admitted" home.

A special, even perfect place within is again the focus in a poem which describes location largely with the language of time:

> There is a Zone whose even Years
> No Solstice interrupt –
> Whose Sun constructs perpetual Noon
> Whose perfect Seasons wait –
>
> Whose Summer set in Summer, till
> The Centuries of June
> And Centuries of August cease
> And Consciousness – is Noon.   (1056)

That Dickinson within could be likened to "a Zone" with "even Years" in the light of poems like "One need not be a Chamber – to be Haunted –" seems unlikely. But the poet speaks precisely; her designated area is merely a zone, not the whole continent. For here, and here alone, does time stop and seasons cease to shift. At this spot, the mind is sealed in perfection, "Consciousness – is Noon," an allusion to the ecstasy of this interior Shangri-la.

The promise of such hallowed places after death left Dickinson usually opting for the certainties of this world, as in:

> The Life we have is very great.
> The Life that we shall see
> Surpasses it, we know, because
> It is Infinity.
> But when all Space has been beheld
> And all Dominion shown
> The smallest Human Heart's extent
> Reduces it to none.   (1162)

"Finite Infinity" then seems to have been her canny preference, particularly since that finitude may be held in the "smallest" heart and be superior to "all Space" and "all Dominion," which are, in truth, nothing outside of consciousness. Nowhere does Dickinson make such a succinct argument for the contained, "little" life.

If such statements of the importance and even the location of interior peace or ecstasy might suggest that Dickinson was sure of these homes, then the poet hampers such expectation by admitting their transient quality:

> In many and reportless places
> We feel a Joy –
> Reportless, also, but sincere as Nature
> Or Deity –
>
> It comes, without a consternation –
> Dissolves – the same –
> But leaves a sumptuous Destitution –
> Without a Name –
>
> Profane it by a search – we cannot
> It has no home –
> Nor we who having once inhaled it –
> Thereafter roam.   (1382)

The nature of this rapture is not given. It might be related to Emily's loved ones or to her swiftly passing seconds of belief. But one thing is certain: Joy's sincerity parallels Nature's and God's;

that is, it is untrustworthy, for both cosmic forces betrayed her. In fact, its departure leaves her in a state of "sumptuous Destitution," a narrowed life. To attempt to enlarge it again through one's own efforts is hopeless. Homeless without this joy, nonetheless, the speaker must wait for its unpredictable return.

A similar respect for the fragility and fugitive nature of joy appears in another poem which plays upon the house image as a shelter for the small in nature. This theme, so akin to Dickinson's own situation, appears in several poems in which the poet focuses on the abodes of the bee, rat, squirrel, frog, spider, or the "residence" of flowers, as in this poem:

> Go not too near a House of Rose –
> The depredation of a A Breeze
> Or inundation of a Dew
> Alarm it's walls away –
> Nor try to tie the Butterfly,
> Nor climb the Bars of Ecstasy,
> In insecurity to lie
> Is Joy's insuring quality.   (1434)[9]

Emily Dickinson's ability to find her special Zone of Noon, even though it be as fleeting as the various moods of her mind, helps to explain her satisfaction secluded in her father's Mansion. Though she might feel imprisoned, she could prefer it so:

> A Prison gets to be a friend –
> Between it's Ponderous face
> And Our's – a Kinsmanship express –
> And in it's narrow Eyes –
>
> We come to look with gratitude
> For the appointed Beam
> It deal us – stated as our food –
> And hungered for – the same –
>
> We learn to know the Planks
> That answer to Our feet
> So miserable a sound – at first –
> Nor even now – so sweet –

As plashing in the Pools –
When Memory was a Boy –
But a Demurer Circuit –
A Geometric Joy –

The Posture of the Key
That interrupt the Day
To Our Endeavor – Not so real
The Cheek of Liberty –

As this Phantasm Steel –
Whose features – Day and Night –
Are present to us – as Our Own –
And as escapeless – quite –

The narrow Round – the Stint –
The slow exchange of Hope –
For something passiver – Content
Too steep for looking up –

The Liberty we knew
Avoided – like a Dream –
Too wide for any Night but Heaven –
If That – indeed – redeem –   (652)

Oddly, the poem appears to begin with the speaker outside the prison facing its façade and recognizing similar features between that façade and the speaker's own face in an architectural parallel of radically different "houses." The prison's "narrow Eyes" recall the poet's, also "narrow," in "Their Hight in Heaven comforts not –" (696). The prisoner thus may see the "Beam" from these eyes with equally narrowed ones, appropriate to the meager "diet" allotted. By stanza three, "We" are inside and listening to the floor respond to footsteps with a wistfulness for release which somewhat belies the affirmation of the poem's first line. Yet this note is quickly lost as the poet goes on to praise her boundaried life of "Demurer Circuit" and "Geometric Joy," echoing her substantial body of poems rejoicing in renunciation or deprivation. Even if her plans are "interrupted" by being under lock, this existence is more real than freedom, whose "Cheek," being soft, suggests unreliability, compared to the steel of this prison, though it be

"Phantasm," fancied. The prison's reduced dimensions shrink expectation to acceptance and the prisoner's vision no longer searches
up for release. By the final stanza, the earlier counterpoint of dis-
satisfaction seems to be heard lightly again as the thought of looking up reminds the poet of a liberty lost and irrecoverable, thus
avoided. Only in heaven could there be width enough for that, if
indeed even there.

The indefiniteness about limitation which weakens Emily's supposed theme in this poem does not afflict another which also sees
this life as a prison:

> Of God we ask one favor,
> That we may be forgiven –
> For what, he is presumed to know –
> The Crime, from us, is hidden –
> Immured the whole of Life
> Within a magic Prison
> We reprimand the Happiness
> That too competes with Heaven.   (1601)

Emily confidently, even flippantly, requires God to pardon her
for misdemeanors only He, certainly not she, knows to have been
committed. For existence here has been Edenic, a life within an
incredible lodging, a magic prison, boundaried but beautifully
mysterious and infused with an unknown spirit. With this attitude
toward Now, Emily's last two lines seem understandable only if
read ironically; her reprimand to happiness cannot be serious unless she has suddenly shifted to acknowledge sin, which does not
seem to be the case.

Emily's refusal to accept guilt, whether for the sins of the fathers
or for her own, established her as a knowing innocent, pleased to
be protected from the world's disillusionments at home. There
she could follow Emerson's advice to build her own house until
the day of her final going home. A retrospective summation of that
life appears in the following poem. No one but she could compose
such a pointed epitaph in biographical, poetic, or spatial terms:

> She staked her Feathers – Gained an Arc –
> Debated – Rose again –
> This time – beyond the estimate
> Of Envy, or of Men –

And now, among Circumference –
Her steady Boat be seen –
At home – among the Billows – As
The Bough where she was born –   (798)

FIGURE 23. *Back hall door of the Mansion, ca. 1916. Courtesy of Priscilla Parke.*

Appendix
A selected list of Emily Dickinson's vocabulary of space

Emily Dickinson often chose words relating either to space generally or derived from domestic architecture. Observing these and noting their frequency gives a rough guide to the centrality of the home image and also to its manifold, shifting nature.

Words	Frequency of Use	Words	Frequency of Use
away	216	low	48
go	152	alone	43
without	140	joy	43
out	114	left	43
home	86	lie	41
within	86	beyond	40
sky	77	near	39
door	76	stand	39
house	74	east	33
world	74	below	31
earth	57	room	31
paradise	57	high	30
further	54	town	30
behind	53	universe	29
gone	51	west	27
back	50	close	27
eternity	50	brain	26

If numbers are significant at all, their significance should not be pressed too far, and it might be questioned whether words used more than 25 times were necessarily special favorites of Emily's. For instance, using a word once, as a painter mixes an uncommon hue never again the same, could make it powerful with ramified meaning for her. As she once said, overcome with the potency of her tools, "I have no grace to talk, my own words so chill and burn me." Such a word wrung into an "essential oil" was *circumference,* used only 17 times.

However, special words on which she leaned, often monosyllabic and strong, ask for speculation. Certainly by coincidence, but what suggestive coincidence, are the two words *home* and *within* used the same number of times. They were as often chosen as *bee, look,* and *thy*. Also by chance, *house* and *world* each are used 74 times. The difference in meaning between *home* and *house* for Emily seems to be clarified by *within* and *world,* their numerical partners. *Alone, left,* and *joy* appear 43 times in the poems, also a matter of computer roulette, but the words are forcefully raised to attention alone and in relation to each other. The *alone* and *left* pair is balanced by *joy,* as if to confirm Emily's habit of translating tragedy into triumph.

The poems themselves, as well as the words, increase the statistical scores. Ones which mention *house* or *home* number more than those which use both words together. Cognates of each, such as *houses, household, housewife* and *homes, homesick, homeless, homestead,* increase the number of poems from 160, the total use of *house* and *home,* to 210, or about 12% of her known poems. But these figures, like those on *circumference,* hardly measure the energy and emphasis which Emily gave the words. To paraphrase her, quantity is no test of depth (her words, "Area – no test of depth"). Of course, the values of these words augment according to context in Emily's letters, indispensable companions to her poetry for comprehending her total concept.

Notes

NOTES TO PREFACE

1. Thomas De Quincey, *Autobiographic Sketches* (Boston, 1853), p. 39.
2. Ibid., p. 41.
3. P I, 397, p. 311.
4. L II, 268, p. 412.
5. L II, 265, p. 408.
6. She may repeat the "I" several times within a poem so that the figure 1682 cannot be directly compared to her total number of 1775 poems.
7. S. P. Rosenbaum, ed., *A Concordance to the Poems of Emily Dickinson* (Ithaca, New York, 1964), p. 865.
8. See appendix 2, of P III, pp. 1197–1200, for a list of the recipients of the 581 poems.
9. Michael Zuckerman, "The Nursery Tales of Horatio Alger," *American Quarterly*, XXIV (May 1972), p. 208. Zuckerman writes, ". . . homes are crucial concerns for Alger even before his heroes consummate their quest, for such lodgings symbolize superbly the fusion of public and private aspiration to passive security and indulgence in their desires. An ample home is, in Alger, the alternative to the real independence and loneliness of the large city. . . . It is a sanctuary, a veritable womb."
10. Susan Sontag, "The Anthropologist as Hero," *Against Interpretation* (New York, 1966), p. 69.
11. Violet Saub de Laszlo, ed., *Psyche and Symbol: A Selection from the Writings of C. G. Jung* (New York, 1958), p. xxv.

NOTES TO CHAPTER ONE

1. William Howard, "Emily Dickinson's Poetic Vocabulary," *Publications of the Modern Language Association*, LXXII (March 1957), p. 246.
2. [Edward W.] Carpenter and [Charles F.] Morehouse, *The History of the Town of Amherst, Mass.* (Amherst, 1896), p. 205.
3. See especially P I, 61, and P II, 520; also P II, 501, 636, 738, 762, 793; P III, 1185. And in June 1862 Emily writes T. W. Higginson,

"Would you have time to be the 'friend' you should think I need? I have a little shape – it would not crowd your Desk – nor make much Racket as the Mouse that dents your Galleries." L II, 265, p. 408.

4. Martha Dickinson Bianchi, *Emily Dickinson, Face to Face* (New York, 1970), p. 3.

5. L II, 330, p. 460.

6. P II, 657, 944; P I, 486.

7. L II, 459a, p. 554.

8. P II, 670, pp. 516–17.

9. L II, 591, p. 634.

10. L II, 220, p. 364.

11. P II, 608, p. 467; P II, 824, p. 624.

12. P III, 1767, p. 1183.

13. L I, 114, p. 239.

14. L I, 118, p. 245.

15. L I, 31, p. 86.

16. One of Erikson's greatest contributions to the psychosociological understanding of identity is this emphasis on the individual's actual environment as an integral part of his sense of himself. *Identity: Youth and Crisis* (New York, 1968), p. 24.

17. Charles Rycroft, "A Great Mother's Helper," *New York Review of Books*, June 1, 1972, p. 18.

18. J. Hillis Miller, *The Disappearance of God* (New York, 1965), p. 306.

19. Ibid., pp. 282–83.

20. Noah Webster, *An American Dictionary of the English Language,* 1st ed. in Octavo (Amherst, 1844), I, 833.

21. Richard B. Sewall, *The Lyman Letters: New Light on Emily Dickinson and Her Family* (Amherst, Mass., 1965), p. 71.

22. P II, 1104, p. 776; P I, 475, p. 365.

23. P III, 1573, p. 1084.

24. P II, 652, pp. 503–4.

25. Ibid.; P III, 1334, p. 922. See Appendix, pp. 229–30.

26. Gaston Bachelard, *The Poetics of Space*, trans. Maria Jolas (New York, 1964), p. 6.

27. L II, 268, p. 411. See also L II, 261, p. 405: "My size felt small – to me."

28. P I, 143, p. 102.

29. Sigmund Freud, *A General Introduction to Psychoanalysis* (New York, 1938), p. 260.

30. Ibid., p. 136. Perhaps borrowing from Freud, C. G. Jung draws a similar plan of the mind, although he does not differentiate between conscious and unconscious parts of the psyche: "We have to describe

and to explain a building the upper story of which was erected in the nineteenth century; the ground-floor dates from the sixteenth century, and a careful examination of the masonry discloses the fact that it was reconstructed from a dwelling-tower of the eleventh century. In the cellar we discover Roman foundation walls, and under the cellar a filled-in cave, in the floor of which stone tools are found and remnants of glacial fauna in the layers below. That would be a sort of picture of our mental structure." C. G. Jung, "Mind and the Earth," *Contributions to Analytical Psychology*, trans. J. G. and Cary F. Baynes (New York, 1928), pp. 118–19; quoted by Bachelard, *The Poetics of Space*, p. xxxiii.

31. Freud, in fact, believed that daydreams form the raw material of poetry. *A General Introduction to Psychoanalysis*, pp. 88–89; see also his "The Relation of the Poet to Day-Dreaming" (1908), in Philip Rieff, *Character and Culture* (New York, 1963).

32. Erikson, pp. 261–94.

33. Jay Leyda, *The Years and Hours of Emily Dickinson* (New Haven, 1960), II, 480.

34. Kenneth Burke, *Attitudes toward History* (Los Altos, California, 1959), pp. 198–99.

35. Kenneth Burke, *The Philosophy of Literary Form* (Baton Rouge, 1941), pp. 20, 24–26, 27. In these pages Burke includes a discussion of synecdoche, which he calls "the figure of speech wherein the part is used for the whole, the whole for the part, the container for the thing contained, the cause for the effect, the effect for the cause, etc. Simplest example: 'twenty noses' for 'twenty men.'

"The more I examine both the structure of poetry and the structure of human relations outside of poetry, the more I become convinced that this is the 'basic' figure of speech, and that it occurs in many modes besides that of the formal trope."

36. Ibid., pp. 10–11.

37. Ibid., p. 10.

38. Bianchi, p. 15.

39. L I, 13, p. 39.

40. L II, 262, p. 405.

41. P I, 199, pp. 142–43.

42. S. P. Rosenbaum, ed., *A Concordance to the Poems of Emily Dickinson* (Ithaca, New York, 1964), pp. 685–87, 447–50.

43. P II, 640, pp. 492–93.

44. For example, see Albert Rothenberg, "The Flesh-and-Blood Face on the Commemorative Stamp," *Saturday Review*, September 11, 1971, pp. 33–38; Charles Rycroft, "The Artist as Patient," *Times Literary Supplement*, September 22, 1972, pp. 1089–90, and Robert Coles,

"Shrinking History – Part I, *New York Review of Books*, February 22, 1973, pp. 15–21, and "Shrinking History – Part II," *New York Review of Books*, March 8, 1973, pp. 25–29.

NOTES TO CHAPTER TWO

1. L I, 89, p. 204.
2. L I, 52, p. 134. Emily told Austin, "I am glad we dont come home as we used, to this old castle. I could fancy that skeleton cats ever caught spectre rats in dim old nooks and corners, and when I hear the query concerning the pilgrim fathers – and imperturbable Echo merely answers *where*, it becomes a satisfaction to know that they are there, sitting stark and stiff in Deacon Mack's mouldering arm chairs." P. 135.
3. Jay Leyda, *The Years and Hours of Emily Dickinson* (New Haven, 1960), I, 4, 13.
4. Ibid., p. 13.
5. L I, 52, p. 134.
6. As Albert Rothenberg quotes Freud, "Before the problem of the creative artist, psychoanalysis must, alas, lay down its arms." "The Flesh-and-Blood Face on the Commemorative Stamp," *Saturday Review*, September 11, 1971, pp. 33–38.
7. John Cody, *After Great Pain: The Inner Life of Emily Dickinson* (Cambridge, Mass., 1971), pp. 102–3.
8. L II, 342b, p. 475; L II, 405, pp. 517–18. Not only does Cody take these comments out of context, but he does not consider the period of Dickinson's life when she uttered them, ignoring, strangely for a psychoanalytic biographer, the psychological matrix of her views. Further, he overlooks the possible extremism of statements which were doubtless designed to evoke sympathy from Higginson, and thus to enlist him not only as a critic-friend but also as an adopted relative, thereby bringing him closer to her. Dickinson's "I never had a mother" becomes, for Cody, a thematic drumbeat for his entire book, which he repeats incessantly and fails to consider critically. On the strength of it, he argues that Emily's neurotic, even psychotic behavior of later years, may be traced almost exclusively to inadequate mothering on Mrs. Dickinson's part. For proof, he refers not only to Emily's scant references to her mother, but to poems about hunger which, he argues, point to a famine of maternal affection because of the association of food, in the creative personality, with the mother's nuturing love. Cody, pp. 45–46.
But other Dickinson scholars, ones more attuned to poets and their liberties, have stressed that Emily cannot always be taken at her word. Thomas Johnson has put this problem in the context of Dickinson's

withdrawal in the Mansion, making a point which dramatically illustrates the many reverberations consequent from her spatial inscape:

The home in which Emily was born she elected to make in a physical sense exclusively her life. She was therefore at times intolerably lonely, and gained a sense of freedom by unburdening herself to outsiders like Higginson who would be understanding but not inquisitive in their responses. Saying to such a person that one's father read lonely and rigorous books, or that one's mother did not care for thought, was intended to stir sympathy for one's isolation. What she said was true, but it was not the whole truth, as she herself well knew.

Thomas Johnson, *Emily Dickinson: An Interpretive Biography* (New York, 1967), p. 31.
9. Leyda, I, 29; see also p. 11.
10. Ibid., pp. 255, 282, 373.
11. Ibid., p. 11.
12. Ibid., pp. 38, 46, 52.
13. Ibid., p. 52.
14. Ibid., p. 31.
15. Ibid., pp. 3, 6.
16. Ibid., p. 4.
17. Ibid., p. 5.
18. Ibid., p. 4.
19. Ibid., p. 10; see also pp. 28, 30, 91, 92.
20. Ibid., p. 81.
21. Ibid., p. 87.
22. L II, 318, p. 453.
23. Leyda, I, 35.
24. Ibid., pp. 76–77.
25. Ibid., p. 21.
26. Ibid., p. 22.
27. Ibid., p. 86. Another letter Mrs. Dickinson wrote Emily the same month is in a similar style and tone, indicating that her manner was consistent:

I leave all my affairs this mor*ning* to say a few words to *you.* presuming you are happy to hear from home often, we were a little disappointed in not getting a letter from you on *Saturday.* but concluded that you was so much occupied that you could not find *time* to write, we hope you are *well* and enjoying your visit *finely,* We are lonely without *you.* and shall be very glad to see you safe home *again.* I suppose Father & Mother & *Cous Emily* are with you.? I thought of them much those two pleasant days they were *out* on their jour*ney*, hope they are all *comfortable*, we are all well, and evry [*sic*] thing moves along about as usual with *us*, I see some of your young friends evry day *or two*. they make many inquiries for *you*, and wish to be remembered to *you*. I suppose Father has written to you with reference to the *time* he thinks it best for you to return, I shall not therfore [*sic*] say any thing about it, Your plants are doing well. Lavinia takes very good care of them. I am in haste and must *close*. We all [join?], in love to *you*. and our dear friends, From your dear Mother

Letter to Emily Dickinson in Boston, May 1844, Dickinson Papers Box 3, Houghton Library, Harvard.

28. L I, 5, p. 10.

29. L I, 76, p. 180. Two years later, however, when Edward was absent, Mrs. Dickinson attended a Lyceum lecture alone. L I, 156, p. 286.

30. L II, 261, p. 404.

31. Charlotte Perkins Gilman, writing on the "Lady of the House" and the social assumption that women belong exclusively at home, reveals the pervasiveness of this sentiment as reflected in such popular proverbs as, "A Woman should leave her house three times – when she is christened, when she is married, and when she is buried," and "The woman, the cat, and the chimney should never leave the house." Mrs. Gilman goes on to deplore the effects of this incarceration. *The Home, Its Work and Influence* (New York, 1903), p. 209. See also her *Women and Economics* (Boston, 1899), p. 65.

32. Sermon for Edward Dickinson by the Reverend Jonathan L. Jenkins, Summer 1874; Dickinson Papers Box 3, Houghton Library, Harvard.

33. Leyda, I, 28.

34. Ibid.

35. Ibid.

36. Ibid.

37. Ibid., p. 50.

38. Ibid.

39. Ibid., p. 56.

40. Ibid., p. 58.

41. Ibid., pp. 61–62. It is true that Grandmother Gunn had a reputation for bad temper, a trait which, appearing in her grandchildren, was explained as her "coming out" in them. Martha Dickinson Bianchi, *Emily Dickinson, Face to Face* (New York, 1970), pp. 87–88.

42. The Dickinson family was known for its determination. Leyda, I, 25. And Edward was known for his soberness, which combined with his determination to make him pursue financial success as well as politi-

cal esteem. On his soberness, see Catharine Dickinson's letter to her parents, June 22, 1835, Leyda, I, 29. On his ambition to be prosperous, if not wealthy, a letter to his wife, September 7, 1835, Leyda, I, 30, reveals how profoundly he wished it; "I must make some money in some way & if I don't speculate in the lands, at the 'East,' I must at the 'West' – and when the fever next attacks me [the desire for wealth, one supposes] – nothing human shall stop me from making one desperate attempt to make my fortune."

43. Cody ignores this aspect of Edward's ambitiousness in relation to his ancestral home and to his attitudes about *any* home. Consequently, he exaggerates one side of Edward's ambivalence about his family responsibilities. And further, he misses an opportunity to reinforce two aspects of Edward's character which he outlines quite well, namely, the tandem operation of two motivations: (1) the unconscious desire to suppress any evidence of weakness or a need for dependency, and (2) the need to be the unquestioned authority figure in which power and control were so rigidly and completely his that the possibilities of revealing any inadequacies were minimized, if not wholly disguised. Cody, p. 84.

Repeatedly, Cody stresses that Edward overcompensated for his resentment toward his family, because of its encroachment upon the time he might give his political and legal career, by an *excessive* concern about his wife and children. As Cody writes:

These obsessive fears (especially about death) that some calamity would befall his family reveal his inner conflict. Consciously, of course, he wished to be a good husband and father. But the need to be a worldly success was evidently a stronger wish, augmented in importance by its role as defense against repudiated and shamefully "unmanly" urges to be dependent and cared for. When it seemed that the demands of his family would preclude the longed-for professional and political triumphs necessary to his self-esteem, the unconscious wish to obliterate the domestic encumbrance became pressing.

Ibid., p. 88.

44. Millicent Todd Bingham, *Emily Dickinson's Home* (New York, 1955), p. 329.

45. Ibid., p. 327.

46. Leyda, I, 41.

47. Ibid., p. 14.

48. Ibid., pp. 27, 35, 39, 40.

49. Ibid., p. 39.

50. Ibid., p. 40.

51. Ibid., p. 42.

52. Cf. Cody, pp. 52, 101–3.

53. John S. C. Abbott, *The Mother at Home* (Boston, 1833), pp. iii–iv.

54. Ibid., p. 62.

55. Ibid., p. 19.

56. Ibid., pp. 149, 164.

57. Ibid., p. 96.

58. Ibid., pp. 60–61.

59. Ibid., p. 101.

60. Ibid., pp. 102–3.

61. P II, 613, pp. 471–72.

62. Leyda, II, 483. Cf. Cody, p. 78; I disagree with the conclusions drawn there.

63. Cf. Cody, p. 77.

64. P III, 1545, pp. 1065–66.

65. L I, 42, p. 111.

66. Leyda, I, 240; see also Lavinia's Diary, July 17, 1851: "Horse whipped!" (presumably by Mr. Dickinson again). Lavinia Dickinson, Daily Pocket Remembrancer, 1851, Dickinson Papers Box 8, Houghton Library, Harvard. Emily's letters abound in evidence which contradicts extreme disciplinary measures from her parents. Once when they surprised her with a visit to Mount Holyoke, she wrote her friend Abiah Root, ". . . I danced & clapped my hands, & flew to meet them for you can imagine how I felt. I will only ask you do you love your parents?" L I, 18, p. 55.

67. L I, 9, p. 24.

68. L I, 11, p. 31.

69. L I, 11, pp. 32–33.

70. L I, 10, p. 28.

71. Bingham, p. 63.

72. Ibid.

73. L I, 118, p. 245.

74. L I, 156, p. 286; see also L I, 145, p. 276.

75. L I, 106, p. 227.

76. L I, 63, p. 156.

77. Richard B. Sewall, *The Lyman Letters: New Light on Emily Dickinson and Her Family* (Amherst, Mass., 1965), p. 12.

78. L I, pp. 257, 258, 282.

79. L I, 22, p. 62.

80. L I, 109, p. 233.

81. L I, 129, p. 258.

82. Bingham, p. 64.

83. Leyda, I, 226; for Emily's views, L I, pp. 157, 272.
84. Sewall, p. 52.
85. L I, 116, p. 243.
86. L I, 88, p. 202.
87. L I, 103, pp. 223–24.
88. L II, 177, p. 315.
89. P II, 609, p. 467.
90. L I, pp. 120, 166, 209, 218.
91. L I, 11, p. 30.
92. L I, 48, p. 124; see also pp. 15, 117.
93. L I, 96, p. 215.
94. L I, 66, p. 162; L I, 67, p. 164.
95. L I, 77, p. 181.
96. Bingham, p. 63; L I, pp. 254, 256, 258.
97. L I, 127, p. 254.
98. L I, 53, p. 137.
99. L I, 58, p. 149; see also L I, 131, p. 261; L I, 132, p. 263.
100. L I, 85, p. 194.
101. L I, 114, p. 239.
102. L I, 44, p. 116.
103. L I, 72, p. 174.
104. L I, 88, p. 201.
105. L I, 115, p. 241.
106. L I, pp. 21, 39, 140.
107. L I, 39, pp. 103–4.
108. L I, 61, p. 154; L I, 124, p. 251.
109. It is important to remember that psychology's treatment of symbols, largely because of Freud's scholarly and imaginative mind, has at its base a rich grounding in folk tales and myths, jokes and witticisms, folklore, manners and customs, sayings and songs, poetic and colloquial use of language – in brief, a wide and deep reservoir in the history of expression. Sigmund Freud, *A General Introduction to Psychoanalysis* (New York, 1938), pp. 135, 148. From this knowledge, Freud realized the limitations to dream interpretation, for he knew that the symbolization process he observed in the unconscious mind clearly operated with even greater range in the conscious psyche. It seems to me that Freud thereby did double service for the literary critic: he pointed to a wealth of references in history and experience as sources in the process of symbol-formation, and he emphasized the function of symbol-formation well beyond the realm of dreams. In Dickinson's case, her pre-poetic, sometimes nascent symbolization of the hearthstone, front door, her chamber, and the garden could be

considered such extra-oneiric expressions. At the same time, though not dreams, nor even daydreams, as symbols they are open to the same sort of analysis Freud introduced in his dream interpretations.

In such analyses, Freud suggests that the womb may be symbolized by objects which, like it, enclose a space or hold something. Rooms, he finds, function this way because, as with the uterus, people are contained in them. He thus refined his theory that, among a limited number of whole items which are represented in dreams, the human body often appears as a house. Logically then, rooms would represent parts of the body and especially those parts with similar form, such as the womb. But even smaller divisions of architecture and household paraphernalia Freud designates as surrogates for female genitalia. He lists the fireplace or hearth, stove, table, cupboard, and bottle (inkstand?), among many objects. Further, he suggests that the garden in blossom is a composite image of female organs, its fruit suggesting the breasts, and woods or thickets (groves?), pubic hair. Feminine genital openings he sees symbolized by the door or gate. Erikson largely builds his views upon Freud's equivalences. At the same time, he agrees with Freud's consideration of the ambiguity present in either male or female symbols, though not in the obvious, striking ones. It seems that Dickinson's areas fall within this latter category. Freud, pp. 139 ff.

110. Sigmund Freud, *The Ego and the Id* (London, 1935), p. 36.
111. Ibid., p. 37.
112. Leyda, I, 229. "Old un" might have been an epithet borrowed from Dickens's *David Copperfield*, an allusion perhaps to Mrs. Gummidge, despite the difference in sex.
113. L II, 265, p. 408.
114. Emily continues, "Little *Emerald Mack* is washing, I can hear the warm suds, splash. I just gave her my pocket handkerchief – so I cannot cry any more. And Vinnie sweeps – sweeps, upon the chamber stairs; and Mother is hurrying round with her hair in a silk pocket handkerchief, on account of dust. Oh Susie, it is dismal, sad and drear eno'." L I, 85, p. 193.
115. L I, 123, p. 249.
116. Ibid.
117. L II, 418, p. 528.
118. Lavinia Dickinson, Daily Pocket Remembrancer, Dickinson Papers Box 8, Houghton Library, Harvard.
119. Leyda, I, 163.
120. L I, 58, p. 148.
121. Sewall, pp. 70–71.
122. R. W. Emerson, *Miscellanies* (Boston, 1860), p. 177.
123. L I, 16, p. 48.

124. Ibid., pp. 48–49.
125. Ibid.; L I, 17, p. 52.
126. See L I, 20, p. 58, for a description of Emily's homecoming at Thanksgiving 1847. The whole scene is a coming to life of contemporary watercolors or embroidered pictures showing a family crowded on the front doorstep to embrace a returning member, perhaps a prodigal son.

At the Houghton Library, Harvard, there is a bound volume of miscellaneous sheet music with Emily E. Dickinson printed in gold on the cover. The index lists the song "Home, Sweet Home!" in duple time, but also a quickstep entitled "Home," in 6/8 time, and three waltzes, "Sounds from Home," "The Home, I love," and "Home." Emily must have been exposed to these pieces soon after she began learning the piano at age fifteen. She could hardly escape the imprint of their sentiment, style, and rhythm. In January 1849, Emily gave Lavinia "Home as a Waltz," the same piece mentioned above, presumably because she liked it. Leyda, I, 104.

127. Leyda, I, 135. Interestingly, Emily was not alone in her condition of "no hope"; in fact, a large group of this category is reported in the *Mt. Holyoke Journal* for October 2, 1847. Leyda, I, 123, 124.
128. L I, 23, p. 67. She also distrusted her emotions. L I, 10, pp. 27–28.
129. Bingham, p. 490.
130. Leyda, II, 200.
131. L I, 23, pp. 66–67.
132. L I, 31, p. 86.
133. Ibid.
134. Ibid.
135. L I, 32, p. 90.
136. L I, 30, p. 82.
137. Ibid., p. 83.
138. Ibid., p. 84.
139. Albert Gelpi, *Emily Dickinson* (Cambridge, Mass., 1966), p. 91.
140. L I, 35, p. 95.
141. Ibid.
142. L I, 36, p. 98.
143. L I, 59, pp. 150–51.
144. L I, 36, p. 97.
145. L I, 56, p. 144; referred to by Richard Chase, *Emily Dickinson* (New York, 1965), p. 50.
146. L I, 36, p. 99.
147. L I, 39, p. 104.
148. L I, 65, p. 161.

149. L I, 42, p. 111.
150. Ibid., pp. 111–12.
151. L II, 207, p. 354.
152. Leyda, I, 213.
153. L I, pp. 197, 293, 298.
154. L II, 178, p. 317.
155. L I, 59, pp. 150–51.
156. L I, 30, p. 84.
157. L I, 69, p. 167.
158. Bingham, p. 369. Emily's concern about her parents' health, increasing in later years, may have been an unconscious counter-resistance to the self which resented, even detested, their authority, or in her mother's case, a dependency upon Emily's attention and help.
159. Emily's undated definition of reality makes it a revelation open only to a few and, even for them, unfathomed facets might remain: "No dreaming can compare with reality, for Reality itself is a dream from which a portion but of Mankind have yet waked and part of us is a not familiar Peninsula." L III, PF 2, p. 911.
160. L I, 126, p. 253.
161. L I, 123, p. 249; L I, 144, p. 274.
162. L II, 180, p. 321.

NOTES TO CHAPTER THREE

1. Erik H. Erikson, *Identity: Youth and Crisis* (New York, 1968), pp. 271–72. Freud noted that a house could represent an entire organism in dreams, or several houses, that is, a row, might stand for a single organ such as the intestines. Also, he observed that separate sections of a house could symbolize separate parts of the human body. Sigmund Freud, *The Interpretation of Dreams,* ed. James Strachey (London, 1954), p. 85. Since the body is involved in this sort of symbolism, it might be thought that only somatic stimuli contribute to it. However, Freud found that not only physical but psychic sources can provide the ideational (wish) material for the content of such dreams. Freud, p. 228. See also Freud's examples of dreams of his own and of his patients, pp. 231, 397–99, 454.
2. The importance of a trustworthy object world to the healthy growth of self-identity, beginning with the confidence of the mother-infant relationship, is explored by Erik Erikson, pp. 71, 103–4.
Emily's relationship with Susan Huntington Gilbert, her future sister-in-law, is relevant to her search for an ideal mother. Most of the time her deep affection for Sue was sisterly, but it was from the perspective of a "little sister," and sometimes Emily attributed maternal qualities to Sue, suggesting that she thought she needed them:

"Oh Susie, I would nestle close to your warm heart, and never hear the wind blow, or the storm beat, again. Is there any room there for me, or shall I wander away all homeless and alone?. L I, p. 177. See also L I, pp. 176, 182–83, 201, 208, 210, 211, 215, 229–30, 304. A certain independence from Sue was possible, however, even in the early 1850s, as one letter clearly shows, p. 306. Emily also noted Sue's attractiveness to Edward Dickinson. Sue's wit and charm must have contrasted sharply with Mrs. Dickinson's well-meaning blandness. L I, pp. 250, 252.

3. Emily's thoughts were clear as early as 1851, when she wrote to Austin, "Prof. Jewett has come and is living with his wife east of Gen Mack and *his* wife. Pretty perpendicular times, I guess, in the ancient mansion. I am glad we dont come home as we used, to this old castle. L I, 52, p. 134.

4. L II, 182, pp. 323–24.

5. Ibid.

6. L II, 318, p. 453; L III, appendix 2, p. 959; L III, PF 80, p. 924.

7. Jay Leyda, *The Years and Hours of Emily Dickinson* (New Haven, 1960), I, 331, 332, 339, 359. A lithograph of 1858 shows the refurbished house in quiet grandeur. It appeared with other views of Amherst homes on a poster advertising the town, now at the Amherst Historical Society.

8. Erikson, pp. 61–62. Erikson describes the case of a domineering grandfather whose conservative, self-immortalizing motivations led him to establish his family mansion as a timeless monument to his clan and especially himself. The mansion so represented him, even after his death, that the place exercised an extraordinary control on his grandchildren, at least those who could not break away from the house. The Dickinson situation was different, but a similar desire on Edward's part for continuing the family's position and power as it was in his own father's heyday seems to have been a factor in his plans not only to repurchase the family homestead but also to enlarge and enhance it stylistically with the front portico and cupola. His influence was successful, too, in enticing Austin to remain in Amherst, partial inducement being the house he gave Austin next door, which might have been included – at least in Edward's mind – as part of the homestead.

9. E. Littell, ed., *Littell's Living Age,* 2nd Ser. (Boston, 1855), IX (7 April 1855), p. 1.

10. R. W. Franklin, *The Editing of Emily Dickinson: A Reconsideration* (Madison, 1967).

11. L II, 265, p. 408.

12. The 1872 version of this poem considerably improves on that of 1862, at the same time that it still seems to refer to the Pleasant Street house. P II, 609, pp. 468–69.

13. Sigmund Freud, *A General Introduction to Psychoanalysis* (New York, 1938), pp. 232–33.

14. L III, PF 69, p. 922.

15. William Howard, "Emily Dickinson's Poetic Vocabulary," *Publications of the Modern Language Association of America,* LXXII (March 1957), p. 246.

16. Howard, p. 230, shows that out of 442 words Emily uses from "special sources," the second largest group is of words deriving from housewifery. (The first is, interestingly, from contemporary technology or science.)

17. Erikson, p. 281.

18. Asher Benjamin, *The Country Builder's Assistant* (Greenfield, Mass., 1805; reprint ed., New York: The Architectural Book Publishing Co., P. Wenzel and M. Krakow, 1917), plate 32, p. 37. The central section of this design for a country residence follows the Mansion's five bay, two-story outline. Further, the Palladian window probably was part of the Mansion's original design, as was the fan-light doorway, both evident by the scars of later brick work. The "First contractor," or builder, for the house may have been the well-known Isaac Damon of Northampton. D. Merrill, "Isaac Damon and the Southwick Column Papers," *Old Time New England,* LIV (October 1963), 48–58.

19. Edward gave Austin the house next door, "The Evergreens," as a wedding present in 1856. Austin's choice of design in the irregular Italian villa style of the sort found in A. J. Downing's work had a tower, similar in style to the cupola. It may have been that Edward did not want to be out-cupola-ed by his son. Also, however, his neighbor to the east and across Triangle Street, Leonard Hills, had an even larger outlook, which may have been incentive for this addition on the Mansion. See A. J. Downing, *Cottage Residences . . .* (New York, 1842), design VI, facing page 124, figs. 49 and 50. Sue noted in an essay, "Society in Amherst," that Downing was an architect "whom [Austin] had long studied." Dickinson Papers Box 9, Houghton Library, Harvard.

20. Today there are still traces of the yellow paint attached to the brick and mortar of the house.

21. Emily described one in "By my Window have I for Scenery," P II, 797, p. 603. Emily was in Cambridge, Massachusetts, for eye treatments in mid-May 1865 and wrote home, "I hope the Chimneys are done and the Hemlocks set, and the Two Teeth filled, in the front yard. . . ." L II, 308, p. 442.

22. Martha Dickinson Bianchi, *Emily Dickinson, Face to Face* (Boston and New York, 1932), p. 22. Henceforth cited as FF.

23. Ibid., p. 23.

24. Ibid., p. 34.

25. L II, 342a, p. 473.

26. L II, 487, p. 572.

27. George Whicher, *This Was a Poet* (New York, 1938), pp. 124–25.

28. FF, p. 86. See also J. B. A., "The Home of Emily Dickinson," *The Packer Alumna* (Brooklyn, New York), VII (December 1891).

29. Unpublished notebook of household furnishings from the Mansion and the Evergreens, Martha Dickinson Bianchi, January 1923. The Evergreens, Amherst, Massachusetts.

30. Mrs. C. M. Badger, *Wild Flowers Drawn and Colored from Nature* (New York, 1859).

31. FF, p. 4.

32. L III, 738, p. 718.

33. Martha Dickinson Bianchi, *The Life and Letters of Emily Dickinson* (Boston, 1924), p. 69. Henceforth cited as LL.

34. FF, pp. 25–26.

35. FF, pp. 5–6; Leyda, II, 478.

36. FF, p. 39.

37. Leyda, II, p. 482.

38. L II, 304, p. 440. The floor plan shows that the only access to the garret was by a spiral staircase just outside Emily's bedroom. This staircase must have resembled the one leading to the cupola.

39. I am indebted to Millicent Todd Bingham's verbal account of visiting the Mansion as a young girl of fourteen, about 1894, after the poet's death but at a period when her room was left intact. Mrs. Bingham could not remember any details about the room other than a double mahogany sleigh-style bed placed on the east wall. She also recalled that the downstairs rooms and hallways were darkened from draperies and closed shutters. Remarks about the house by M. T. Bingham, June 1967.

40. P I, 375, p. 298.

41. L II, 204, p. 351.

42. P I, 83, p. 67; P I, 228, p. 163.

43. FF, p. 46.

44. P II, 636, p. 489.

45. For instance, years after she had begun her self-isolation only friends like the Hollands, Helen Hunt Jackson, and Maria Whitney were welcomed in the Mansion.

46. FF, p. 66.

47. P II, 1090, p. 769.

48. Allen Tate, "New England Culture and Emily Dickinson," *The Recognition of Emily Dickinson* (Ann Arbor, 1964), p. 158.

49. Erikson, p. 268.

50. Erikson more fully qualifies himself, "Nothing in our interpretation, then, is meant to claim that either sex is doomed to one spatial mode or another; rather, it is suggested that in contexts which are not imitative or competitive these modes 'come more naturally' for natural reasons which must claim our interest." Ibid., p. 273.

51. Kate Millett, *Sexual Politics* (New York, 1970), pp. 210–20.

52. Erikson elaborates upon his starting point, the womb, in several ways, two of which are particularly relevant to Dickinson: 1) its ability to produce anxiety and 2) its sufficiency as an organ to satisfy female self-identity as opposed to possession of a phallus.

On the first point, Erikson argues that the womb has great portents of fear and danger, as revealed in dreams, myths, and cults of various cultures. These appear awesome to men as well as women. The vagina can be an aggressive organ ("a devouring mouth"), or a rebuffing, excluding one ("an eliminating sphincter"), or a gaping, ugly one ("a bleeding wound"). Erikson, p. 267. These negative aspects of femininity are associated only with the *opening* of the womb and not with that central space *per se*. Erikson does not make this distinction, but it is important in this study for its association with Dickinson's frequent reference to windows and doorways, accesses to her inner, often hidden and "little" self. Typically, she expresses an ambivalence, as in the two contrasting poems, "The Soul selects her own Society – / Then – shuts the Door" and "Doom is the House without the Door." But it is the womb's *entrance* which is fraught with potential accident, and thus anxiety, while at the same time, the womb itself remains the core of physical satisfaction for a woman.

Erikson's second suggestion is a challenge to the attention given the problem of penis-envy, traditionally thought to be a central trauma in female psychology. This point makes him sound more like a supporter of women's liberation, or at least that part of its philosophy celebrating feminine potency and patience, than the enemy its most vocal adherents have heretofore made of him. In any case, Erikson's thesis appears to speak to Dickinson's situation. For him, feminine characteristics, especially "passive-masochistic" roles and the ability to tolerate and comprehend pain, are manifestations of an early awareness of a "productive interior" rather than functions of a "trauma" over lacking a penis. He sees that the woman's role is determined by a sense of "vital inner potential" and not by envy of the male. Ibid., pp. 274–77. Erikson implies that women who are not able to satisfy instincts fulfilling the demands of this inner space develop neurotic symptoms either denying or exaggerating their womanliness. In Dickinson's case, perhaps the latter circumstance predominated. Her withdrawal, sense of insignificance, frequent testimony to her contests with acute pain, and above all, her concentration on the inner life, would all suggest that sexual frustration focused her attention upon her own femininity.

If she exhibited an element of enviousness relating to the male perhaps it was less, or not at all, for his appendage but for the privileges which his size and strength earlier demanded and which tradition and society reinforced. Male superiority has been customarily symbolized by the phallus (that is, by towers and obelisks in monuments and by weapons and tools in literature). But curiously, apparently ignoring the symbolization process with which it constantly deals, psychoanalytic theory, beginning with Freud, has too literally interpreted the female desire for equality with men as, at base, a desire to possess a phallus *per se*. Not only Kate Millett but Karen Horney, one of Freud's students, and other women in literary criticism or psychology are arguing that this attributed desire profoundly misunderstands and misrepresents the feminine psyche. Karen Horney, *Feminine Psychology* (New York, 1967), pp. 57–59, 77. Erikson is scientific support in their behalf.

53. See P I, 393; P II, 574, 685, 855. Emily had particular problems in overcoming her adolescence. She had to remain at home as part-time housekeeper, the atmosphere encouraging her to delay adulthood. Further, she needed home for protection to preserve her intellectual freedom and to shield her emotional dependencies. Thus, at the moment when she might have been concluding childhood, which Erikson defines as "the mental and emotional ability to receive and give fidelity" and become an adult, which he defines as "the ability to receive and give love and care," she was asked not to change the "objects" of her nascent fidelity, love, and care, but to give the same objects *more* of such attention. The choice was hardly hers; it was a demand. The stasis resulting, or partially resulting, seems understandable. See Erikson, ibid, pp. 33, 155, 203, 265.

54. L III, PF 21, p. 914.

55. This image seems to be strikingly masculine, according to both Freud and Erikson; see Freud, *The Interpretation of Dreams,* p. 354. Perhaps it was borrowed from the Brownings.

56. L II, 261, p. 404.

57. This impression is supported by Erikson's observations of a young man who, in the severe throes of withdrawal and aloneness, made a comment strikingly like Emily's: "I was a majority of One." Another patient, a woman, expressed herself in a similar phrase, speaking of her "right to oneliness [*sic*]." Erikson, pp. 78–79. See also pp. 97, 101.

58. P I, 306, p. 227.

59. Erikson writes, "When the human being, because of accidental or developmental shifts, loses an essential wholeness, he restructures him-

self and the world by taking recourse to what we may call *totalism*. As pointed out, it would be wise to abstain from considering this a merely regressive or infantile mechanism. It is an alternate, if more primitive, way of dealing with experience, and thus has, at least in transitory states, certain adjustment and survival value. It belongs to normal psychology." P. 81. The poems quoted above are from a period of radical shift in Dickinson's life. Others, to be studied later, are less authoritarian and indicate that the poet was able to readapt herself to a more flexible objective synthesis of feelings in interplay with her experience.

60. P II, 642, p. 494.

61. L II, 281, p. 424.

62. LL, p. 83.

63. P I, 216, p. 151.

64. P I, 449, p. 347.

65. P I, 465, p. 358.

66. See also L I, 103, p. 223.

67. The substitution of two of Emily's words in this poem for the way they are printed in the Johnson edition of the poetry changes the entire meaning of it. In making a printer's copy of the poem, Mabel Loomis Todd substituted "mighty" for "timid" in line two and replaced "fallow" in line four with Emily's alternate suggestion, "shadows." (Dickinson had no alternate for "timid.") Cf. Franklin, fig. 16, facing page 99, with Johnson's form of the poem, P III, 1767, p. 1163.

68. Sewall, p. 65.

69. Ibid.

70. Ibid., p. 67.

71. Although this poem exists only as a transcript made by Sue, it does not necessarily mean that she added the last line, as some critics have argued. Even if she did, she would have done so not to protect Emily from psychoanalytic scrutiny but rather to make the poem more meaningful. Without the last line a reader could infer it was a dream but also read it as an exercise in the absurd.

72. Sigmund Freud, *Delusion and Dream and Other Essays* (Boston, 1956), p. 132.

73. Erikson, pp. 22, 197.

74. Freud, *The Interpretation of Dreams,* pp. 347, 356–57.

75. Ibid., p. 347. To call Emily neurotic, or even psychotic, should hardly be considered an insult in a contemporary world when this condition is one definition of a "sane" response to crisis or pressure. Also, neuroticism is no disqualification for the poet; in fact, it may be a prerequisite to the insight required of one as introspective as Emily.

See Lionel Trilling, "Art and Neurosis," *The Liberal Imagination* (New York, 1953), esp. pp. 172 ff. To say this, of course, is not to state that madness is an integral part of creativity, only that it may be.

76. L I, 31, p. 88.

77. L II, 193, p. 339. Emily wrote to Samuel Bowles, "Our Pastor says we are a 'Worm.' How is that reconciled? 'Vain – sinful Worm' is possibly of another species."

78. Cf. Clark Griffith, *The Long Shadow* (Princeton, N.J., 1965) pp. 177 ff. John E. Walsh, leaning too heavily on his thesis that Emily borrowed extensively from *Aurora Leigh,* again attributes this poem to lines of E. B. Browning's. His argument remains unconvincing. Walsh, *The Hidden Life of Emily Dickinson* (New York, 1971), pp. 260–61.

79. Freud, *Delusion and Dream,* p. 97.

80. P II, 986, p. 711.

81. For the Puritans, the snake was an emissary of the devil. In Emily's poem the snake combines both evil and overpowering male force. A quaint description of the "devil's" visitation to a synod meeting in Cambridge is given in John Winthrop's *Journal* for August 15, 1648:

> It fell out, about the midst of his [Mr. Allen's] sermon, there came a snake into the seat, where many of the elders sate behind the preacher. It came in at the door where people stood thick upon the stairs. Divers of the elders shifted from it, but Mr. Thompson, one of the elders of Braintree, (a man of much faith,) trode upon the head of it, and so held it with his foot and staff with a small pair of grains, until it was killed. This being so remarkable, and nothing falling out but by divine providence, it is out of doubt, the Lord discovered somewhat of his mind in it. The serpent is the devil; the synod, the representative of the churches of Christ in New England. The devil had formerly and lately attempted their disturbance and dissolution; but their faith in the seed of the woman overcame him and crushed his head.

Perry Miller and T. H. Johnson, eds., *The Puritans* (New York, Harper Torchbooks, 1967), I, 142–43. Winthrop's reference to "faith in the seed of the woman" probably refers to Gen. 3:15 in which God speaks to the serpent, "I will put enmity between you and the woman, and between your seed and her seed . . ." (RSV).

82. Clues to Emily Dickinson's education on sexual matters include Professor Hitchcock's lectures at Amherst College "on Physiology with the Manikin," lectures open to Academy students while the poet was enrolled there. Leyda, I, 84. At Mount Holyoke in 1848, she reported studying "Cutter's Physiology." And if one may believe Karen Horney, some knowledge of sexual function is probably "learned" by the givens

of male or female structure and their respective sensations. As Horney writes, "It may be asked whether such instinctive knowledge of the processes of penetration into the female body necessarily presupposes an instinctive knowledge of the existence of the vagina as the organ of reception. I think that the answer is in the affirmative if we accept Freud's view that 'the child's sexual theories are modelled on the child's own sexual constitution.' For this can only mean that the path traversed by the sexual theories of children is marked out and determined by spontaneously experienced impulses and organ sensations." See Horney, p. 155.

83. It could be that the string's significance also derives from her use of it to tie the fascicles and packets of poetry together, keeping them safe as she was physically, both "opened" truly only by posterity. All of Dickinson's eight poems about snakes hold the creature suspect, and in one, "Sweet is the swamp with its secrets," Emily sighs "for houses" because "A Snake is summer's treason, / And guile is where it goes." P III, 1740, p. 1170. See also P I, 11; P II, 606, 1136; P III, 1298, 1500, 1670, 1740. In contrast, her ten poems about the worm are appreciative when they are not neutral. See P I, 1, 66, 70; P II, 871, 885, 893, 913, 1034, 1058; P III, 1134, 1670.

84. P I, 475, p. 365.

85. L III, PF 120, p. 929.

86. Erikson's explanation of the basic meaning of anxiety is relevant to this sense of deprivation. He notes that it derives from *angustus*, meaning to feel hemmed in or choked up. Erikson, *Young Man Luther* (New York, 1958), p. 39.

87. P II, 679, p. 525.

88. P II, 855, p. 641.

89. Richard Chase, *Emily Dickinson* (New York, 1951), pp. 119–21, 140–41.

90. P II, 641, p. 494; P II, 675, p. 522; P III, 1308, p. 908; P III, 1382, p. 952.

91. P I, 207, p. 146.

92. R. W. Emerson, "Compensation," *Essays, First Series* (Boston, 1861), p. 107.

93. P I, 165, p. 120.

94. P III, 1589, p. 1096.

95. P III, 1603, p. 1104.

96. L II, 342a, p. 474.

NOTES TO CHAPTER FOUR

1. L III, index; also Harvard List of Books in Dickinson Library, hereafter referred to as HL.

2. Ibid.

3. Jack Capps, *Emily Dickinson's Reading, 1836–1886* (Cambridge, Mass., 1966), p. 27.

4. HL; Austin and Lavinia also received Bibles at this time. Each child's copy contains his name, the date, and Edward Dickinson's signature.

5. L II, 395, p. 511.

6. Capps, p. 30. An enormous number of references to house and its cognates, well over 2000, appear in the Bible. James Strong, *The Exhaustive Concordance to the Bible* (New York, 1890), pp. 489–90, 494–500. Home and related words occur much less often but usually with the same meanings. To list them reveals both Webster's sources and the ecclesiastical emphases of the Judeo-Christian tradition. At least eight definitions appear: a dwelling place (Gen. 19:3), its inhabitants (Acts 10:2); kindred, stock, or lineage (2 Sam. 7:18); wealth, riches, or estates (Matt. 23:14); the grave (Job 30:23); the mortal body in which the immortal soul dwells (2 Cor. 5:1); the church of God (1 Tim. 3:15); and heaven (John 14:2). By far, the everyday, so-called secular meanings of house, roughly the first four definitions above, occur most often in the Bible. Of the other four, theologically figurative uses, God's house is most frequently mentioned. The "long home" of Eccles. 12:5 and heaven as "my Father's house" of "many mansions" are less often used, while home or house as man-in-the-flesh is rather rare, as in "whilst we are at home in the body, we are absent from the Lord" (2 Cor. 5:6). A more positive reading of the body as a spiritual house dedicated to God appears only with "temple," a divine house, as in John 2:21: "But he spake of the temple of his body," and in 2 Cor. 6:16: "For ye are the temple of the living God." Ibid.

7. P III, 1545, pp. 1065–66.

8. P III, 1657, p. 1131.

9. P I, 249, p. 179.

10. P I, 211, p. 148.

11. P I, 61, p. 46; P I, 127, p. 90.

12. L II, 180, p. 321.

13. L II, 593, p. 635.

14. L I, 57, p. 146.

15. David T. Porter, *The Art of Emily Dickinson's Poetry* (Cambridge, 1966), p. 58. See also Capps, pp. 73–74.

16. P II, 964, pp. 697–98.

17. L III, 947, p. 847.

18. L III, 979, p. 871.

19. P I, 488, pp. 372–73.

20. Capps, p. 63.

21. John E. Walsh, *The Hidden Life of Emily Dickinson* (New York, 1971), pp. 190–91. In Higginson's notes to his wife about Emily in 1870, he incorporated into his own remarks one of the poet's: "After long disuse of her eyes she read Shakespeare & thought why is any other book needed." L II, 342b, p. 476.

22. Capps, p. 63.

23. Ibid., pp. 182–85.

24. Alexander Schmidt, *Shakespeare-Lexicon* (Berlin, 1902), I, 548.

25. Ibid.

26. For example, Robert Chambers, ed., *Cyclopaedia of English Literature*, 2 vols. (Edinburgh, 1844); Charles A. Dana, *The Household Book of Poetry* (New York, 1858); and Rufus W. Griswold, *The Sacred Poets of England and America* (New York, 1850).

27. Byron's prisoner stated, "My chains and I grew friends," which may have prompted Emily's thoughts toward, "A Prison gets to be a Friend." Capps, p. 79.

28. Walsh, especially chapters 3 and 4 and their notes, pp. 255–65.

29. As quoted by Helen Vendler, "The Wasteland," *New York Times Book Review*, November 7, 1971, p. 45, from T. S. Eliot, "Philip Massinger," *The Sacred Wood* (London, 1920), p. 125. Eliot continues, . . . bad poets deface what they take, and good poets make it into something better, or at least something different. The good poet welds his theft into a whole of feeling which is unique, utterly different from that from which it was torn. . . ." On this scoring, Dickinson would have been one of Eliot's applauded thieves.

30. And the lines Walsh attributes to Browning as inspiration for Dickinson seem to be insubstantial evidence, pp. 257–60.

31. It is sheer speculation, but possible that "He" in this poem refers to Samuel Bowles. Sue Dickinson had recommended *Aurora Leigh* to him and he reported that he took a copy of it and the Bible on his first trip to Europe. Bianchi, FF, p. 283. See also chapter 5 of this book for the role of Bowles in Emily Dickinson's life.

32. L II, 261, p. 404.

33. Capps, p. 87.

34. HL.

35. Capps, pp. 88, 91.

36. Leslie N. Broughton and B. F. Stelter, eds., *A Concordance to the Poems of Robert Browning* (New York, 1924), pp. 1006–8.

37. Ibid., pp. 994–96.

38. Ibid., pp. 995, 1007–8.

39. Robert Browning, *The Ring and the Book* (Boston, 1869), p. 176.

40. Ibid., p. 168.

41. Capps, pp. 94–95, 99, 95; HL.

42. Sol Holt, *The Dictionary of American History* (New York, 1963), pp. 295, 291, 181.

43. Richard Poirier, *A World Elsewhere: The Place of Style in American Literature* (New York, 1966), p. viii.

44. Quoted in Harry Levin, *The Power of Blackness: Hawthorne, Poe, Melville* (New York, 1958), p. 3.

45. Ibid., chapter 1.

46. L II, 622, p. 649.

47. L I, 62, pp. 155–56; L II, 290, pp. 431–32; L II, 542, pp. 604–5; L II, 593, pp. 635–36; L II, 622, pp. 649–50.

48. L II, 662, p. 649.

49. Perhaps Hilda, in the last work, gave Emily another literary reason for wearing white – an earlier one could have been *Great Expectations'* Miss Havisham – although by 1860, she would probably have been appalled by Hilda's unmitigated and pious purity. Aurora Leigh's white, morning dress may have been more inspiring. HL. Higginson's *Studies* (1879) included a chapter on Hawthorne.

50. Seymour L. Gross, "Hawthorne's Revision of 'The Gentle Boy,'" *American Literature*, XXVI (May 1954), 196–208.

51. Ibid.

52. L I, 62, p. 155.

53. If Hawthorne's characters kindled imaginative identifications in Dickinson, could his house *per se* also have been suggestive, again "in a relative sense?" In 1851, the Dickinsons were at the Pleasant Street house, but as indicated earlier, the pattern of life which developed there for Emily continued and solidified in later years at the Mansion. Hawthorne's tale clearly separates house from street, and both Dickinson residences were shielded by gates or hedges but were also situated on main arteries (Pleasant Street, then North Street, was the principal road leading north from the center of town; the Mansion was on Main Street). Thus their general prospects were identical to Hawthorne's house. But beyond physical setting and its significance of separating house from world, in what ways did the seven-gabled house find nonfictional similarities to the poet's own?

Only hindsight gives us the chance to draw certain parallels. At twenty, Emily would hardly have been able to foresee that her future would indeed be akin to Hepzibah's, a recluselike life in her ancestral home. Yet that life would not include the role which made Hepzibah's worth living, that is, the custodial care of her brother. Nor would Emily then have been able to know that in fact her family, like the Pyncheons, would wither, with no progeny at all from Emily or Lavinia and, in Austin's case, the death of his three children without issue. The other side of the family in Hawthorne's story, the Maules, also had a trait for which the Dickinsons were famous, an "hereditary character of reserve." Emily early cherished this habit as her own.

The complex symbolism of Hawthorne's house, outlined by Roy R. Male in *Hawthorne's Tragic Vision* (Boston, 1964), in its relation to time, the word, and darkness bears a certain resemblance to the actual history of the Dickinsons. See especially pp. 124–26.

54. Hyatt H. Waggoner, ed., *Nathaniel Hawthorne: Selected Tales and Sketches* (New York, 1959), p. 374.

55. Ibid., pp. 374, 400.

56. Ibid., p. 374. Ripley was also an ancestor of Emerson's.

57. Ibid., p. 385.

58. Ibid., p. 391.

59. Ibid., p. 392.

60. Ibid., pp. 392–93. Hawthorne then speculates about the seasons and their analogy to human life, especially autumn and the approach of death. He speaks about the cricket's song as an early token of fall. Dickinson's poem, "Further in Summer than the Birds," P II, 1068, p. 752, develops the same theme.

61. P I, 186, p. 134. In "This Consciousness that is aware," the poet again acknowledges her inner division, concluding that the Soul is condemned to be pursued by "a single Hound/It's own Identity." P II, 822, pp. 622–23.

62. Waggoner, pp. 322–23. In a "newspaper" Hawthorne circulated among his friends entitled "The Spectator," his poem "My Low and Humble Home" was published August 21, 1820. Richard E. Peck, ed., *Nathaniel Hawthorne: Poems* (Charlottesville, Virginia, 1967), pp. 8, 33.

63. Waggoner, p. 325.

64. L II, 320, p. 455.

65. L III, 691, p. 692. Capps quotes a cousin of Emily's, Mrs. Ellen E. Dickinson: "Thoreau was naturally one of [Emily's] favorite authors from his love of nature and power of description in that direction. On one occasion when a lady recently introduced in the family by marriage quoted some sentences from Thoreau's writings, Miss Dickinson recognizing it hastened to press her visitor's hand as she said, 'From this time we are acquainted'; and this was the beginning of a friendship that lasted till the death of the poetess." Capps, p. 119.

66. Henry David Thoreau, *Walden, or Life in the Woods* (New York, 1960), p. 30.

67. Ibid., pp. 30–31.

68. Ibid., p. 32.

69. Ibid., pp. 35–36.

70. P I, 84, p. 68.

71. Thoreau, pp. 36–37.
72. P I, 196, 366; P II, 631, 950, 961; P III, 1743.
73. Thoreau, pp. 29, 43, 44, 52, 59.
74. Ibid., 163. See also *Walden* (Boston, 1862), pp. 261–62.
75. Capps, p. 118.
76. HL. Emerson visited Amherst at least twice, in 1855 and 1879, and was a guest at the Evergreens, but it is not known if Emily met him. Ralph L. Rusk, *The Life of Ralph Waldo Emerson* (New York, 1949), pp. 385, 498.
77. Hyatt H. Waggoner, *American Poets: From the Puritans to the Present* (Boston, 1968), p. 213.
78. R. W. Emerson, "Self-Reliance," *Essays, First Series* (Boston, 1861), p. 47.
79. Emily might have felt vindicated by Emerson in her decision not to pursue study at Mount Holyoke, or even to trust exclusively in her own rationality. He wrote in "Literary Ethics," "The Vision of genius comes by renouncing the too officious activity of the understanding, and giving leave and amplest privilege to the spontaneous sentiment." *Miscellanies* (Boston, 1860), p. 159.
80. Emily might have agreed with Emerson's statement in "The Poet" that ". . . we use defects and deformities to a sacred purpose, so expressing our sense that the evils of the world are such only to the evil eye," at least in moments when she toyed with this theory of compensation. But her rebellion and sense of estrangement from Nature and God left her ultimately more convinced than Emerson that evil existed apart from the observer as an absolute, independent force, even though she names the devil in only two poems: P III, 1479, p. 1023 and P III, 1545, p. 1065.
81. Emerson, *Miscellanies*, p. 167.
82. Ibid.
83. L II, 268, p. 412.
84. Emerson, "Nature," *Miscellanies*, p. 42.
85. Emerson, "The Poet," *Essays, Second Series* (Boston, 1862), p. 23. Emily's wavering pencil line extended down the margin to include the following three sentences: "It does not need that a poem should be long. Every word was once a poem. Every new relation is a new word."
86. Ibid. Emerson's aesthetic appreciation of house-building and house-keeping raised to philosophic heights recurs again and again in other writings. In the essay "Fate," he indicates why each new generation, or even the same mind taking on fresh views, is impelled to find new forms: "Every spirit makes its house, but afterwards the house confines the spirit." In *Conduct of Life,* he versifies to confirm his admonitions in "Literary Ethics":

Cleave to thine acre; the round year
Will fetch all fruits and virtues here.
Fool and foe may harmless roam,
Loved and lovers bide at home.

Then in his *Journals,* unknown to Emily, Emerson has a thought which would have won her instant assent:

My idea of a home is a house in which each member of the family can on the instant kindle a fire in his or her private room.

Bruce Bohle, ed., *The Apollo Book of American Quotations* (New York, 1967), pp. 197, 200.

87. Melville, *Moby Dick,* I, 133, quoted in William Braswell, *Melville's Religious Thought: An Essay in Interpretation* (New York, 1959), p. 87.

88. Emily's eclectic reading tastes included several other Americans whose use of the image may well have contributed to her own thinking but whose works are not scrutinized here: Lowell, Longfellow, Howells, Holmes, James, and Helen Hunt Jackson. In England, Tennyson is a large omission, especially since Sue's copies of his best-known works are marked and since Tennyson has an impressive number of references to house and home. In the Dickinson Library at Harvard are nine listings of works by Tennyson, including a ten volume edition of his works (Boston, 1871). But the Brownings overshadow Tennyson in Emily's affection, and for interests of brevity, he is left unexplored. Howells and James do not seem to be omitted with such danger. Emily knew serialized novels of both men which appeared in *The Atlantic Monthly.* But those which would have given her imagistic materials in architectural or object reference of quantity did not appear until either near her death or after it: in James's case, *The Portrait of a Lady* (1881) and *The Spoils of Poynton* (1897); in Howells's, *A Modern Instance* (1882) and *The Rise of Silas Lapham* (1885).

NOTES TO CHAPTER FIVE

1. Martha Dickinson Bianchi, *The Life and Letters of Emily Dickinson* (New York, 1924), pp. 39, 53. See also M. D. Bianchi, *Emily Dickinson, Face to Face* (New York, 1932), p. 4.

2. Bianchi, *Face to Face,* p. 60.

3. Bianchi, *Life and Letters,* p. 69.

4. Leonard Hills owned this house, directly east of the homestead.

5. L II, 304, p. 440.

6. P II, 832, p. 631.

7. L II, 459a, p. 554.

8. She wrote her cousins Louise and Fannie Norcross in early February 1863, the time of year beyond doubt requiring "garden" to be read "conservatory": "Would it interest the children to know that crocuses come up, in the garden off the dining-room? and a fuchsia, that pussy partook, mistaking it for strawberries. And that we have primroses – like the little pattern sent in last winter's note – and heliotropes by the aprons full, the mountain colored one – and a jessamine bud, you know the little odor like Lubin – and gilliflowers, magenta, and few mignonette and sweet alyssum bountiful, and carnation buds?" L II, 279, p. 422.

9. Bianchi, *Life and Letters*, pp. 42–43.

10. L II, 513, p. 588.

11. In 1873, she noted, again to her Norcross cousins, "That was my 'pipe' Fanny found in the woods." L II, 394, p. 510. A fuller testimony of her lifelong familiarity and feeling for this exquisitely delicate, almost translucently white plant which grows only in the shadows of the forest and lives from decaying roots (did she know this last fact?), is found in a letter she wrote in 1882 to Mabel Loomis Todd. Mrs. Todd had sent Emily a wooden panel of a group of Indian pipes, finely handpainted by herself, their fragile forms almost transparent but still silhouetted against a black background. Emily kept it displayed in her bedroom. She wrote an exuberant letter thanking Mrs. Todd: "That without suspecting it you should send me the preferred flower of life, seems almost supernatural, and the sweet glee that I felt at meeting it, I could confide to none. I still cherish the clutch with which I bore it from the ground when a wondering Child, an unearthly booty, and maturity only enhances mystery, never decreases it. To duplicate the Vision is almost more amazing, for God's unique capacity is too surprising to surprise." L III, 769, p. 740. See also Mabel Loomis Todd, ed., *Letters of Emily Dickinson* (New York, 1962), p. 368.

12. Occasionally, Emily wound a verse around the stem of a flower sent a friend, perhaps part of a larger bouquet, suggesting more than unity with it. MacGregor Jenkins, *Emily Dickinson, Friend and Neighbor* (Boston, 1939), p. 91. Her intimacy with flowers may again demonstrate her fundamental femininity. Blossom and poem emerge from her center, the fruit of profoundest culture of heart, mind, and hand. (She once ended a poem, "To be a Flower, is profound / Responsibility – " P II, 1058, p. 746).

13. L II, 388, p. 505. She pressed the identification even further in the poem "Essential oils are wrung," studied in chapter 3. There the theme of immortality, at least for her poetry, is explicitly paired with the attar extracted from the rose, lasting after the flower dies. It had

long been developing as a botanical analogue to her own expectations of an eternal life, probably more forcefully than any theological doctrine could have been. In 1877, she commented to T. W. Higginson, "When Flowers annually died and I was a child, I used to Read Dr. Hitckcock's [sic] Book on the Flowers of North America. This comforted their Absence – assuring me they lived." L II, 488, p. 573.

This sentiment was reinforced by her intimate care of the conservatory's plants, where beyond practical requirements of sun, soil, and water, Emily could observe: "Flowers are not quite earthly. They are like the Saints. We should doubtless feel more at Home with them than with the Saints of God." L II, 417, pp. 527–28. See also L II, 213, p. 359. Their attraction seemed so simple and direct. Surely, then, they were "vices"? One thinks of Zenobia's flower in reading Emily's observation, "Flowers are so enticing I fear that they are sins – like gambling or apostasy." L III, PF 923. The supposition of their afterlife became almost a fixed assumption so that she could state with a tone of surety, "The immortality of Flowers must enrich our own, and we certainly should resent a Redemption that excluded them." L II, 528, p. 597 (see previous letter, no. 527, as well).

14. L II, 354, p. 482.

15. L II, 391, p. 508.

16. Allen Tate, "New England Culture and Emily Dickinson," *The Recognition of Emily Dickinson: Selected Criticism Since 1890* (Ann Arbor, 1964). Tate discusses how Emily's "poetry of ideas" is ultimately a fusion of mind and heart because of the poet's peculiarly immediate, nonintellectual approach to experience. Pp. 161, 164.

17. P III, 1354, p. 935.

18. William R. Sherwood, *Circumference and Circumstance: Stages in the Mind and Art of Emily Dickinson* (New York, 1968), pp. 139 ff.

19. Ibid., p. 140.

20. Tate and others are correct when they state in effect that Puritanism supplied key words in Emily's vocabulary. They are right, too, in saying that by questioning this culture she invented her own definitions, because on balance she uses theological terms originally or casually more often than she does traditionally. See Emily's unique use of despair in P II, 505, 756, 799; P III, 1299. See also her meaning of justification, P I, 313; P II, 427, 510, 569, 591, 663, 698, 709, 713, 745; P III, 1388. Such theological concepts as communion and sin are treated in only two poems each: P I, 130, P III, 1452, and P II, 801, P III, 1545 respectively. Regeneration is not a word she used at all.)

They may be wrong, however, when they suggest that her satirical or critical use of such words illustrates an attitude which is simple heresy. Her religious quest, to support Sherwood, was deeply authentic, even *through* the satire, it seems, and quite naturally it was, on the whole, conventionally structured or conditioned (see " 'Houses' – so the Wise Men tell me" P I, 127, p. 90). The several series of evangelical revivals in Amherst in her early adulthood could not help but challenge her to think and react to a faith and in a manner which John Winthrop would still have recognized. But Sherwood is incorrect when he moves from this point first to argue that Emily manifestly experienced conversion, adopting an abiding faith in the benevolence of God and, finally, to state with what seems alarming ease, "After 1862, she, like her father, was pledged to God, her loyalties and her assumptions fixed." Sherwood, 179.

21. P II, 906, p. 666.

22. L III, PF 53, p. 920.

23. Perry Miller, *The New England Mind: The Seventeenth Century* (Cambridge, Mass., 1954), p. 25.

24. L II, 193, p. 339.

25. P II, 885, p. 654.

26. P III, 1545, p. 1066.

27. P II, 1601, p. 1102.

28. See P I, 420, 432; P II, 816, p. 618; P III, 1207, 1547, 1556.

29. "For the comprehension of Suffering One must ones Self have Suffered." L II, 416, p. 527.

30. See P I, 203, 225; P II, 571, p. 436. There are only one or two firm assertions of the consoling power of Jesus (though she does speculate), as in a rare poem in which he assures her of immortality by affirming, "Death was dead." Rather, on the one hand, she cannot find him: "Oh Jesus – in the Air – / I know not where thy chamber is"; or on the other, he raps at her door, and searches for her soul with no response, just as she knocks for "Heart" to answer, referring either to her own stubbornness or to a beloved's reserve. See P I, 317, 432; P II, 502, p. 385.

Moving toward skepticism, Emily compares her devotion to her beloved as greater than Jesus' love for mankind, because she loves "So well that I can live without." Jesus' promise has the proviso that men follow him. More ominously, in another moment he "strained" her faith, "hurled" her belief, "wrung" her with anguish, and "stabbed" when she sought him. One wonders how she could end the poem still relatively drawn to him: "Jesus – it's your little 'John'! / Don't you know – me?" P I, 456, p. 352; P II, 497, p. 380. It is hardly a surprise then to find her questioning his invitation: " 'Unto Me?' I do not know you – / Where may be your House?" P II, 964, pp. 697–98. She avows, "I am spotted," which is answered by his pardon. Her assertion that "I am small" receives his assurance, "The Least / Is esteemed in

Heaven the Chiefest – / Occupy my House." But Emily's response here and elsewhere is not given. The most it seems she can do is question, "Say, Jesus Christ of Nazareth / Hast thou no Arm for Me?" P II, 502, p. 385.

31. L III, 932, p. 837.

32. A turn on this meaning is the achievement of grace through extended suffering, a Puritan notion, though not signified as a divine requirement but rather as a felt happening. "To vitalize the Grace," a tooth is needed. "Wo" bends sight "Best Beauty's way" just as the cost of grace is the Cross, "no Extravagance" for Jesus. The temporal and painful bases of grace, fairly obviously directed to a beloved, re-appear in "Fitter to see Him, I may be / For the long Hindrance – Grace – to Me." The same poem equates grace with benevolence, "He left behind One Day," the lover now gaining God's bestowing role. The definite dissent from dogma strongly arises in Emily's view of "The Sweetest Heresy," two lovers converting each other to each other, a "Grace so unavoidable," paralleling the irresistible power of regeneration but decidedly natural, not supernatural. P I, 296, 259, 387, 459; P II, 471, 968. See also Perry Miller, p. 28.

33. P I, 473; P II, 508, 640.

34. L III, PF 50, p. 919.

35. The same theme of the soul's self-awareness of a new life following death recurs predictably as a question, nowhere truly forthrightly. The point is that there is no assist from above (God) or from immanent divinity (Christ). On the threshold of heaven, "the Grace in sight," Emily's query, "Do we die – / Or is this Death's Experiment – / Reversed – in Victory?" probes and thus challenges Paul's rhetoric, "O death where is thy sting, O grave where is thy victory?" Heaven for the comprehending poet seems "too difficult a Grace – / To justify the Dream" because it requires death of the consciousness, and for Emily, the poet's eye was "All." While certain illuminations of this world, literally, spectacular natural scenes at dawn, noon, or sunset, might mimic the enlightenments of paradise, still "how Ourself, shall be / Adorned, for a Superior Grace – / Not yet, our eyes can see."

Yet the very act of death could be the ecstatic moment whether life beyond was promised or not: "There is no Gratitude / Like the Grace – of Death –" or the "Capacity to Terminate / Is a specific Grace." It is as if the moment in which she could become at once the "Convex & Concave Witness" was the "superior Grace" she could recognize as her own. It came only in the imagined process of dying, which allowed her a transcending insight or appointment to eternity, never fast but fleeting when the vision receded.

Her splendid paean to the "minor Nation" of the cricket in "Further in Summer than the Birds" speaks of a "gradual" grace descending on the scene of "unobtrusive" and innocent insects, whose sounds haunt and prophesy the end of human life as well as their own. They conjure up the spirit of death and invest nature with a "Druidic Difference," precisely because they are unseen. In the same way, summer in October is "graphicker for Grace" than June, because it is dying and more precious, "finer" for its going. Renewed life as immortality then remained for Emily only an imperceptible atmosphere inhaled at the premonition of decease, received as a "courteous, yet harrowing Grace," so reluctantly did she surrender breath, and so unsure was she of the character of heaven. P II, 550, 569, 575, 614, 1068; P III, 1196, 1422, 1540. See also L III, PF 114, p. 928.

36. P I, 476, p. 365. Also, Richard B. Sewall, *The Lyman Letters: New Light on Emily Dickinson and Her Family* (Amherst, Massachusetts, 1965), pp. 70–71.

37. L II, 261, p. 404.

38. P III, 1247, p. 866. See also Thomas Johnson, *Emily Dickinson* (Cambridge, Mass., 1955), p. 146.

39. P II, 595, p. 456; P II, 643, p. 495.

40. L II, 355, p. 483.

41. If Emily had been struck by the divine light of grace in 1862, then one would think that prayer would be almost an involuntary response on her part and that in some way she would know it had been heard. But her poetry of this year testifies to an opposite fact, her unanswered voice. First, her expectations of the efficacy of prayer are not what a convert anticipates but what a child demands as she notes almost in self-mockery, "Of course – I prayed – / And did God care? / He cared as much as on the Air / A Bird – had stamped her foot – and cried 'Give Me.' " But she can imagine how "prayer would feel – to me" if she as God were asked to explain "parts of his far plan," the "mingled side of his Divinity." She wants the assurance of God's strength "to hold my life for me," but alone she has to support her own "Balance," and "then – it does'nt stay." P I, 376, p. 299; P II, 576, p. 440.

From dethroning God in the act of empathy for his irritation with probes into his mystery, she moves to state her longing for his sustaining power. But he does not appear, leaving her ultimately "unbalanced." Is this the state of mind a believer "would understand as the apprehension of the position death, suffering, and tantalizing uncertainty occupy in God's beneficent plan," as Sherwood states? Sherwood, p. 160; also L III, 830, p. 780.

42. Perhaps her rock bottom view of God was a vestigial belief combined with a personal hope, stated in two contrasting ways; "God did not ignite this world to put it out" is basically more optimistic than the resigned, "God cannot discontinue [annul] himself. This appalling trust is at times all that remains." L III, PF 34, p. 916.

43. P I, 476, p. 365.

44. P III, 1320, p. 913; L II, 410, p. 523. See also L III, 976, pp. 866–67.

45. L III, 750, p. 728. See also L III, 694, 727, 746, 808, 866, which all show Emily's continuing religious consternations.

46. P II, 668, p. 515.

47. P I, 364, 400; P II, 668, 786–90, 986; P III, 1215, 1330, 1740, 1757, 1775.

48. Sherwood states that Emily's poetics developed during the year 1862, in the process of her correspondence with Higginson. P. 207. One may at least agree that her earliest surviving comments date from this time, although she may have thought or expressed them before. If this were true, then she may have used her sister-in-law's editions of Emerson's essays, which bear pencil markings or have corners turned up, typical of Emily's notations. Probably she had previously known some of the essays. But in writing Higginson, she may have wanted recent sources from which to extract thoughts. "Circumference," for instance, was a standard Emersonian word, although it is true that the Brownings and Carlyle use it, too. None of Emily's poems before 1862 mention this word, and at least half of the ones which do are within the period from 1862 to 1864. S. P. Rosenbaum, ed., *A Concordance to the Poems of Emily Dickinson* (Ithaca, New York, 1964), p. 133.

49. R. W. Emerson, "Experience," *The Selected Writings of Ralph Waldo Emerson* (New York, 1950), p. 352.

50. R. W. Emerson, "The Over-Soul," *Selected Writings*, pp. 262, 269.

51. P I, 378, p. 300.

52. P I, 420, p. 326; L II, 342a, p. 474.

53. P II 1075, p. 760.

54. P III, 1412, p. 980.

55. Cf. Clark Griffith, *The Long Shadow: Emily Dickinson's Tragic Poetry* (Princeton, 1964), p. 25.

56. P II, 668, p. 515.

57. P I, 49, p. 38.

58. One also thinks of her request to T. W. Higginson to comment on her poetry, because " 'twould be control, to me.' " L II, 265, p. 409. More completely, she confessed to him in another letter, "I had no

Monarch in my life, and cannot rule myself, and when I try to organize – my little Force explodes – and leaves me bare and charred." L II, 271, p. 414.

59. Referring to Sue, with whom Emily once felt a mother-daughter relationship, she wrote her nephew, "Did you know, Mama was a precious Inn, where the Fair stopped?" L II, 398, p. 513.

60. P I, 488, p. 372.

61. L II, 591, p. 634.

62. Emerson, "Experience," *Selected Writings,* p. 357.

63. P II, 1054, p. 744.

64. P II, 894, p. 659; also P II, 822, pp. 622–23.

65. P III, 1323, p. 915; also P II, 822, pp. 622–23.

66. Albert Gelpi, *Emily Dickinson* (Cambridge, Mass., 1966), pp. 105–6.

67. Tate, pp. 159, 161.

68. Ibid., p. 162.

69. P I, 384, p. 304.

70. P II, 956, p. 745; P II, 777, p. 588.

71. P II, 553, p. 423.

72. P II, 680, pp. 256–57.

73. L II, 288, p. 430.

74. Emerson, "Circles," *Selected Writings,* p. 281.

75. Ibid., p. 282.

76. Ibid., p. 279.

77. L III, 950, p. 850.

78. See section 1, chapter 4, in this book.

79. L III, 904, p. 825; also L III, 683, p. 686.

80. Gelpi, p. 108.

81. L II, 268, p. 412. "Centre" and "circumference" were polarities used by Sir Thomas Brown, Carlyle, both Brownings, and Melville, among others whom Dickinson read.

82. P II, 802, p. 607.

83. Gelpi, p. 120; see also Charles R. Anderson, *Emily Dickinson's Poetry* (New York, 1960), chapters 3, 4.

84. L III, 807, p. 765.

85. P I, 378, p. 300.

86. P II, 967, pp. 699–700.

87. P II, 943, p. 685.

88. P II, 515, pp. 395–96.

89. P II, 632, p. 486.

90. P II, 889, p. 656.

91. P II, 658, 892, 1090; P III, 1718.

92. P III, 1620, pp. 1111–12.

93. Emerson, "Experience," p. 360.
94. P II, 633, p. 486.
95. Emerson, "Nature," p. 19.
96. L III, 1004, p. 882.
97. L II, 342a, p. 474.
98. L III, 946, p. 847.

NOTES TO CHAPTER SIX

1. The dating of Emily Dickinson's manuscripts may forever remain somewhat conjectural, but in his assiduous study of Thomas Johnson's work on her manuscripts, R. W. Franklin does not criticize the dates assigned her poems. R. W. Franklin, *The Editing of Emily Dickinson* (Madison, 1967). John E. Walsh comments convincingly that 250 of the 366 poems Johnson attributes to the year 1862 were more than likely written over a longer period of time, about 1857–61, with "peak production in the latter year." These 250 poems, then, were possibly copies of drafts composed earlier, but not a great deal earlier. Walsh suggests that Dickinson's quantity of fair-copying, which he dates in early 1862, was to prepare the poetry for submission to Higginson. Walsh, *The Hidden Life of Emily Dickinson* (New York, 1971), pp. 264–65.
2. L II, 191, p. 337.
3. L I, 36, p. 97.
4. L II, 397, p. 512.
5. The Mansion was painted yellow, probably at the time of renovation in 1855, which may have faded to an off-white; or it may have been covered with snow. Either explanation could account for the reference to "Alban" house.
6. L II, 261, p. 404.
7. Walsh, pp. 264–65.
8. David Porter, *The Art of Emily Dickinson's Early Poetry* (Cambridge, Mass., 1966), chapter 1.
9. Rosenbaum, pp. 358–60, 363–64.
10. L II, 228, p. 370.
11. Rosenbaum, p. 117.
12. P I, 365, p. 289.
13. P II, 528, p. 405.
14. The door figure is a favorite and an elastic one, used in 82 poems, a third of which were written between 1861 and 1863. *Concordance,* pp. 201–2.
15. Emily's cup cannot be filled; neither can she, as in the closing lines of the psalm, "dwell in the house of the Lord forever." She stopped going to church sometime in the early 1860s. See "Some keep

the Sabbath going to Church" (P I, 324, p. 254), and "Who has not found the Heaven – below – " (P III, 1544, p. 1065).

16. L II, 438, p. 540.

17. Their work in identifying Bowles was preceded by Winfield Townley Scott, "Emily Dickinson and Samuel Bowles," *Fresco: The University of Detroit Tri-Quarterly*, X (Summer 1960), 3–13. See David Higgins, *Portrait of Emily Dickinson: The Poet and her Prose* (New Brunswick, New Jersey), chapters 4 and 5. Also Ruth Miller, *The Poetry of Emily Dickinson* (Middletown, Connecticut, 1968), chapters 5–7.

18. Bowles came to Amherst much more frequently than did Wadsworth, who may have visited Emily three times, although only two visits are definitely known. Not only was Bowles an intimate friend of Austin and Sue Dickinson, but he also became a trustee of Amherst College in 1866, and annually attended Commencement "Gravities," as Emily described them. L II, 266, p. 410. Only one letter from Wadsworth to Emily remains, although there doubtless were others. It shows pastoral, not romantic, concern for a major problem which oppressed her. L II, 248a, p. 392. In contrast, Emily's letters to Bowles imply a delicate understanding probably accomplished by his attempts to protect himself and at the same time prevent injuring her, and by her efforts to control, but not conceal, at least from him, an overwhelming devotion.

Emily tried to interest Bowles in printing her poetry and occasionally sent him verse, although she doubtless early sensed that her dominant melancholy and his athletic optimism would eventually leave him cool to her offerings. Miller, p. 128. Interestingly, and ironically, it was this very buoyancy, Bowles's generosity of life to others, for which Emily constantly thanked him as a personal antidote to her anguish. See L II, 275, p. 418; L II, 300, p. 437; L II, 415, p. 526; L II, 438, p. 540. And further irony, this suffering was caused in large part by his rejection of her poems and by her lonely love for him. Bowles did publish five of her poems (see P III, p. 1207, appendix 9), a mere token in comparison to the banal sentimentalities of contemporary young poetesses which he seemed much happier to print. Miller, pp. 121–26. Nonetheless, he obviously respected Emily's intellect and wit and her repeated affection for him. Ebullient, gregarious, intelligent, and articulate, he was attracted not only by comeliness but also by the New England mind in feminine form, as his letters and his biographer reveal. Higgins, p. 108; Miller, p. 118; also Jay Leyda, *The Years and Hours of Emily Dickinson* (New Haven, 1960), II, 463.

Admiration evokes production and so it was with Emily's correspondence, if not with her poems, which probably puzzled as well as depressed him. However, he did enjoy his correspondence with her and wanted her to remember him. How could he forego the pleasure either of her thought or of her flattery? His comment to Austin in a letter of late March 1859 indicates what was the essential nurture he received from Emily: "My properest remembrances to the ladies of your household, permanent & temporary, & let there be something over for the sister of the other house who never forgets my spiritual longings." Leyda, I, 366; quoted also in Miller, p. 119. (I disagree with J. E. Walsh that "spiritual longings" necessarily refers to the wine Emily was known to have sent Bowles. Her letters are full of theological queries or comments.)

Further, Bowles has been identified by both Higgins and Miller as the probable "Master" to whom Emily drafted three rather abject admissions of devotion, though they may never have been sent. In these and in other letters Bowles is known to have received, she identified herself both as "Daisy" and "your *Queen*," combining her total self, small but royal, secular but sacred. L II, 249, p. 393. The two letters addressed "Dear Master" and the third with no salutation but similar substance are dated roughly 1858, 1861, and early 1862, respectively. L II, 187, p. 333; L II, 233, p. 373–75; L II, 248, pp. 391–92. (Although the personalities and apparent roles of Edward Dickinson and Bowles differed widely for Emily, she found their eyes singularly similar, calling them "those isolated comets." L III, 830, p. 780.) In her correspondence with Bowles Emily used other images to emphasize the enormous value of this relationship, especially of gold and jewelry, of the East and purple, of the sun and day, but most revealingly, of home or cup.

19. L II, 193, p. 338.
20. Ibid.
21. Ibid., p. 339.
22. P I, 132, pp. 94–95. The same year she did try to send him wine with a flower. L II, 205, pp. 351–52.
23. L II, 205, p. 352.
24. See L II, 219, p. 363; L II, 220, p. 364; L II, 223, p. 366.
25. L II, 229, pp. 371–72.
26. L II, 247, p. 390.
27. One can compare these sentences with an undated poem, not only because of the same theme of offered love but also because of the underlined personal pronoun and possessives:

Proud of my broken heart, since thou didst break it,
Proud of the pain I did not feel till thee,

Proud of my night, since thou with moons dost slake it,
Not to partake thy passion, *my* humility.

Thou can'st not boast, like Jesus, drunken without companion
Was the strong cup of anguish brewed for the Nazarene

Thou can'st not pierce tradition with the peerless puncture,
See! I usurped *thy* crucifix to honor mine!   (1736)

Whether this poem was intended for Bowles or not cannot be said. But the similarity of religious overtone to the sentences cited is striking. Here the cup is not Emily's, of course, because it is "for the Nazarene." But Emily has "saved" the subject from assuming Christ's crucifix (the "peerless puncture") by taking his cross, an act which enhances her own cross through her resignation to reality and her subsequent humility.

28. L II, 189, p. 334.

29. L II, 205, p. 352.

30. L II, 259, p. 402.

31. L II, 272, p. 416.

32. See also L II, 515, pp. 589–90.

33. There is a hiatus in the remaining correspondence between Emily and Bowles from 1864 to 1870.

These key metaphors, which Emily reportedly used in letters or poems to Bowles, also illustrate her radically shifting religious attitudes and Bowles's connection with those attitudes. In her second letter to him, Emily had raised rather facetious questions about the resurrection, original sin, and God. L II, 193, pp. 338–39. At the same time, she spoke of friends as her most valuable earthly possessions: "The Charms of the Heaven in the bush are superseded I fear, by the Heaven in the hand, occasionally." Ibid. This theme of uncertainty and preference for the sureties of this life rather than of that beyond was a constant, even dominant, one. She began one letter to Bowles with the quatrain: "Faith is a fine invention / When Gentlemen can *see* – / But *Microscopes* are prudent / In an Emergency." Empirical life, observation, or experience perpetually wooed or bothered her, as in the statement following the poem, "That *Bareheaded life* – under the grass – worries one like a Wasp." L II, 220, p. 364.

In early December 1861, she admitted her special nonconformity: "We told you we did not learn to pray – but then our freckled bosom bears it's friends – in it's own way – to a simpler sky – and many's the time we leave their pain with the 'Virgin Mary.'" Then followed the poem, "Jesus! thy Crucifix," in which she asked Bowles to be reminded of her in heaven when he saw Christ's "*second* face" (a transformed one?). L II, 242, p. 383.

I have noted that in her letter to Bowles in January 1862, Emily could imagine herself administering the communion wine on that unspecified Sabbath, refashioning traditional theology so that she might perform the sacrament, not Christ or one of his ministers. L II, 247, p. 390. Assuming this role, she hinted that the terms of the bond they gave each other were actually hers alone. Then, when she sent him the poem "Title divine – is mine! / The Wife – without the Sign!" she again assumed Christ's authority without becoming Jesus' bride, nor relinquishing her femininity. L II, 250, p. 394.

At the time Bowles was in Europe later in 1862, Emily wrote his wife (rather illogically considering Christ's earthly role), "I often wonder how the love of Christ, is done – when that – below – holds – so." L II, 26, p. 406. Simultaneously, she assured Bowles, still abroad, that she was "taking lessons in prayer," but that was "so to coax God to keep you safe"; no other reason was given. L II, 266, p. 410.

And again, in 1864, she admitted, "We pray for you – every night – a homely shrine – our knee – but Madonna looks at the Heart – first." L II, 300, p. 438. She still suspected prayer as ineffectual. The felt, not spoken, word was what counted. Then ten years later, following her father's death, she conferred her Christ-like role to Bowles, "Resurrection can come but once – first – to the same House. Thank you for leading us by it." No doubt the Bowleses, present at Edward Dickinson's funeral, had momentarily left Emily convinced that her father now knew immortality. L II, 415, p. 527.

The familiar figures of cup, home, and house in the Bowles letters then show not only the depth of Emily's personal costs but also her religious hesitations and her theological adaptations. They are penetrating simultaneous codes to Emily's emotional and spiritual restlessness. Questions of faith and private love appear in a quatrain whose self-deprecatory tone repeats the oppressively apologetic messages Bowles was sent: "If Blame be my side – forfeit Me – / But doom me not to forfeit Thee – / To forfeit Thee? The very name / Is sentence from Belief – and Home" (775). Further, poems which mingle religious theme with romantic confession show Emily as suffering servant and Bowles as her savior. They are "united" by imitating two sides of Jesus' role. Some of her poetry referring to "he" or "thee," previously read as signifying Christ, may then have a more surely earthly referent, as suggested in chapter 5, namely Bowles.

In certain poems, ambiguities obscure the nature of "He" enough so that either a lover or Jesus may be identified with the addressee or subject of the poem. There are clues, however, which help to place "Him" as human. In P II, 1053, "It was a quiet way – / He asked if I was his," Emily offers herself, and though the two rise above this world, the ecstasy is still within time and life: "Eternity – it was – before / Eternity was due." Though this might be read as the moment of conversion, the exclusiveness and height achieved by the pair suggests earthly love, not the traditional humbling of a freshly formed believer. The whole poem seems to state a wish, so that the otherworldliness of it hints of a dream rather than of life beyond.

For examples of other poems which seem to speak to a beloved, see P I, 236, 272, 463, 603, 616, 643. P III, 1435, "Not that he goes – we love him more," is the beginning of a stanza sent to Mrs. Bowles in late January 1878, following Bowles's death. It illustrates that "he" at one moment clearly signified Bowles. Capitalizations or lower case "h's" make no difference in identifying "He."

The same problems are connected with Emily's reference to "Thee." Again, however, certain hints help to place the other. For example, P I, 275, "Doubt Me! My Dim Companion!" echoes Bowles's "near, but remote" position. Also she "poured" herself as from a cup, "The whole of me – forever /What more the Woman can." Identifying sex should have no real consequence with Christ. In a love affair, it is everything. In fact, many of the poems speaking of "Thee" seem more certainly addressed to a lover than do those referring to "He." They often end on the word, as "in Thee," "for Thee," or "no Thee." Or, as in P II, 577, Emily explicitly names, "Think of it Lover! I and Thee," united in eternity. Also, in a few poems, the references to Christ and "Thee," clearly the beloved, are distinct: P I, 203, 394, 456. Or in one poem, P III, 1461, beginning "Heavenly Father," God is without doubt the "thee" (note lower case).

Sample poems for pondering this problem are P I, 106, 203, 209, 212, 235, 275, 279, 284, 339, 343, 368, 470, 474, 480, 482; P II, 549, 564, 577, 587, 589, 597, 611, 646, 738, 788, 815, 831, 869, 881, 908, 918, 939, 961, 966, 1007, 1028; P III, 1231, 1237, 1305, 1534, 1559, 1625, 1664, 1666, 1689, 1736, 1737, 1743, 1754.

34. L II, 262, p. 406; L II, 308, p. 442.

35. Scott, p. 12.

36. L III, PF 58, p. 921 (appendix 3). Even earlier, she told Higginson, "Shame is so intrinsic in a strong affection, we must experience Adam's reticence." L II, 318, p. 452.

37. L II, 207, p. 354.

38. For her mother's continuing ill health, see L II, 406, p. 442; for Emily's eye problems, see L II, 430–35; for her father's wishes, see L II, 450–53; for Emily's annoyance with housekeeping, see L I, 318, p. 453.

39. L II, 330, p. 460.

40. L II, 333, p. 464.

41. Charles R. Anderson, *Emily Dickinson's Poetry* (New York, 1960), p. 56. Other poems which state or suggest completeness in the word "adequate" are P I, 290, 370, 422 (where Emily's life is in proportion

to her "Anthracite" nature), 508, 726, 744 (where remorse is the "Adequate of Hell"), 822, 1221, 1262, 1400, 1709.

42. L II, 342, p. 475.

43. L II, 355, p. 483. Just a few months later, she wrote Perez Cowan on the news of his engagement, "Home is the definition of God." But for Emily, since God was beyond comprehending or trusting, this statement was more hopeful than sure.

44. L II, 342b, p. 475.

45. Ibid.

46. L II, 405, pp. 517–18.

47. L II, 260, p. 403.

48. Millicent Todd Bingham, *Emily Dickinson's Home* (New York, 1955), pp. 176–80.

49. L II, 414, p. 526.

50. L II, 432, p. 537.

51. Ibid.

52. L III, 785, p. 750.

53. P III, 1573, p. 1084.

54. L II, 441, p. 542.

55. L II, 450, p. 548.

56. Millicent Todd Bingham, *Emily Dickinson: A Revelation* (New York, 1954).

57. L II, 600, p. 638.

58. L II, 586, p. 632.

59. L II, 591, p. 634.

60. L III, 645, p. 664.

61. L II, 353, p. 481.

62. P III, 1732, p. 1166.

63. L III, 1040, p. 901.

64. L III, 890, p. 815; L III, 968, p. 861.

65. L III, 1046, p. 906.

66. L II, 487, p. 572.

67. P II, 1119, p. 787.

68. P I, 127, p. 90.

69. L I, 59, 150–51.

70. L III, PF 96, p. 926. See also L III, PF 69, p. 922: "Consummation is the hurry of fools (exhiliration of fools), but Expectation the Elixir of the Gods."

71. L III, 819, p. 773.

NOTES TO CHAPTER SEVEN

1. Emily felt ashamed that she "smiled at women," she once admitted to Samuel Bowles. Presumably she was referring to the feminist

movement and women such as Susan B. Anthony, whom she probably would not have classified among the "holy ones" she "revered," namely, Elizabeth Fry and Florence Nightingale. L II, 223, p. 366. Her conventional femininity seems predicted in a prose fragment of about 1850, supposing these words applied to herself: "With the sincere spite of a *Woman.*" L III, PF 124, p. 929.

2. L II, 225, p. 368.

3. L II, 567, p. 620.

4. L III, 737, p. 717. For similar references sent to Samuel Bowles, see L II, 272, p. 416; to Helen Hunt Jackson, L III, 1015, p. 889.

5. L III, 976, p. 867.

6. L III, 989, p. 875. The sentence which followed suggests that Emily referred to herself in both, "In childhood I never sowed a seed unless it was perennial – and that is why my Garden lasts." P. 876.

7. L II, 564, pp. 618–19; L III, 751, p. 729.

8. L II, 205, p. 352; L II, 534, p. 600; L II, 559, 614–15; L III, 656, p. 670; L III, 750, p. 727. See also L III, 890, p. 816; there she calls her few nearest friends "each a World." Emily's cousin, Clara Newman Turner, remembered that Emily called "me her little *World.*" Jay Leyda, *The Years and Hours of Emily Dickinson* (New Haven, 1960), II, 481.

9. Among her closest friends in Amherst during the 1850s were Edward S. Dwight, pastor of the First Congregational Church, and his wife, Lucy. Perhaps their departure from Amherst in 1860 was one of the reasons Emily stopped attending church. See L II, 243, pp. 383–84; L III, appendix 1, p. 941. Jonathan L. Jenkins and his wife, Sarah, did not come to First Church until 1866, perhaps too late to interest Emily in coming to services again. Nonetheless, they were close family friends, especially beloved by Emily, as she mentioned in a letter to Mrs. Holland. L II, 492, p. 576; L III, appendix 1, p. 947.

10. Such sorts of disdain are registered in P III, 1207, p. 839 and P I, 401, p. 314. Leyda, I, 163.

11. L III, 1045, p. 905. See also Washington Gladden's answer to Emily's question, "Is immortality true?" L III, 752a, 731.

12. Brita Lindberg-Seyersted, *The Voice of the Poet: Aspects of Style in the Poetry of Emily Dickinson* (Cambridge, Mass., 1968).

13. David T. Porter, *The Art of Emily Dickinson's Poetry* (Cambridge, 1966), chapter 4.

14. Lindberg-Seyersted, p. 161.

15. Ibid., p. 138.

16. Ibid., p. 81.

17. Ibid., pp. 63, 64, 110.

18. P II, 885, p. 654; also, Lindberg-Seyersted, p. 69.

19. George Jackson, ed., *Spiritual Folk-Songs of Early America* (New York, 1964). Jackson studied folk songs recorded in books appearing largely in southeastern states, but at least one of which was known in New England, Jeremiah Ingalls's *Christian Harmony* (New Hampshire, 1805). Many of the hymns he discusses have lyrics attributed to Watts. It seems justified to compare Emily's work with his own studies and to say that the hymns which inspired the form of her poetry were also "part and parcel of the ancestral folk-melodism of the English speaking people." P. 19. The adoption of such tunes for church purposes is clearly datable only after the Norman Conquest. P. vii.

On this same theme, Emily also foreshadows the folk-rock and "soul" or gospel threads in contemporary beat music, both in her message – protest and search – and in her style – fresh and, though from the heart, crafted and practiced. One thinks of such current songs as Bob Dylan's "Dear Landlord" or "No Destination – Home" in relation to a poem like " 'Houses' – so the Wise Men tell me." (P I, 127, p. 90).

20. L II, 591, p. 634.

21. Higginson's Diary, May 1886, Leyda, II, 474–75.

22. Mrs. Jameson to her son, Frank, May 23, 1886, Leyda, II, p. 475. In September 1883, Emily's thoughts on eternity again found expression in the figure of a dwelling place, "The first Abode 'not made with Hands' entices to the second." L III, 866, p. 797.

23. L III, appendix 1, p. 947; Leyda, II, 475.

24. Mrs. Todd to her mother, May 23, 1886, Leyda, II, 474.

25. Ibid., II, 475.

26. Ibid., II, 476.

27. Ibid., II, 474; Martha Dickinson Bianchi, *The Life and Letters of Emily Dickinson* (Boston, 1924), p. 61.

28. Jay Leyda, "Miss Emily's Maggie," *New World Writing* [ed. Arabel J. Porter] (New York, 1953), pp. 266–67.

29. P III, 1360, p. 940. Jonathan Jenkins, pastor of First Church, delivered Edward Dickinson's funeral sermon, comparing Edward to the Old Testament Samuel: "With the good prophet of Israel our friend and Father shares the rare distinction of being buried where he was born and lived in what was most truthfully his own place." Jenkins might have said exactly the same words for Emily and been equally accurate. Jonathan Jenkins, Funeral Sermon for Edward Dickinson, MS, Dickinson Papers Box 3, Houghton Library, Harvard, p. 6.

30. Leyda, *Years and Hours*, II, 474.

NOTES TO CHAPTER EIGHT

1. L III, PF 66, p. 922.
2. Cf. P II, 1090, p. 769.

3. Also P II, 564, p. 431.

4. Also P I, 98, 115; P II, 499, 575, 892.

5. L II, 330, p. 460.

6. See also P I, 456, p. 352.

7. P II, 1099, pp. 772–73; see also P I, 103, pp. 78–79, and in relation to Jesus, P I, 502, p. 385.

8. P II, 1052, p. 742; cf. P I, 106, pp. 80–81.

9. See also P II, 605, 612; P III, 1298, 1338, 1356, 1374, 1423, 1586.

Bibliography

MANUSCRIPTS

Bianchi, Martha Dickinson. Notebook of Household Furnishings from the Mansion and the Evergreens, January 1923. The Evergreens, Amherst, Massachusetts.

Dickinson, Emily Norcross. Letter to Emily Dickinson in Boston, May 1844, Dickinson Papers Box 5 (Norcross Family and Correspondence). Houghton Library, Harvard University.

Dickinson, Lavinia. Daily Pocket Remembrancer for 1851, Dickinson Papers Box 8 (Emily and Lavinia Dickinson). Houghton Library, Harvard University.

Dickinson, Susan H. G. "Society in Amherst Fifty Years Ago," Dickinson Papers Box 9 (Susan H. G. Dickinson). Houghton Library, Harvard University.

Jenkins, Jonathan L. Funeral Sermon for Edward Dickinson, Dickinson Papers Box 3 (Family Correspondence and Papers). Houghton Library, Harvard University.

Music: a bound volume of miscellaneous sheet music without title page; Emily Dickinson's name on flyleaf and "Emily E. Dickinson" printed in gold on the cover, autograph signature of Emily Dickinson on sheet of "Louisville March," p. 101; perhaps a.s. of Lavinia Dickinson on sheet of "Home, a Waltz," January 15, 1846. Houghton Library, Harvard University.

ARTICLES AND BOOKS

Abbott, John S. D. *The Mother at Home; or, the Principles of Maternal Duty*. Boston: American Tract Society, 1833.

Anderson, Charles R. *Emily Dickinson's Poetry: Stairway of Surprise*. New York: Holt, Rinehart and Winston, 1960.

Bachelard, Gaston. *The Poetics of Space*, trans. Maria Jolas. New York: The Orion Press, 1964.

Badger, Mrs. C. M. *Wild Flowers Drawn and Colored from Nature*. New York, 1859. Introduction by Mrs. L. H. Sigourney.

Benjamin, Asher. *The Country Builder's Assistant*. Greenfield, Mass., 1805. Reprint. New York: The Architectural Book Publishing Co., P. Wenzel and M. Krakow, 1917.

Bianchi, Martha Dickinson. *Emily Dickinson, Face to Face.* New York: Archon Books, 1970.

———. *The Life and Letters of Emily Dickinson.* Boston: Houghton Mifflin, 1924.

Bingham, Millicent Todd. *Ancestor's Brocades: The Literary Debut of Emily Dickinson.* New York: Harper and Bros., 1945.

———. *Emily Dickinson's Home: Letters of Edward Dickinson and His Family.* New York: Harper and Bros., 1955.

Blake, Caesar R. and Carlton F. Wells, eds. *The Recognition of Emily Dickinson.* Ann Arbor: University of Michigan Press, 1964.

Bohle, Bruce, ed. *The Apollo Book of American Quotations.* New York: Apollo Editions, 1967.

Braswell, William. *Melville's Religious Thought: An Essay in Interpretation.* New York: Pageant Books, 1959.

Broughton, Leslie N. and Benjamin F. Stelter, eds. *A Concordance to the Poems of Robert Browning.* New York: G. E. Stechert and Co., 1924.

Browning, Elizabeth Barrett. *Aurora Leigh.* New York: Francis, 1857 (Sue's copy); 1859 (Emily's copy).

Browning, Robert. *The Ring and the Book.* Boston: Fields, 1869.

Capps, Jack L. *Emily Dickinson's Reading, 1836–1886.* Cambridge, Mass.: Harvard University Press, 1966.

Edward W. Carpenter and Charles F. Morehouse. *The History of the Town of Amherst.* Amherst, Mass.: Carpenter and Morehouse, 1896.

Chambers, Robert, ed. *Cyclopaedia of English Literature.* 2 vols. Edinburgh: W. and R. Chambers, 1844.

Chase, Richard. *Emily Dickinson.* New York: Dell, 1965.

Cody, John. *After Great Pain: The Inner Life of Emily Dickinson.* Cambridge, Mass.: Harvard University Press, 1971.

Coles, Robert. "Shrinking History, Part I." *New York Review of Books,* XX (February 22, 1973), 15–21; "Shrinking History, Part II." *New York Review of Books,* XX (March 8, 1973), 25–29.

Dana, Charles A. *The Household Book of Poetry.* New York: Appleton, 1858.

De Quincey, Thomas *Autobiographic Sketches.* Boston: Ticknor, Reed, and Fields, 1853.

Downing, Andrew Jackson. *Cottage Residences.* New York: Wiley and Putnam, 1842.

Eliot, T. S. *The Sacred Wood: Essays on Poetry and Criticism.* London: Hogarth Press, 1920.

Emerson, Ralph Waldo. *Conduct of Life.* Boston: Ticknor and Fields, 1861.

------. *Essays, First Series.* Boston: Ticknor and Fields, 1861.
------. *Essays, Second Series.* Boston: Ticknor and Fields, 1862.
------. *Miscellanies.* Boston: Phillips, 1860.
------. *The Selected Writings of Ralph Waldo Emerson,* ed. Brooks Atkinson. New York: Modern Library, 1950.
------. *Society and Solitude.* Boston: Fields, 1879.
Erikson, Erik H. *Identity, Youth and Crisis.* New York: Norton, 1968.
------. *Young Man Luther.* New York: Norton, 1958.
Franklin, R. W. *The Editing of Emily Dickinson: A Reconsideration.* Madison: University of Wisconsin Press, 1967.
Freud, Sigmund. *Delusion and Dream.* Boston: Beacon, 1956.
------. *The Ego and the Id.* London: Hogarth, 1935.
------. *A General Introduction to Psychoanalysis.* Garden City, New York: Doubleday, 1938.
------. *Inhibition, Symptom and Anxiety.* Stamford, Conn.: The Psychoanalytic Institute, 1927.
------. *The Interpretation of Dreams.* London: Hogarth, 1954.
Gelpi, Albert J. *Emily Dickinson: The Mind of the Poet.* Cambridge, Mass.: Harvard University Press, 1966.
Gilman, Charlotte Perkins. *The Home: Its Work and Influence.* New York: Source Book Press, 1903.
------. *Women and Economics.* Boston: Small, Maynard and Co., 1899.
Griffith, Clark. *The Long Shadow: Emily Dickinson's Tragic Poetry.* Princeton: Princeton University Press, 1964.
Griswold, Rufus W. *The Poets and Poetry of America.* Philadelphia: Parry and McMillan, 1855.
------. *The Sacred Poets of England and America.* New York: Appleton, 1850.
Gross, Seymour L. "Hawthorne's Revision of 'The Gentle Boy,'" *American Literature,* XXVI (May 1954), 196–208.
Higgins, David. *Portrait of Emily Dickinson: The Poet and Her Prose.* New Brunswick, N.J.: Rutgers University Press, 1967.
Hitchcock, Edward. *Catalogue of Plants Growing Without Cultivation in the Vicinity of Amherst College.* Amherst: J. S. and C. Adams, 1829.
Holt, Sol. *The Dictionary of American History.* New York: Macfadden-Bartell, 1963.
Horney, Karen. *Feminine Psychology,* ed. Harold Kelman. New York: Norton, 1967.
Howard, William. "Emily Dickinson's Poetic Vocabulary," *Publications of the Modern Language Association of America,* LXXII (March 1957), 225–48.

Jackson, George P., ed. *Spiritual Folk-Songs of Early America*. Locust Valley, N.Y.: J. J. Augustin, 1964.

J.B.A. "The Home of Emily Dickinson," *The Packer Alumna*, VII (December 1891), n.p.

Jenkins, MacGregor. *Emily Dickinson: Friend and Neighbor*. Boston: Little, Brown, 1939.

Johnson, Thomas. *Emily Dickinson: An Interpretive Biography*. Cambridge, Mass.: Harvard University Press, 1955.

————, ed. *The Poems of Emily Dickinson*. 3 vols. Cambridge, Mass.: Harvard University Press, 1963.

———— and Theodora Ward, eds. *The Letters of Emily Dickinson*. 3 vols. Cambridge, Mass.: Harvard University Press, 1958.

Levin, Harry. *The Power of Blackness: Hawthorne, Poe, Melville*. New York: Alfred A. Knopf, Vintage, 1958.

Leyda, Jay. "Miss Emily's Maggie." *New World Writing*. [Ed. Arabel J. Porter]. New York: Mentor, 1953, pp. 255–67.

————. *The Years and Hours of Emily Dickinson*. 2 vols. New Haven: Yale University Press, 1960.

Lindberg-Seyersted, Brita. *The Voice of the Poet: Aspects of Style in the Poetry of Emily Dickinson*. Cambridge, Mass.: Harvard University Press, 1968.

Littell, E., ed. *Littell's Living Age*. 2nd ser. Boston, 1855 (7 April 1855).

Lowell, James Russell. *My Study Windows*. Boston, 1872.

Male, Roy R. *Hawthorne's Tragic Vision*. New York: Norton, 1964.

Merrill, D. "Isaac Damon and the Southwick Column Papers," *Old Time New England*, 54 (October 1963), 48–58.

Miller, J. Hillis. *The Disappearance of God*. New York: Schocken Books, 1965.

Miller, Perry. *The New England Mind: The Seventeenth Century*. Boston: Beacon, 1954.

———— and Thomas Johnson, eds. *The Puritans*. 2 vols. New York: Harper Torchbooks, 1967.

Miller, Ruth. *The Poetry of Emily Dickinson*. Middletown, Conn.: Wesleyan University Press, 1968.

Millett, Kate. *Sexual Politics*. New York: Doubleday, 1970.

Peck, Richard E., ed. *Nathaniel Hawthorne: Poems*. Charlottesville, Virginia: University Press of Virginia, 1967.

Poirier, Richard. *A World Elsewhere: The Place of Style in American Literature*. New York: Oxford, 1966.

Porter, David T. *The Art of Emily Dickinson's Early Poetry*. Cambridge, Mass.: Harvard University Press, 1966.

Rosenbaum, S. P., ed. *A Concordance to the Poems of Emily Dickinson*. Ithaca, New York: Cornell, 1964.

Rusk, Ralph L. *The Life of Ralph Waldo Emerson.* New York: Scribner's, 1949.

Rycroft, Charles. "The Artist as Patient," *Times Literary Supplement* (September 22, 1972), 1089–90.

————. "A Great Mother's Helper," *New York Review of Books,* XVIII (June 1, 1972), 17–18.

Schmidt, Alexander. *Shakespeare-Lexicon.* 2 vols. Berlin: Georg Reimer, 1902.

Scott, Winfield T. "Emily Dickinson and Samuel Bowles," *Fresco: The University of Detroit Tri-Quarterly,* X (Summer 1960), 3–13.

Sewall, Richard. *The Lyman Letters: New Light on Emily Dickinson and Her Family.* Amherst, Massachusetts: University of Massachusetts Press, 1965.

Sherwood, William R. *Circumference and Circumstance: Stages in the Mind and Art of Emily Dickinson.* New York: Columbia University Press, 1968.

Sontag, Susan. *Against Interpretation.* New York: Dell, 1966.

Staub de Laszlo, Violet, ed. *Psyche and Symbol: A Selection from the Writings of C. G. Jung.* New York: Anchor, 1958.

Strong, James. *The Exhaustive Concordance to the Bible.* New York: Abingdon, Cokesbury, 1890.

Thoreau, Henry David. *Walden.* Boston: Ticknor and Fields, 1862.

————. *Walden; or, Life in the Woods.* New York: New American Library, 1960.

Todd, Mabel Loomis, ed. *Letters of Emily Dickinson.* New York: University Library, 1962.

Trilling, Lionel. *The Liberal Imagination: Essays on Literature and Society.* New York: Anchor, 1953.

Waggoner, Hyatt H. *American Poets: From the Puritans to the Present.* Boston: Houghton Mifflin, 1968.

————, ed. *Nathaniel Hawthorne: Selected Tales and Sketches.* New York: Rinehart, 1959.

Walsh, John E. *The Hidden Life of Emily Dickinson.* New York: Simon and Schuster, 1971.

Ward, Theodora. "The Finest Secret: Emotional Currents in the Life of Emily Dickinson after 1865," *Harvard Library Bulletin,* 14 (Winter 1960), 82–106.

Warren, Austin. "Emily Dickinson." *The Sewanee Review,* LXV (Autumn 1957), 565–86.

Webster, Noah. *An American Dictionary of the English Language.* 1st ed. 2 vols. Amherst, Massachusetts: Adams, 1844.

Whicher, George. *This Was A Poet.* New York: Scribner's, 1938.

Wilner, Eleanor. "The Poetics of Emily Dickinson." *English Literary History*, 38 (1971), 126–54.

Woolf, Virginia. *A Room of One's Own*. London: Hogarth, 1929.

Zuckerman, Michael. "The Nursery Tales of Horatio Alger," *American Quarterly*, XXIV (May 1972), 191–209.

General Index

Marriage, 97, 113, 177, 179, 187, 197–98, 216

Martyrdom, 190

Masochism, 190, 246 n. 52

Matthew, Gospel of, 117, 118, 119

"Me" (ED), 7, 55, 56, 65, 98, 99–100, 156, 159, 171, 220

Melville, Herman, 2, 14, 116, 127–29, 142–43

Memory, 3, 4, 57, 77, 105, 108, 122, 190, 191, 216, 224

Men, 35, 53, 60, 94, 103–8, 123, 141–43, 159, 166, 226, 246–47 n. 52, 247 n. 55, 249 n. 81

Middlemarch, 126

Miller, J. Hillis, 10–11

Miller, Perry, 249 n. 81

Miller, Ruth, 182

Millett, Kate, 96, 247 n. 52

Milton, John, 120–21

Mind, 3, 7, 9, 10, 14, 17, 21, 23, 60, 66, 97, 98, 111, 116, 122, 127, 131, 133, 134, 135, 164, 192, 207, 221, 232 n. 30, 239 n. 109. See also Consciousness and Psyche

Ministry, 171, 172, 216

Mitchell, D. G., *Reveries of a Bachelor*, 68

Monson, Mass., 30, 31

Montague, Jemima, 26

Morphology, 15, 95, 97, 142, 147, 185

Mother, 2, 9, 27, 32, 42, 43, 75, 192, 234 n. 8, 242 n. 2

Motivation, 17, 20

Mount Holyoke Journal, 241 n. 127

Mount Holyoke Seminary, 5, 48, 62, 64, 70, 75, 103, 151, 193, 238 n. 66, 255 n. 79

Mouse, 3, 19, 174, 190, 230–31 n. 3

Music, 10, 241 n. 126

"My Spirit" (ED), 7, 55, 56, 65, 98, 99, 104, 220

Nail, 101, 189

Narrow, 12, 108, 175, 188, 210, 212, 215, 224, 225

Nature, 1, 6, 8, 10, 13, 19, 48, 82, 89, 122, 132, 133, 141, 147, 150, 151, 160–64, 170, 171, 175–76, 198, 223, 255 n. 80, 261 n. 35

Neighbor, 212

Nest, 13, 14, 16, 121, 136, 209

New England, 49, 135, 192, 249 n. 81, 265 n. 18, 262 n. 19

Newmans, the (cousins), 7

Newton, Benjamin, 57, 137

Night, 49, 122, 141, 175, 211, 216, 217, 225

Nightingale, Florence, 271 n. 1

Nims, Seth, 62, 104

Noon, 48, 82, 122, 165, 179, 213, 222, 224

Norcross, Elizabeth (grandmother), 29, 34

Norcross, Emily L. (cousin), 64

Norcross, Lavinia (aunt) 30–32, 46

Norcross, Louise and Frances (cousins), 100, 193, 195, 198, 257 n. 8, 257 n. 11

North Sunderland, 38

"Northwest Passage, The," 88

November, 131

Nowhereness, 12, 127, 131

Nun, the Amherst, 179

Oak, 86, 189

Objects, 1, 8, 9, 13, 19, 45, 54, 55, 56, 70, 84, 89, 92, 103, 110, 126, 135, 140, 141, 143, 159, 169, 170, 175, 182, 196, 207, 240 n. 109, 242 n. 2, 247 n. 53

October, 51, 261 n. 35

Oils, 92, 112

Orpheus, 167

Pain, 20, 168, 170, 177, 183, 186, 191, 217, 246 n. 52, 266 n. 27, 267 n. 33. *See also* Suffering

Paradise, 12, 114, 117, 150, 157, 181, 188, 194, 195, 229, 260 n. 35. *See also* Heaven

Parents, Dickinson, absence of, 64, 69; Dickinson, Emily E., as child with, 19, 97, her health and, 193, 206, 218, influences of, 41, 43, 44, her love of, 238 n. 66, her perplexity and hurry because of, 173–74, 189–90, her resentment of, 242 n. 158, her separation from, 59; mistakes with children of, 42; objects and, 55; sexual models, 26. *See also* Dickinson, Edward and Emily Norcross

Parlor, 87, 198

Peace, 11, 12, 80

"Peninsula, My Blue," 12, 171

Penis-envy, 53, 246–47 n. 52

Phallus, 106, 246–47 n. 52

Philadelphia, 182

"Philadelphia," 198

Physiology, 22, 54, 249–50 n. 82

Physique. *See* Body

Pleasant Street house: barn at, 52, de-

Index of First Lines